Dedication

Without a question of doubt,,,if it weren't for the constant back-up and guidance from our best friends, Zabro and Shanola,,,and Bob and Betty,,,who just happen to be our parents,,,well, we would not have had the heart to do what is being done here at Philoxia.

Then,,,there's the rest of you,,,which makes our little bubble look like nothing,,,and it's because of yawl that we have grown to love and care to be right here, alongside you and your's.

My goodness,,,you people are somethin' else,,,and we love you.

Chaum'd For Sure,,,

Iilah and Tawlia

Acknowledgments

We wish to thank the following people whose
interest, friendship, and dedication in this
timely project have helped to make this book
so very extra special.

First of all,,, if it weren't for the artis-
tic talents and patience of our devout friend,
colleague, and fellow Philoxian,,, "From Grits
to Gourmet" would not have turned out as it did.
Awanota, once again we are indebted to you, and
are happy to have you here, caring to share your
life and multi-faceted talents with us.

At first, when talked of,,, this seemed like an
easy project, but then came the many other facets
needed to produce such a complexity of invalued
information. This is where our sincere gratitude
goes out to Sheilah Hintz who donated so much of
her time and masterful skills in helping with all
the typing, set-up, and layouts. Sheilah,,, from
the bottom of our hearts,,, "Mmmmmmmmmah!"

And to Andrew McKay, a trusted friend and resident
of Philoxia, we'd like to thank you for your dili-
gence in helping to keep Philoxia running, and especially for the caring, preparation, and thought-
fulness given to our kitchens and guests,,, allowing Iilah and I the freedom to complete these long
awaited for projects.

Most of all,,, we'd like to thank the thousands of
people and friends who encouraged us to produce
"From Grits to Gourmet" as a result of having eaten
in the dining halls of our Pheylonian Cookery.

My God,,, what would Heaven be like without the likes
of yawl in it, forever after.

Published in Canada by:

    Pheylonian Publishing Kohr
    R.R.#1
    Marlbank, Ontario
    K0K 2L0
    CANADA

    COPYRIGHT 1988   #350802

    TAWLIA AND IILAH CHICKALO.

International Distribution by:

    Pheylonian Production Kohr, CANADA.

PRINTED IN CANADA

Contents

INTRODUCTION
by
Kjo Dindee

Introduction

'Tis a rare treat indeed,,,, as well as being a special honour for me to partake and introduce this amalgamation of invalued treasures to the likes of yawl. It's about time, such an enchanting collection of gastronomic delicacies be shared with the greatest civilization ever to be graced birth onto the soreface of this here wee little planet. ii,,, there are so many yearning and unripened souls who must be properly guided in order to simply be able to relate to the common sensed care needed to develop their own budding intellect along with their eternal character worth having. The real rewards and wizdoms of why one should begin and continue to eat proper cannot commence,,, until one's peaceful, deepened senses are strong enough to realize the tremendous limitations one has imposed onto one's self, through lack of konkshus actions, deeds, and diet,,, all being relative. Since the time of man's earliest advent upon the Earth, dualistic miskonceptions have bin goin' on hand in hand, along with all else of value. It's pleazen to see, where man's Link be reachin' the limboh of oneness. ii,,, with the center being the cauze of duality,,, more and more people are coming to realize how there are those who are doin' it all too fast, while some are goin' way too slow,,, and, of course, yawl know of those who have had to manifest this time and do it halph-fasstedly.

These restrictions are put upon man's own subkonkshus minds, in order to be dealt with by one's own maturing sense, as part of the ultimate lesson needed to teach one all about life's simple and true meaning beginning at grit levels. This lesson is one which must finally be learnt by the self,, for the self,,, otherwize, all the knowledge acquired, bears no realistic, spiritual value. When the aurik gasses of one's own gritty digestion puts a polish onto one's inner and outer spirited complacency,,, man will have finally evolved beyond religion, economics, and the pseudo duality of it all. ii,,,, problem is,,, half the population spends so much of its precious time practising the gruelsome art of one-up-manship, having a good time and making lots of money doin' it. While on the other hand,, the other half are being starved, enslaved, etc.,,, or are having to fight for their country in order to defend their right to stay poor, homeless, and undernourished,,, all for the sake of those who think only about economics. How many free people cause war on the other in God's name and His teachings, fighting about just who His people really are. In all, so many are forgetting to put into a peace loving practice just what it is that they should be doing at grit levels in order to joyously complete the real reason of why people are born one and alike onto this aching planet.

     Before we get into this fine book of cookin' for life and konkshusness,,, know ye well that the Great Family has absolutely nothing to do with aggressive acts of terrorism, war, greed, ego, starvayshun, and all the so called devastating, cataklismik events soon to happen, reflective of the price of man's doings. They're the Acts of God, as the insurables call it. ii,,, for these things they should happily pay, rather than call them Acts of God, which they are not.

        Why,, the Great One bee telling me Himself,,, "Kjo,, if I had all the resources and finances given the governments to play with,, I'd hire the military mights of each country to immediately deploy their brave troops into tilling the soil, and adopt their machisimo-ships towards betterment, supplying the nutritionative foods needed for nourishment and preventive medicine, while there is just enough time left to make it worthwhile for everyone". Many have said,,, "Why,, there's no big bucks in it". Wrong,,, it's a lot cheaper to plant, harvest, feed, and heal the world's populace than it is to bankrupt, starve, and finally blow up each country for the mere sake of the sinpathetik, agorik commodities being allowed to pollute all the lands, lakes, rivers, and bloodstreams of the Earth. When will the masses come to realize that there was no money in the beginning,,, nor will there be any six, sick, six financial strongholds forever after, either.

It is time they get on up to the freedom of 7,,, ate it all up,,, nine,,, don't look back,,, and ten-us anyone? Fact is,,, the Great One had often told me,,, "Kjo,, from Christian to Heathen, Athiest to the devil himself,,, every-one from all beliefs and all walks of life have an equal right to what is being offered by mine hand alone". He went on to say, "Kjo,, remind everyone that the little devil used to be a personal friend of mine,,, and as it is, everyone has a bit of the little stinker in themselves,,,, so what should I do,,, take haum the son of a Bombastian, Belfastian Irish Catholic and say to Hell'en high water to the so called brave, terrorizing Protestants who are snipin' and blowin' up my children as well"?

No,, Noh,, Noh,,, the Great One is coming for the whole kit'n-kah-bootle (keetan-ka-ha-boutle, as was said in ancient tongue). All what should remain after the galactic departure is the shell and afterbirth of this giant solar egg called Earth. Know ye well,,, He don't have the time to get technikil, philosophize, or match wits, grammars, and egos with seven billion individual concepts of what it's really all about,,, until, en mass, at grit levels, man's kind comes to peace loving common sense, and qualifies to play the real game of God, in a realistic way, with the Great Ones above us all. Why, it's been said over and over again by the ancient masters,,, "God ain't comin' to make no one man, religion, cult, or sect right about all what's bin done for kreashon,,, nor is he comin' to wrong no one, either". Now there's a sense, with humour, compassion, and love for all, in it.

The Great Family be readying to absorb all who come to an honest peace within the morfessis of their own modulative, solarized cell. Be ye dead or alive,, konkshus or not,, don't really matter none to them what know better,,, only to you it should matter. Unless the spirit within your personal self has grown to be a peace loving, conscientious one,,, it is impossible to achieve and fulfill such an enlightening virtue at grit levels. As long as the gasses of one's auro-nik self are intoxified to such heights & depths with all the chemikilled, neurotic pollutants,,, man's kind shall remain suckilled to the cold heart'd, soulless grind of the great machine known as the Beast. Thank God it's not too late,, and man still has the power to honestly make the necessary adjustments.

This here very special book of cookin' for real with one's life is precisely what is needed for all families to adopt a joyous new frame of mind,, along with a healthy enough body to keep one going on the right track. Without a konkshus input at grit levels,,, the output is but an ever changing concept which can hold no water for real. Regard-less of the depth or height to one's expanding konkshus-ness,,, the same lesson has to be equally learnt by all. Ever ask yourself why it is so very difficult for a man and a woman to simply accept an actual Kreator who kreated people to be just like Himself and Herself, amidst all that is omni-potent, present, and niffty? Why?,,,, because with knowledge alone, people have not yet reached the wizened awareness and peace needed to qualify to play the game of God,, as revealed by the Great Ones. Yet,, it's all so very simple. Even the aborigine could accept and understand the simple truth of this here little kreashon, because they are lucky enough to be plugged into the real jungle, and not the one modern man has built around himself. The Great Chef, who mustered up this whole kreative experiment in the beginning, says,,, "People en mass still have to learn a little more about pure simplicity, being reflected through honest digestion, before they can freely curtail the necessary alterayshons needed to bring about change for true world betterment".

Like people,, this aching planet needs its greens and grains soh's an honest break can manifest itself before the last and final blow-out. ii,,, no matter what is said, pros or cons,,, the Earth is hurting bad,,, and in order for it to be of any further use, it must be replenished with the vital essences needed to attract the kreative force once again. Remember the basic law of physics: Actshun's - reactshun'd,,, where proper actshons reap accordingly, for all who choose to do so.

For example,,, take a small piece of fresh water-crescent and plant it in your aquarium for 24 hours. Oy chi-wa-Wah! It's amazing to see such a healthy growth take place. Now,,, take any piece of meat you want - Grade A to Zee-Chaud-Chiens - and do the same thing,,, remembering all along that the Earth and your body consist of some 90% water. ii,,, right away you'd think,,, eehh gadds,,, what's this guy trying to do,, kill my fish? Heck noh,,, and besides, with meat costing a arm and a leg (and quite a few stomachs),, why waste it on such a dumb old experiment when I could fry up that sucker for supper. Unfortunately,,, most people don't realize that man and beast did not eat meat or each other in the original beginning,, nor during that time of restockment within the last Eden of Kreashon.

Izzn't it ironik how people take better care of their car motors, factories, and tools, than they do their own bodies. Ask yourselves,,, why do so many still remain skeptical and think that the eating of this new polyester and petrolium food makes no difference to their spiritual, physical, and mental growth? I sure wish they'd all do this here little experiment:

Grind up a pound of fresh killed, dead, decaying flesh and taste it as it is. Ah, go on,,, try it,,, eh, eh,,, no bayonaise or sauce vinegreete,, just plain, in its unnatural, adulterated, decaying state,,,, Yuk! Next,, wash your grinder and repeat this procedure with a pound of your favourite fresh veggie and grain mix. Now taste this mixture. Are there not good yuks and bad ones? Of course there are. Be honest now,,, which would you prefer to eat raw each day for the rest of your life?

Ahhhh,,,, c'est bien,,, your humbling machisimo-ship is finally beginning to reflect a sense of honesty. Bon! Now, take both these grain and dead flesh mixtures out front to your flower garden where plenty of 98° sun can get to them. Make two shallow holes and plant each mixture separately,,, then, plant your favourite seeds into these two experimental plots and let them be for a couple of days. Folks,,, the astounding microscopic facts of such an experiment, as proven by scientists in top universities around the world,,, showed, without a doubt,, that most of the seeds planted into the dead flesh mixture died within 12 hours,,,, where the same experiment completed with the energized grain and veggie mixture turned out to be quite different. ii,,, you guessed it,,, where one was a total loss,, the other grain experiment was a tremendous success,, and most seeds sprouted within 24 hours and grew to be high-yielding, healthy plants,,, while the other batch began to smell so bad after a day in the sun,,, one would recommend that it be buried or sprayed with a deodorant of a sorts.

While on the subject of truth and grit facts worth discussing,,, there's one other little experiment which is a must. Take a fresh piece of meat, approximately 1 pound, and sit in your favourite lawn chair facing the 98° sun, holding this fresh morsel of dead, decaying flesh under your nose, about neck level, for some 8 hours. Truly,,, this is my favourite experiment,,, for throughout my world lectures people have always reacted for the worst when asked to do this. "Why, that's morbid", some have bin heard to say. Very well,,, I then told them to lower it some 10 inches and stick it into their stomachs at 98° for 24 hours. Always,, an awesome hush of eerriness could be felt afterwards.

Now remember,,, be it spiced, cooked, or not,,, when taken internally as food,, this decaying, dead, foul flesh mixture reacts accordingly in the 98° human body as it does in the sun at 98°. Soh,,, you see why the deodorant business is one of the biggest in the world. And,,, while on the subject of this smelly business,, there is another experiment worthwhile doing. Take your favourite household living plant and put makeup onto its flowers, underarm deodorant onto its leaves, crotch sprays on its stem, and foot sprays on its roots. Go ahead,,, don't be afraid to learn before it's too late. Here again,, people will not do to their plants what they do each day to their God-given bodies. To prove to yourself just how fast these oxides, etc., travel to your brain and nervous system,,, at bed time, wrap your feet in a damp towel filled with crushed garlic against your skin. Guaranteed that you will have garlic on your breath in the morning. These horrible chemicalized sprays get absorbed into your pores exactly the same way.

When people feed themselves a devitalized pile of decrepid pultch, chemically vitaminized and preserved to look like decent, nutritious food,,, each tiny little living cell in their bodies reacts and cringes accordingly. As well,,, be guaranteed that one's subconscious mind remains shut tight until the day when one's juices flow throughout with the harmonious nutrients needed to reflect one's wizening maturity. Thusly,,, the repulsive putridities and the toxic gasses formed from these toxic foods are what governs one's Psyche and destructive lifestyle,,, no matter how much of a spiritual or religious sweetheart you believe yourself to be. ii,,, to know better and not to change while it's still available,, is the greatest sin next to killing an other.

From an orbital viewpoint,,, it is easily seen that wherever cities and big bucks are being made unnaturally upon the face of the Earth,,, a repulsive, brownish-gray aura of chemical, cancerous growth seems to have manifested itself. From the moon,, these spots on Earth equivalate what a single human cancerous cell looks like when observed through a laboratory microscope. Like,,, who needs it,, sure,,, in the past 24 years, 87% of the North American population have become aware of what they are doing to themselves,,, yet only some 23% have begun the logical transformashon from a non-sensible diet to one involving a more humanistic approach.

There are soyton invalued scromatics about life's true meaning what don't come from knowledge alone. Remember,,, far greater than the angels, spirit, and space beings,,, are the human beings. Reason being,, as well as having what they have,,, throughout all mythologies, the so called immortals have given up their immortality to be wed as mortals, with full senses. The God-like components kreated just for the likes of Earth people are designed in such a manner soh's as to be able to reflect the original full and complete image, which is being taken soh easily for granted. One has to change one's own aura in order to understand and appreciate what's bin bistowed with a great deal of grace. Both the konkshus and subkonkshus circuitries of the brain are ingenious masterpieces of kreashon,,, especially when you think of how they are connected to the delicate nervous system. And my,,, don't forget the heart, which perpetually pumps millions of gallons each year. As good and holy as one thinks one is,,, when one feeds one's face without care or thought,, the blood runs impure throughout the system, as does the type of energy it brings to the swollen, hurtin', malfunctioning organs. Ever wonder who gets credit for all these perfectly engineered components? By the way people spray, oil, and feed themselves with emulgeon'd foods,,, one would think man was a product of the oil refineries, instead of who should really be getting credit for such a phenomenal kreashon. In fact,,, when treated properly with tender love and care,,, people were originally designed to last an erah,, instead of a few cancerous years. From the early beginnings on through the Mu's,,, entities would live healthily for hundreds of thousands of years on natural foods. Here again,,, the Holy Ancients from the second and third empires lived for thousands of years on diets comprised of whole grains, flower pollens, unadulterated veggies, nuts, seeds, and fruits. Even later, during the Atlantian and Egyptian erahs,,, Noah still lived to be a thousand, and Moses reached 700.

Ironically,, in ending this Omegan erah,, we have come to a very short life span of review, where such terms as astral awareness, natural foods, fertilizers, preventive medicine, herbs, organically grown grain and fruit, have become dull and dirty words to so many,,,, while such terms as irradiation, microwave, fun foods, emulsifire, preservatives, stabilizers, artificial colourings and flavourings, deodorants, etc., seem to blend in well with the economically unstable empire of this timing. Of course, all are respected as being the proper mode and expressions of the day. One thing good about the diet being fed to the youth of today is that the machine that runs all governments won't have to pay out any more old age pension cheques, because kids will never reach 50 on this simulated, humane diet. My goodness,,, for one to buy a pound of organic grain, which may take half an hour to cook and prepare enough to last three or four days,, becomes a disaster in most micromotized kitchens. It's unfortunate how most of modern society are too lazy or too busy to realize that cooking and spirituality go hand in hand. Without a shadow of a doubt,,, when people eat these quick cooked, processed foods, which are coloured and garnished with emulsions, white sugar, artificial flavourings, etc., they generally wash it down with chemically flavoured beers, pops, teas, and coffees. Already, it has bin proven many times over that hypertensionness, stress, manic depressiveness, false anxieties, malfunctioning organs, etc., etc., stem from one's basic upkeep and fuel intake. As a matter of fact,,, all problems within the world today stem from the same instability at grit levels. A perfect example of this can be seen on the tropical islands where sugar cane and rum are the main sources of economics. There are three or four diabetic clinics in each small village, and several on each street in the major cities.

If this is what it means to be an edgemakated North American,,, again,, who needs it,,, unless something of true value comes from it all. Look at what it's really done to nature and the peoples of the world. Those who know, live, and exemplarate the simple meanings of the woid, are far happier and poorer than those who care only for the spelling and economics of it. Heck,,, if it's good for the economy,, it's got to be good for you too. Pooh bah,,, the cold, heartless machine that computes and prepares this sinpathe- tik, simulated pultch made to look like humane food, don't give a damn about you or your children. Why,,, if this stuff they produce with the long shelf life doesn't kill the expe- rimental guinea pig or rat in two years,,, it's good enough for your family. This emulgeon'd, chitty stuff is allowed in all commercial processed products,,, yet, with the limited amounts they put in each one,, no one company can actually be held liable or responsible for the suffering and death of your loved ones years later. I've actually heard some people say,, "But I'm only eating 2% of that stuff", in accordance with the F.D.S. something-or-other code of ethicks. True,,, yet, when all the small percentages within each one of these foods you eat throughout the day get added up,, it then becomes a much larger amount than what was given to the poor little mouse in the laboratory.

"Thy will be done on Oith foist, before the acts get took haum". Meaning: If enough individuals come to their common sense,, sanity will once again manifest itself, and will be witnessed from the Heavens. Be it that the world's policy builders were right or wrong to begin with, matters no more,, providing a liberated sense of basic values is once again instigated, upheld, and exemplarated. Common sense and a grit, wholesome, unrefined grain and veggie diet must be shared equally with a wizened tear and a smile before any real miracle of miracles can be activated. Askin' your leaders to feed the poor starving masses with most of your taxes, rather than letting them falter along, allowed to play the heartless game of greed and economics for the good of those who got far too much, ain't really a bad idea. These are not really bad people in power,,,, they just ain't fully come to a calming awareness yet. For a fact,,, if they had a Godly way out of what they don't like about what they were all allowed to be a part of,,, they too would like to redeem themselves in the eyes of the Great Family what be watchin' from above. Only thing is,,, the masses have to let them know what they need, rather than to play the economic game of not enough or too much.

When goodness and abundance are not being shared with those in honest need,,, they're simply wasted. Fact is,,, even our unemployed and welfare families could eat and live like kings and queens compared to our native friends who are born into starvation around the world. Yet, this money is spent on all the fun things, rather than a sensible, simple life. As observed by the Man Upstairs,,, when both rich and poor alike are allowed to be brought up in a simple, God-like fashion,, their ecological worth and spirited progressiveness are the same in any given career or birth-rite. Where all else has failed, and with what little time there is left,,, people should begin to think of why it is they were all put here in the first place,,,, otherwize, they'll never be able to grasp or experience such realities as astral travel, déjà vu, preventive medicine, self fulfill-ment, and eternal peace.

Only when the proper grains are eaten with the right vegetable, does this produce an energy surge throughout your personalized, galactic massouppulah,,, causing each and every cell to come alive with the harmonious etheric gasses so needed to be shared with your highly sensitized nervous system and dormant subconscious brain. When your machine is hoanin',, it's like "Ou" and "Ah" all the time. ii,,, when one does not know the truth of life while alive,, death will also have its uncertainties, dualities, and unkonkshusness.

When fed properly,,, the human cellular structure will always reflect, as does a light bulb. A proper balance of positive and negative energy is most necessary at this time,,, and it only takes seven weeks to honestly change and revitalize one's physical character and cosmic awareness. Having taken the initiative to do so,,, one can rejuvenate one's whole molecular structure within seven months into one which is more conducive to the universal, non-dualistic flow,,, and within seven years, one's spiritual immunity to old age, emotion, and sickness will be easily witnessed by all who know and love you. Only when it's working for you, will friends and loved ones have the chance and good fortune to do as well,, or better. One's comfort must finally be at peace with reality,,, rather than caught up in the wrongs and rights of it. People have to copy something of value in order to do better for themselves,,, especially if they want to experience a universal change throughout.

So many have bin heard to say,,, "The world is beyond saving", or,, "Let's party till the end". Well,,, I tend to agree to a point,, yet people can change, as have 47 million on the North American continent alone,,, and there are two ways to party. One is pseudo and self-destructive,,, while the other reflects one's ability to extend the constant happiness which flows from within. To feast, dance, and sing are all God-like characteristics when done in a true spirited fashion. Why,, it's bin said many a time in the Heavens,, "God can't wait to party and feast with his people".

"To dine own self, ye must be true". But foist: With how easily the governments could deploy their military mights for war,,, imagine what the great leaders, their countries, and companies could do with the help of all of these military giants and personnel when it would come to plantin', feedin', and properly distributin' all what's worth havin' to save face, honour, and eternal redemption. Machineries could be easily adapted somewhat, as do the ever-changing car manufacturers, soh's as to restructure the food industry before it's absolutely too late to change, by utilizing whatever common sense still remains. Think about it,,, what could be wrong about doin' something decent for a change? Imagine,,, for your gastronomic pleasure, they already have a chemically vitaminized polyester food supplement ready to market as the latest craze for all who have become too busy to cook. My God,,,, don't let this happen to you, cuz it ain't comin' from the Heavenly Kitchens. No one man or woman is responsible for this; it is but a hard and dirty lesson all have had to learn from. When the world shakes and the plug is pulled on the Beast,,, even the eleven or so who are allowed to think they own the world will be needin' proper help,,, because being up there in those satellites while the presidents are sent underground, ain't goin' to do them or the presidents no good when the Earth blows out of orbit. Before the time allotted for Kreashon comes to an end,, don't let anyone fool you to think otherwize,, because the world could easily feed and comfortably house seven billion people. ii,,, the killing and stealing from each other,, whether it be done legally or not,, must stop, and everyone should look at what people, rich and poor alike, are afraid to give up in exchange for what's being offered by the Great Family. Yawl know it don't make no sense the way it is,,, yet because those who are affected with a false sense of power haven't bin able to properly develop their digestive tract,,, their egos don't allow them to be simple, happy, and for real. They still argue and work for money instead of truth, while blaming others for all what's goin' wrong,, rather than doin' what they should really be doin' them-selves, their families, and their people.

Soh many people blame God for the pain and suffering goin' on in the world,,, when all along they should look more closely at what it is that they are into which lacks Godli-ness at grit levels. It takes real guts to admit what you're eating is doing the same thing to your government's blood-stream, konkshusness, arteries, and organs as well,,, being the reason they allow it to happen to the creeks, rivers, lakes, oceans, and air of our kreative module. The real value of such a worthwhile change comes about when you do it for yourself before it's too late to help the world to help itself honestly.

Folks,,, the people who own and run these giant cartels are dying of the same dreaded diseases you are,,, and I'm sure if they were given an honest chance for a new life,, they, including the devil himself, would want to help others so they can come to a final konkshus peace for ever after. As it stands,, they who run the governments and syndicates don't do better because they too are fooled by their own heracy,, thinking you really do enjoy what's being allowed to happen. They're all dying of the same diseases, as well as those who are movin' and groovin' out of sync with reality. Obviously,,, the aids needed are not the aids presently being spread throughout. Everybody, be they good or bad, right or wrong, strong or weak, rich or poor,, excluding no living being,, needs a proper diet. While alive,,, one cannot reach a wizened state when one is out of wak with the universal movement of it all. Those who run this thing called the Beast, over in Luxenburg, are all born to an Earth mother,, meanin', whether they be liked or not, the Great One's got to love 'em as well,,, while offering them the same equal chance as everyone else. Mind you,,, those of the Great Family are not too tickled pink about what the creators of this "Beast" are planning to do with that microscopic chip implant. On the other hand,, it's still not too late for them to use this monstrous machine to actually benefit man's kind, along with themselves, without having to actually implant that sick, six, six chip into man's hand or forehead. After they take over all the countries they have bankrupted to begin with, and have introduced the E.C.U. (European Currency Units) throughout,,, wouldn't it be nice to see these people in power honestly come to their senses, and honestly help those who paid so dearly to put them on top. Millions of good people will not take this chip implant, causing them to be enslaved to them who have it. My goodness,,, must it be so? Noh,,,, of course not,, because man has the power to change his destiny.

To be able to spiritually justify one's own character, along with all the rest, is the greatest achievement known throughout the universe. With a little honest, sincere effort from the good, bad, and ugly,,, such a holy impression like the world has never seen could be put into effect, through food consumption alone. ii,,, make love clean once again by sharing the unspoiled leftovers with those not so fortunate,, rather than plough it under because the market price is not right. Think about it,,, to the winner always goes the spoils,,, so with what little time there is left,, better to play fair and square,,, for rich or poor, high or all powerful,, ye are all in the same kettle of soup, heading towards the same engulfment. As I've been told by the Great Ones,,, there are several ways to sum up this here little kreashonal experiment,,, and for what it's worth,, those who believe they can be saved without having to die this time are correct,,, yet let it be known that there are no slaughter houses or beef joints aboard ship,, so best get used to a sensible diet while having both feet on the ground. Because sure as heck,,, if a massive pick-up does take place,,, they aren't gonna be pickin' up those who are going to kill the first deer they see and bar-be-cue it! Again, I repeat,,, one of the nicest ways the Great One could think to have it happen is if every great army were to plant and cultivate the Earth soh's as to feed the rich and poor alike a nutrishus, enlightening diet, prepared with the specific variables required,, allowing everyone the time, dignity, and peace to prepare for a joyous end to this erah. Why,,, with such an enactment,, I believe the Earth's populace could borrow itself enough time to allow all of those who died of starva-tion and warfare to come back as healthy babies and leave this place in such a manner more conducive to the God-like senses people were born to have and enjoy.

Regardless of the fact that an arrogant few might take the liberty to blow up the world,,, the Great Kreashonal Experiment of Humanity has been a success. Problem is,,, if it's allowed to blow,,, certain spirits will float to the surface, konkshus or unkonkshus of what hit them,,, yet they who caused and helped such a thing to happen shall remain sunk, soulless, and without awareness or reflection for ever after.

The Great One is no fool. All the other spirits, be they conscious or not,,, who cherished peace, truth, and simplicity with a common sense to it,, will be scooped up and revived to become the interesting characters worth having to share Heaven with in friendship for ever after. Incidently,, for what it's worth,,, once in Heaven, there are no more religious or athiizzoms,,, so best get used to the peace and oneness of it all from here first, reflective of your particular teaching. As explained in the book, "Alpha, Mu, and Omega",,, when the solid modules of human-type people were finally cloned during the grandearistic erahs of Alpha,,, the same Kreative Movement has continued to help everyone along through the Mu's, to this brief period of review,, ending that of the short erah of Omega. All throughout these times allotted for people's individualized development,, people have always been what they ate,, today being no different. Y'are what chew eat,,, and the truth of your actions and deeds reflects accordingly. Bee ye a scientist, alchemist, theosophist, to great white hunter,,, you're all fooling yourselves when you think that the toxic gasses which emanate from these modern, chemically treated foods are good for your hurting families.

Since yer hearts and minds be open,,, allow me to reveal some more startling facts about the false foods most people are condishund to believe in.

Remember when ice creams didn't have antifreeze or lice killer in them, and would melt to liquid, creamy substance in the sun. Now it just sits there like a glob. How about when beer didn't have some 80 odd chemicals in it, and one could smell an open bottle at 30 feet. Remember when bread had real substance with no wood fibres in it,,, and peanut butter and cheeses melted in your mouth,,, and fruits and veggies weren't being irradiated, and had no sulphide crystals sprayed on 'em. Remember when cookies were bought by the pound and eaten quick, or they would spoil within a week. Why,,, I remember when sugar and salt used to stick together in dampness. Now, I hear tell they bleach it with a borax type of stuff,,, and later when dried, they spray each granule with an emulgeon'd coating so's it don't stick no more. How about when fresh foods lost their colour and spoiled easily,,, and raspberry jams had real raspberry seeds in it. Well,,, after they learnt to bleach, colour, and assimilate real food products,,, the economy simply soared when a revolutionary new petrolium product called BHT, or emulsifire, came to be. It is also known throughout the world by a thousand different names,,, and it all comes from the spotless, inspected, bugless kitchens of the oil refineries. ii,,, it revolutionized the food and drug industries overnight,,, and now they can obtain insurance on their product when shipped and stored so long in warehouses throughout the land, or across the seas.

For some 80 years or so,,, man's been drilling for oil, and has developed such products as jet fuels, clothes, makeup, plastics, napalm, to axle grease and gunk. Now,,, with the billions of tons of stuff left over,,, what couldn't be utilized in any way, shape, or form,,,, this cold and heartless monstrosity created a food product for human consumpshun which more than merely retards spoilage,,, ii,,, amazingly, it builds up texture, fills in for bulk, and can be chemically assimilated to look like edible food. Yuk!! Why,, some cream whipped toppings have the same chemicals in them as do shaving creams,,, and some candies have the same chemicals as do their wrappers. Chocolate bars are now laced with paraffin wax along with the rest of the garbage put on and into them,, so they don't melt or sag in the sun or hands. For example,,, when thousands of pounds of fresh peanuts get their natural oils chemically extracted and sold as pure peanut oil,,, do you think for a moment that the thousands of pounds of devitaminized, grayish peanut pultch left over gets thrown away? Noh way, Jose!! This is when the 55-gallon drums of emulgeons are brought in from the back warehouse and are added to replace the oil,, along with colouring, icing sugars, stabilizers, flavourings,,, and then some approved forms of edible oils are reintroduced to make it look like real peanut butter once again. In truth,,, you would be feeding your child less chemicals if you gave them a piece of white styrofoam lathered with axle grease, instead of these spongy white breads shhmeeered with these particular kinds of assimilated peanut butter and other processed foods.

Throughout my travels abroad and my rewarding experiences at Philoxia,,, I have seen people cured from every
major disease known to man, including cancer, when caught
early enough. Only through diet, herbs, and spirited faith
working hand in hand, can these natural, healthy healing
methods work without fail. I have seen massive third-degree
burns painlessly healed within a few months without the need
for grafting, and afterwards no scar tissue remaining.   I
have seen three-quarters of an inch of finger grow back
totally anew, nail and all, to regular shape and size within
three months after it had been completely cut right off and
unable to be remounted. I have seen livers, kidneys, hearts,
stomachs, etc., all heal and function properly in people who
were given up for lost causes,,, simply because they started
to be fed properly, or had the strength to change to a common
sensed, alkaline diet on their own. The chemical pasifukay-
shun methods of modern society simply prelude the inevitable
surgery, where they must cut out the damaged organ,, never
knowing and caring enough to cure the reason why such
diseased parts came to be.

Most important,,, when the level of growing expanshon allows you to realize your body is a temple,,, you will
want to keep it as clean and as fit as possible, regardless
of age or social standing. In truth,,, there is no such
thing as Earthly perfection. Simply, to be clear minded, and
strong enough soh's as to be able to continue to supply your
families the material and spirited care needed at grit
levels, to sustain and remain as a konkshus entity for ever
after. Soh,,, with what grace and life there is left,,, do
for yourselves and your families what no one else or computerized system will ever care to do for you,,, thus resetting
the proper guidelines,, allowing others who might care to
learn, to do as well or better for themselves. It is your
right to do so,, and don't be so afraid to ask for more
things of real value.

Dang,,, I be sayen enough about what could be. It's
time to go for it,,, and in order to help make it a lot

tastier, easier, and more fun for everyone,,, allow me to introduce these wonderful people who have developed a marvelous recipe for life. It's one worth sharing with everyone, regardless of social standing. Like many who are readying themselves to partake in the miracle of miracles,,, they too are busily at work with their antiquated, respected works in medicine, music, and natural cuisine.

Having been gifted with a sense of why we are here,,, they have mastered and compiled a treasure house of exquisite recipes to be shared internationally with everyone. Besides knowing and loving God,,, life itself has no real substance until you've tasted and delighted in the real gastronomic bliss of it all. ii,,, from mother's milk onto the cream of nature's bussom,,, these talented friends of mine have not only mastered the ancient arts of cooking and preventive medicine through a tasty, nutritional diet,,, they are readying a song and dance routine what should put a tear and a smile onto the faces of everyone who encounters it. Such a joyful, constructive, meditative attitude is rarely experienced in this so called know-it-all age. These fine, hard workin', simple folk have done wonders with what they have learnt through experience, travel, and special teaching. This book is appropriately called "From Grits to Gourmet" because it manifests from the hearts of those who were train'd from the old school of sensible moderayshon in all things of relative value. It is designed to deal with the finer, more wizened details of the inner you,,, the one which has to acquire a taste for itself,, in order to qualify and truly understand the meaning of "As a child of God, ye shall reap accordingly".

Presently,,, there is a very good reason why thousands upon thousands of fine folks and their families keep returning to the kitchens and dining halls of Philoxia. It's because the food not only looks and tastes great,,, it is also fulfilling in more ways than one could imagine. It's also designed to please the great Western palate first,,, then onto the rest of the world, who are beginning to ready

for it as well. One of the nicest things I've ever heard
said about their cookery came from an old timer who frequents
their kitchens. "You know", he says,,, "I don't know what
ch'yawl got in this here food,, but it sure goes in good,
sits well,, and it comes out fantastic!!

Their ancient Pheylonian way of life is truly one
worth observing, bettering, keeping up to, or just rolling
along with the essence and principles of it... your own way.
Diet reflects the truth and depth to one's actual spiritual
perceptions. In other words,,, you don't really know the
silent joy of one hand clapping, nor the taste of real ice
cream,,, until your mode of character qualifies you to experience such phenomena. Who ever is heard to say that macrobiotic and other worthwhile vegetarian cuisines are dull and
unsatisfying, don't have their taste buds in tune,,, nor have
they bin fed proper. It takes the necessary oompf and practice needed to keep a meal well balanced as well as tasty.
Perhaps many were misguided by some who meant well yet
weren't quite ready enough to pass on such a bonafide ful-
fillment. This book of gastronomic pleasures has bin
designed by Iilah and Tawlia to make one proud of one's cuisine,,, be it served daily as a quick, efficient base of
loving nourishment at grit levels,,, or altered organically
in such a manner soh's as to present a delicious royal feast
for any occasion to family, friends, and relatives of all
sorts,,, be they conscious or not of who they really are, or
of what they eat.

Mes Amies,,,, tis time now to bid farewell,, and might I
wish all your spirits the peace your soul was born with.

                    Chaum and Bon Apetite,,,

                    Kjo Dindee

Cooking Abbreviations and Terms

ABBREVIATIONS

tsp.	- teaspoon	**ext.**	- extract
tbls.	- tablespoon	**grd.**	- ground
c.	- cup	**grt.**	- grate(d)
fl.	- flour	**ch.**	- chop(ped)
oz.	- ounce	**min.**	- minute(s)
lb.	- pound	**hr.**	- hour(s)
temp.	- temperature	**cl.**	- clove

COOKING TERMS

Most cooking terms are readily understood and self-explanatory. Here are definitions for any which may be new to you:

Singe-Frying

This is a technique that Iilah taught me which is designed to seal in the flavour with a tamari-flavoured crust. This enhances the natural flavour and gives everything a gourmet flare.

Vegetables:

To singe-fry vegetables,, sauté raw, sliced vegetables in a skillet with a little oil. Cook on a medium heat till vegetables are cooked, yet still retain a crispness. At this point, raise the heat, sprinkle with tamari, and cook, stirring frequently for 1-3 minutes more, depending on what you're frying. When nicely browned and the pan is dry, remove from heat.

To achieve the best effect with this method,, it is good to have no more than one layer (about 1/2 inch) of any one or combination of vegetables cooking.

Vegetables best suited for a singe-fry:

onions	celery	peppers
mushrooms	zucs	carrot slivers

Grains:

Similarly,, singe-frying grain is designed to enhance and seal in the flavour of the grains while adding a tamari taste. Useful primarily with seitan, tempeh chunks, or individually textured grains like crumbly buckwheat, crumbled three-grain (not ground) bulghur and rice.

In a skillet or wok, heat a little oil. When hot, add the grain and stir constantly till good and hot. Be sure to scrape the bottom of the skillet well. Tamari two or three times while cooking. That which cooks onto the bottom of the pan really adds a delicious flavour.

Steam-Frying

This is a more healthful way of frying vegetables using little or no oil. Start vegetables frying with a little oil and a spoonful or two of water,,, or just water. Cook with a cover till the vegetables are half cooked,, tender, yet still crisp. (Cooking with a cover produces moisture from the vegetables themselves.) Remove cover at this point, tamari lightly, and simmer till the vegetables are cooked dry.

Unlike singe-frying,, you can cook a larger quantity of vegetables (1/2 to 1-1/2 inches thick in a skillet) at one time.

Sauté

This means to fry in a skillet with a moderate amount of oil,, stirring as needed to prevent burning.

Steamed

Steaming usually applies to vegetable cooking. It means to cook in a stainless steel or bamboo steamer so the vegetables are not immersed in water. The vegetables are cooked by the rising steam. Always use a lid, or they will not cook properly and the pot will run out of water very fast.

Deep Fry

This means to cook in a deep enough quantity of oil so the vegetables float. Tasty, but usually heavy on the oil.

Tempura

This is a type of cooking that involves dipping vegetables or grain (tofu, tempeh, seitan, millet cubes, etc.) in a batter,, then deep frying them till browned.

Glossary of Terms for Vegetable Cutting

PREPARE:

This is a general term I have used often which means to wash, clean, peel, skin, remove any bad spots,, or whatever is logically needed to prepare a vegetable for cooking or eating.

CHOP:

Refers to using a knife to repeatedly cut a vegetable till it is the approximate size desired.

SLIVERS:

This refers to a very thin slice,, usually 1/16th to 1/8th of an inch thick.

LARGE GRATE:

Graters can be purchased in many sizes,, the most common being an 1/8" or 1/4" hole. The term "large grate" refers to one which has a 1/2" hole. This cuts vegetables into a 1/2" wide by 1/8" thick slice suitable for quick cooking in casseroles, soups, or for stir frying,, and in some cases, raw in salads. Carrots, zucchini, parsnips, beets, potatoes, diakon, squash, and turnips are the best suited to be used in this fashion.

REMOVAL OF SEEDS:

As a general rule,, people remove the seeds from vegetables such as squash, peppers, etc., because they are undigestible. Likewise,, people should remove tomato and cucumber seeds for the same reason. If eaten,, they are irritating to the stomach and intestines, plus they can get lodged in the appendix. It's best to not put in one end what simply has to come out the other.

ONIONS

How you cut an onion will determine if it has a sweet or bitter taste.

HALVED - Slice from top to bottom.

WEDGES - Lay onion halves face down
and cut in lengthwise
chunks. Ideal for
stew or
roasts.

THIN SLICES - Lay onion halves face
down. Cut across the
middle, then cut into
1/4" wide, lengthwise
slices. Ideal for
soup or frying.

DICED - Lay onion halves face down. Make a lengthwise cut
4/5ths of the way from the top towards the
bottom. Do not cut all the way through the
core. Then slice crosswise. Ideal
for salads, frying, or
casseroles.

DIAGONAL SLICES - Cut the vegetable at a 45° angle into
                  slices varying in thickness from 1/8" to
                  1", depending on what and how it will
                  be cooked. Ideally suited to
                  carrots, lohbok, zucchini,
                  parsnips, celery, burdock,
                  etc.

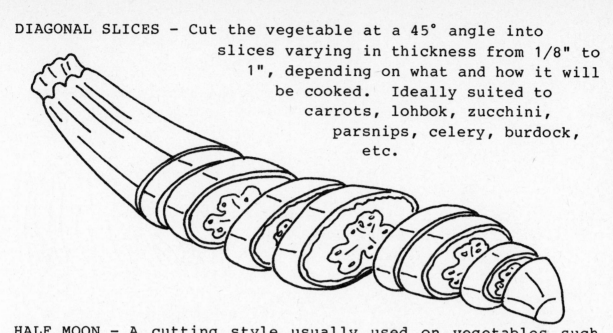

HALF MOON - A cutting style usually used on vegetables such
            as carrots, zucchini, parsnips, etc.   Cut
            vegetable in half lengthwise. Lay face down on
            the flat surface and cut straight across. Vary
            the thickness of each slice according to what you
            are making.

SHAVED - This is an interesting way of cutting any long type
         of vegetable. The shavings can be as thick
         or long as desired. Start cutting
         at the thin end and shave
         away from you as
         you would
         sharpen a
         pencil,
         rotating the
         vegetable
         with each cut.

SMASHED - This term is usually used in reference to garlic. It is an ideal way to prepare garlic when you need it pulverized very finely. Ideal for salad dressings, dips, soups, etc.

Slice each whole clove of garlic in 1/4" thick, crosswise pieces. Place 3 or 4 slices flat on a bread board close together. With your left hand hold the blade of a wide knife over the garlic,, sharp edge away from you. With a closed right fist, give the blade a good pound using the soft heel of your right hand.

Repeat till all is smashed,, then chop it lightly to break it up. This really brings the juice out of the garlic. You can use a garlic press, but this is quicker and doesn't dirty another kitchen tool.

QUARTERED - Refers to cutting vegetables lengthwise into four even sections.

Sometimes you may use quartered vegetables at their full length,, however, they are usually cut into 2" chunks.

Cut in this fashion for stews, casseroles, and for steaming.

Quartered vegetables may be cut in smaller pieces (1/4" to 1") for soups.

MATCHSTICKS - A method of cutting (julienne style) usually
used for carrots. Is very attractive and cooks
quickly.

Cut peeled carrots into 1/4" thick diagonals.
Stack 3 to 4 slices at a time and cut into
1/4" sticks.

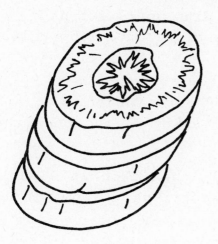
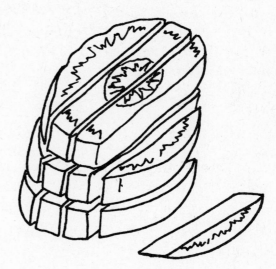

Kitchen Implements

Most kitchens which are cooked in daily have an assortment of different, necessary tools such as measuring cups and spoons, bowls, pots, pans, trays, graters, peelers, knives, etc.

These are a few additional items you may not have which are called for within some of the recipes in our book.

FLAME TAMERS: These are known by various names,, however, what they all do in general is deflect the direct heat to the pots they are placed under. Very useful for cooking foods which are prone to sticking such as porridge, whole grains, sauces, puddings, cream soups, etc. They are inexpensive and will pay for themselves by saving the first pot of rice which may otherwise have burned.

STEAMER: Steamers can be purchased that are made of stainless steel or bamboo. Either is sufficient. Ideally they are used for steaming vegetables,, a method which retains the flavour and nutrition better, as opposed to boiling,, however, they are very useful for reheating leftovers.

GRAIN GRINDER: A grain grinder is an inexpensive tool,, usually costing $24 to $39 for a good hand grinder. Having one allows you to mix and grind your own grain mixtures for porridge. It is also useful for grinding nuts and seeds or for refining some store-bought grains,, i.e., stone ground cornmeal is sometimes quite coarse and needs to be finer for some recipes.

MEAT GRINDER:

This may seem like an odd tool to be had in a vegetarian kitchen,, but it is an essential tool in producing the unique texture as described in our three-grain blend (page 67). It converts the crumbly texture of the grain to one that resembles and does everything that ground-round does. Meat grinders can be purchased for between $18 and $25. The different attachments which usually come with each one are useful for various purposes. An electric coffee mill is an alternative choice which is less expensive for a small family.

BLENDER AND/OR FOOD PROCESSOR

These are pricier implements,, yet they are invaluable for preparing many recipes. Blenders are best suited to prepare nut milks, sauces, puddings, beverages, dressings, etc.

Food processors are better to use when preparing items like dips, mayonnaise, and humus, because they have a thicker consistency and the processor handles this better. That's not to say you can't make these in a blender,,, you can,, you just have to do it in smaller batches. For blending grain, seeds, and nuts,, a blender will do a finer job than a processor will. If you can only afford one of these implements,, a blender is the better all-round tool.

SURIBACHI

This is a traditional Japanese kitchen tool used for grinding seeds,, particularly sesame seeds,, to make gomasio.

Suribachis can be purchased in macrobiotic oriented natural food stores and in Japanese food stores.

GRATERS

Graters of certain sizes are standard in most kitchens,, and I only bring it up here because there is a particular size of grater which we use frequently because it produces a thin, wide slice which is ideal for soup, stir frying,, or even for eating raw. The grater which produces this has a one-half inch wide hole.

Glossary of Foods

AGAR AGAR   A clear, colourless seaweed which is an excellent jelling agent. It has no taste, jells even at room temperature, and is much healthier than animal gelatin or pectin. Can help relieve constipation.

AMASAKE   A sweetener produced by fermenting cooked sweet rice with a Koji enzyme. This makes a thick grain gruel which may be used in baking, cooking, or even in drinks.

ARAME   A delicate seaweed that is blackish-brown and comes in long, thin, curled strands. Very nutritious and a rich source of minerals.

ARROWROOT FLOUR   A nutritious food high in minerals. It is a flour made from the beaten roots of a tuberous root grown in the southern states. Is used as a thickener, the same as you would use cornstarch or flour for desserts, soups, sauces, gravies, etc.

ADZUKI BEANS   Small, dark, red beans with a white spot. Primarily grown in Japan. Very nutritious and tasty.

BURDOCK   A long, dark root vegetable which is an excellent blood purifier.

CAROB POWDER   Resembles a chocolate or cocoa taste. It is produced by finely grinding the budded pod of a tree bearing a pod called "St. John's Bread". It is highly alkaline, a rich source of natural sugar which is low in starch and fat, plus high in minerals: calcium, potassium, phosphorous, iron, silicon, and magnesium.

DIAKON
A large, white Japanese radish. Delicious raw or cooked. Excellent in soups, niskimi, or stir fry.

DULSE
A red seaweed high in minerals and protein. It can be eaten fresh, dried, or powdered. In powdered form it can be used as a substitute for salt in dressings, soups, etc.

FLAX SEED
Untreated flax seed is high in unsaturated fatty acids and aids in the elimination of fatty acids. Is high in fibre and is beneficial to intestinal health.

GOMASHIO
A condiment made of roasted sesame seeds and sea salt, finely ground.

HONEY
A natural product from bees. It is twice as sweet as sugar and is high in minerals. Honey does not seem to cause tooth decay when consumed in its natural, unpasteurized form, having been harvested from bees which are not fed sugar. Honey is a nutritious, energized food,, while white, refined sugar is a poison.

HIZIKI
A dark brown (blackish), stringy seaweed native to Japan. It has a delicious flavour and has been likened to tasting like noodles. Very rich in minerals.

KASHA
Roasted, whole buckwheat groats.

KELP
A seaweed which grows in long, thin fromes. Usually eaten in powdered form. Has a salty

flavour and is useful in sauces, dressings, and casseroles.

KOMBU   A seaweed of the brown algae family. Grows in long, thin, wide streamers. It is the heartiest of the seaweeds and requires a longer soaking and cooking time. Useful in bean dishes, stews, and vegetable dishes.

KUKICHA   A healthful tea, traditionally Japanese, made from the roasted twigs of a three-year old bush.

KUZU   A starch made from the root of a plant which originally grew in Japan. It now grows abundantly in the southern States. It can be used as you would cornstarch. It is very alkaline and beneficial to health. (Also see Page 103).

LECITHIN   A natural food extracted from soybeans. It acts as an emulsifier and preservative in breads and other baked goods. Lecithin will break up and remove fat deposits within arteries and organs and reduce cholesterol. Is useful as a condiment (see page 309).

MALT   A sweetener produced from grains, usually barley. Made by converting its carbohydrate content into its natural sugar state.

MISO   A highly nutritious food product made of cooked soybeans, salt, and grains (usually rice, barley, or wheat),, which has been fermented with a special enzyme for anywhere from a few months to a year or so. Very high in minerals.

MOCHI	A food product made of cooked sweet rice which has been pounded and shaped into cakes or balls. Nutritious and tasty.
NIGARI	A by-product of sea salt used as the curdling agent when preparing tofu.
NORI	A very delicate, tasty seaweed which is harvested and processed into thin sheets. Used in sushi, nori rolls, soups, etc.
SEA SALT	Produced by vacuum drying sea water at low temperatures. Unlike commercial salt, sea salt contains all the natural minerals found in sea water, including a healthy proportion of calcium.
SEITAN	Wheat gluten which has been cooked in a tamari-ginger-kombu broth.
SOBA	Noodles made of buckwheat flour.
SURIBACHI	A ceramic bowl with a ridged inner surface used for grinding roasted seeds and other foods.
TAHINE	A pourable sauce made of roasted sesame seeds. An excellent food high in protein. It makes delicious sauces to serve with vegetables and grains.
TAMARI	Traditional soy sauce which is made by fermenting a blend of cooked soybeans, wheat, and sea salt for a year or more.
TEKKA	A delicious, hearty condiment made from slow-cooking miso and vegetables for a long time.

TOFU   A curded, pressed food product made from
                soybean milk. A good source of protein which
                is very nutritious and easy to digest. Also
                very versatile and useful as a substitute for
                eggs, cheese, cream, and oil in many recipes.

UMEBOSI   See page 103 .
PLUMS

WAKAME   Kelp-like seaweed which is delicate and cooks
                quickly with a short soaking time. Very good
                for soups. Is also very good powdered.

A Note about Ingredients

Everyone varies their standards of what they eat in accordance to their own conscience and knowledge. You should strive to use the best ingredients available. Here are some everyday products with some alternatives worth considering:

GENERALLY USED	PREFERRED	REASONS
Commercial Oils	Cold Pressed Oils	Commercial oils are generally extracted using heat processes which alter the digestability of the oil and diminish the nutritional value. Other processes using chemicals to break down the food and separate the oil devitalizes the product and leaves chemical residues which are detrimental to health. Cold pressed oils retain much of the natural properties they have in their whole state.
Soy Sauce	Tamari or Shoyo	The latter is made from soybeans, wheat, and salt. It is aged to produce a naturally fermented, flavourful product. Commercial soy sauce is oftimes manufactured using processed salt, caramel, roasted wheat, artificial flavourings, plus other chemicals to preserve it. Most of

GENERALLY USED	PREFERRED	REASONS
		these have never seen a soybean.
White Vinegar	Apple Cider Vinegar, Brown Rice Vinegar, Ume Plum Vinegar, Wine Vinegar	Commercial white vinegar has no nutritional value and is very detrimental to your health because of the bleaching stages and other processes it goes through. The other vinegars are of a more wholesome source and are naturally produced. They are beneficial to general health with moderate use.
Cornstarch	Arrowroot	Cornstarch is made from a vegetable which is grown very chemically and is processed in such a fashion that it has little or no nutritional value. Arrowroot, on the other hand, is nutritious,, high in calcium and minerals,, plus it is not a refined product.
Gelatin	Agar Agar	Commercial gelatin is generally an animal-based product. Remember the old grey mare who gets sent to the glue factory? Well, they also made gelatin out of her. Agar agar is

GENERALLY USED	PREFERRED	REASONS
		simply a clear, colourless, tasteless seaweed which works just as well.
Commercial Baking Powder	Alum-Free Baking Powder	Baking powder is not a healthy product to be used a lot, either way. The latter is, however, minus the alum which creates an aluminum oxide when cooked and ingested. This is very harmful and collects in the system, as it is near impossible to eliminate.
Artificial Flavours	Pure Extracts	Pure extracts are just as they say, while artificial flavours are doubling as such, when in reality they are the same chemicals that are used as textile and leather cleaners (pineapple flavouring), as part of rubber cement (nut flavours), as an oil paint solvent (banana flavour), a product used as lice killer (vanilla), a flammable liquid used in antifreeze and paint removers (emulsifier used to replace eggs), a nitrate solvent (strawberry flavour), and many more.

GENERALLY USED	PREFERRED	REASONS
Canned and Frozen Vegetables	Fresh Vegetables	Everyone knows that fresh vegetables are certainly the best source to choose from,, however, many people assume that frozen vegetables are almost as good,, which is basically true except for the fact commercially frozen produce is sprayed with an emulsified product to keep the individual pieces separate and to put a gloss to em. Canned vegetables are usually overcooked,, hence they have little nutrition,, plus they can have any number of chemicals, additives, sugars, and unnecessarily high salt contents.
Iodized Salt	Sea Salt	Commercial salt is chemically bleached and is then sprayed with emulsifier to coat each granule so that the granules do not stick together in dampness. The source of commercial salt is void of the natural minerals which are present in sea salt. The need to synthetically iodize salt wouldn't be necessary if people ate a little seaweed each day.

When buying any prepared foods such as bottled or canned sauces, pickles, fruits, juices, etc.,, be a cautious consumer. There are a fair number of new brands available on the market, both in natural and commercial food stores, which offer fairly unadulterated, pure products.

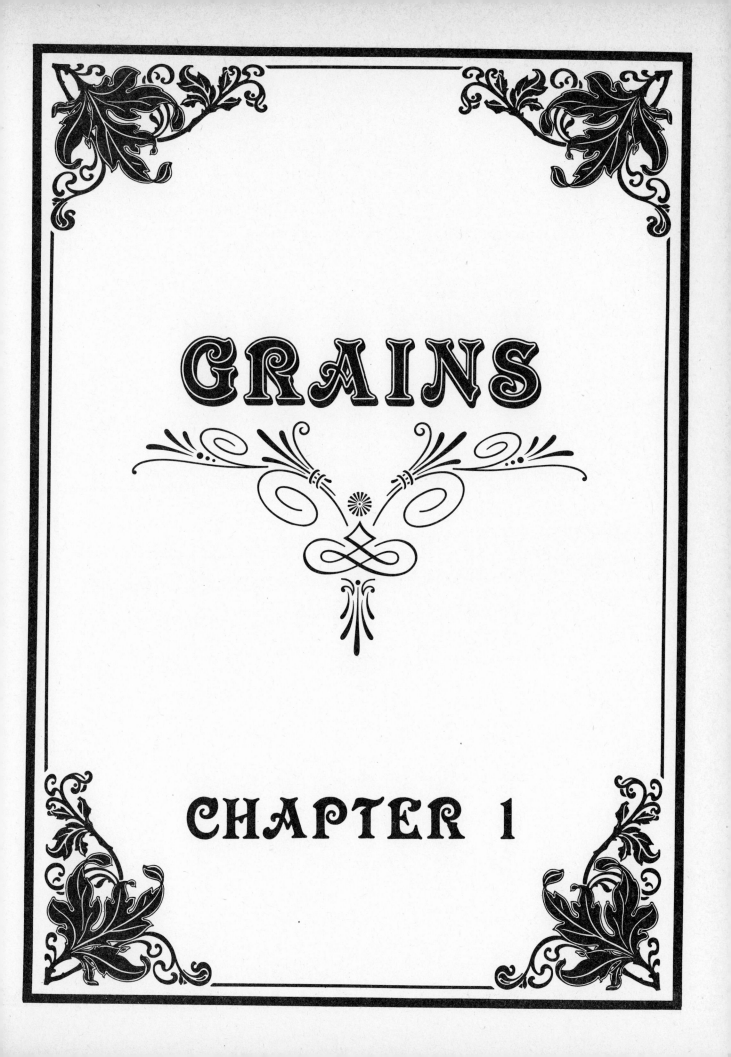

GRAINS

CHAPTER 1

Grains

Grits and Grains

For the millennium of man's time upon this earth, fresh grains and vegetables have been the mainstay of most civilizations. The ancients lived to be thousands of years old on such a diet which was of a pure and unadulterated source. Meats, fowl, and fish are foods which man evolved to eating. The primary reason for this change of diet was due to the cataclysmic changes which took place on earth (see Alpha, Mu, and Omega, Chapter 4 ,, for more details). During these traumatic times, the cultivation of grains had been severely disrupted and the natural and cultivated vegetation was of a scarcity. Out of necessity, humans reverted to consuming animals, birds, and fish,, all of which could survive on the more menial forms of vegetation and insects.

Even as natural wild growth and cultivated crops were re-established,, these alternative diets were maintained, partly out of habit, but also out of lack of knowledge.

Nowadays,, about two-thirds of the world's people still rely on grain as the main staple of their diet,, accompanied by fresh or preserved vegetables, supplemented with fish, fowl, and meat on occasion,, along with seasonal fruits.

The other third is represented by the more civilized countries of the North American and European continents, and most major cities of the so called "third world" countries. In these societies,, beef, pork, poultry, dairy, and processed food products are the main staples. Grains are primarily consumed in the form of fancied, easy to serve cereals,, and bleached, emulsified, commercial breads. Each of these products are bleached, refined, and devitalized to the point where the government insists upon the use of chemical supplements in order to assimilate a nutritious product.

In learning to eat a whole grain, natural diet,, one has to come to a completely new understanding of grains and what grain represents in your daily intake. Grain is the basic cement foundation and structural fortitude needed to maintain our uprooted beings. All the other necessary foods such as fresh veggies, nuts, and fruits are what keep the electrical and water systems of our cosmic structure in working order.

It is surprising how many vegetarians don't even understand how important grains are,, or what constitutes a "whole grain food". Eating whole grain bread and granola each day does not supply the body with the energy one can derive from a properly prepared meal using millet, tempeh, brown rice, tofu, buckwheat, etc.

We really are what we eat, and grains are the very stepping stones which lead back to this common sensed way of eating. The principles behind this way of eating have many different names and technicalities to express the balance one can derive from understanding foods. They are called positive and negative, yin and yang, acid and alkaline. In simplicity, relevant to grains,, I have heard Iilah explain to people, "If you weigh that which you have on your plate visually, and see approximately 50% cooked whole grains and 50% vegetable, be they fresh and/or cooked,, varied daily according to the season and your habitat,,, then that's good enough". The simplicity of this balance has no high falutin technicalities to it.

Some grains are suited to be eaten more in the fall and winter time,, while others are better as spring and summer foods. Grains such as short grain brown rice, tempeh, oats, wheat, rye, and pasta create much more body heat when eaten and are therefore more beneficial to eat during the colder time of the year. Millet, tofu, long grain brown rice, barley, cornmeal, etc. are lighter, cooler to digest, and better during the summer months. Each can be eaten in all the seasons,, but the frequency should reflect the time of year.

The specific properties of each grain will be brought out as we go over them.

In this chapter we would like to acquaint you with the many different grains and how to properly cook them so your family and friends will be delighted with the variety of meals you can prepare. Once you have mastered the basic preparations of these grains, you can easily make any of the recipes within this book, plus many others which will come from your own imagination.

Before we start,, a couple of notes about grains and beans in general.

1. They should always be well rinsed,, usually 2 to 4 times, or until the water is clear. (Bulghur is the exception because it is already par cooked). If time allows,, soak grains before cooking (4 to 24 hours). This reactivates the live energy lying dormant in all grains.

2. Always buy whole grain,, preferably organic. Look for clean, uniform, and properly hulled grain.

3. Some grains such as millet, legumes, and beans sometimes have small stones. Look quickly before washing.

4. Grains should be stored in sealed buckets or jars,, preferably kept in a cool, dry place, out of direct sunlight.

5. Unlike organic vegetables and fruits which are often very hard to find and are usually expensive,,, organic grains are available in most natural food stores for just a little more than what

the others sell for. Eating organic grains helps to counterbalance what you can't get away from in store-bought produce.

6. Each mouthful of cooked grains should be well chewed,, from 30 to 50 times. The initial stage of digestion takes place in the mouth where you break up and masticate your food, mixing it with the natural saliva. This aids and prompts easy digestion once the food gets to your stomach.

7. Grains in general are high in sodium, phospherous, natural carbohydrates,, and are an excellent source of B vitamins. They contain six of the eight essential amino acids. The other two are supplied by vegetables, legumes, and soaked and germinated nuts and seeds.

Before we get into cooking each grain,, I would like to delve into the particular health benefits of each whole grain.

Millet

Millet is the most alkaline of all grains and is a good source of protein. Yellow millet is excellent for the nervous system and mental fatigue, it aids the digestive system, and helps repair gastro-intestinal problems.

Millet is rich in Vitamin A and B complex, phospherous, magnesium, iron, manganese, silicone, and florine. The stomach and spleen are benefited the most by the consumption of millet because of its alkalizing effect.

Rice

Rice is the most balanced grain and is an easily digested starch beneficial for building overall good health. A good food source for people in a weakened condition. It has a high B complex content which calms the nervous system and can help overcome allergies. Rice used regularly in your diet can lower blood pressure, diminish arteriosclerosis, and eliminate toxins and poisons from the body. Rice is ideal as a main dish,, in desserts, sauces, etc.

Barley

Barley is primarily a fall food, yet can be eaten in moderation throughout the year. It is easily digested, imparts strength and endurance, and creates much heat and body energy. It contains Vitamin B and B2 and is beneficial for the lungs and intestines. It is helpful for people with weak digestion. Barley is used in soups, main grain dishes, breads, and in making barley miso.

Corn

Corn is primarily a summer grain. It is rich in calcium, Vitamins B, C, A, F, and E. Corn is beneficial for the small intestines, as it aids digestion and the heart because it imparts good vitality and develops rich, red blood. It also helps build strong bones, teeth, and muscles. Many civilizations have thrived on a main staple of corn for centuries. Because of corn's natural sweetness, it creates quick energy and promotes endurance. Corn can be eaten on or off the cob,, in soup or porridge, as mamalega or in bread.

Rye

Rye may be used in moderation year round in breads or porridge,, however it is primarily a spring food.

Rye strengthens and purifies the gall bladder and liver. It improves circulation, cleans blood vessels, tones muscle, and imparts high energy and endurance. It is also low in gluten.

Wheat

Wheat is a year-round grain which is high in protein and gluten. It has the highest vitamin and mineral content of all grains. The "germ" in wheat is particularly high in Vitamin E, good for your heart and for endurance. In general,, wheat is beneficial to the liver and gall bladder.

Many people find they have an allergy to wheat. This is usually caused by improperly functioning liver, kidneys, and intestines. This may be caused by a system filled or toxified with milk, cheese, fats, and sugars. Wheat eating cultures who have a dairy free diet with little fatty foods and no sugar, experience no such allergy.

Durham Wheat

This is a wheat also, which has a golden colour and is larger than whole wheat. This grain does not have the gluten as does wheat,, making it ideal for people with wheat allergies.

When ground to a flour,, it has a golden colour and is as equally useful for making bread, buns, etc.

Buckwheat

Buckwheat is primarily a winter grain, as it imparts much heat and high energy. It is a good blood builder,, rich in minerals and vitamins (particularly Vitamin C),, and is very beneficial on the kidneys and bladder.

It has the highest protein count of all grains, plus contains a high quantity of lysine, an amino acid which makes it comparable to the nutritive protein value found in animal foods.

Buckwheat is high in manganese which builds good posture by strengthening nerves and muscles. It is also important for metabolism and the control of the reproductive system.

In general,, it helps balance blood quality, has a calming and relaxing effect,, and can help overcome environmental radiation poisoning and anemia.

Buckwheat can be eaten in cereals, main course meals, and in noodle form.

Oats

Oats can be eaten year round,, however they are primarily a fall and winter food. They help eliminate stored proteins and toxic wastes from the body, and are a valuable food in cases of sterility, sexual impotence, underactive thyroid gland, and obesity.

Oats are high in silicone which add to one's healthy appearance (sparkling eyes, skin, hair, strong and healthy nails). The also have a beneficial effect on the lungs and intestines.

Oats are popular in porridge, granolas, cookies, and breads.

MILLET, THE GOLDEN GRAIN

Without a doubt,, millet is one of the most exciting and rewarding grains to use in any natural cookery. First of all,, it is an exceptionally good tasting grain,, as well as being the most alkalinizing whole food known to man.

Here at Philoxia we use it daily within many combinations. It is an excellent source of iron, calcium, and protein,, and can be used a thousand and one different ways. It has a natural, aromatic sweetness to it,, allowing it to also be used as a tasty, nutritious breakfast cereal, with little or no sweeteners,, except some fresh fruit or currants.

We have used this grain to make four, five, and six course meals,, beginning with hors d'oeurves, cream'd soups,, onto several main courses, with sauces, and an array of desserts, from puddings to creamy pastries.

Why,, in Guatemala,, we were able to purchase millet still in its kernel,, and we made some of the best popped millet you ever tasted. It was just like popcorn, except it was only about one-quarter of an inch big. It is a peasant food,, yet throughout our world travels, we have learned that the ultimate gourmet dishes worth eating all originated in the small peasant, or gypsy villages,, only to be found later, as the main course, in the exclusively designed Auberges of the city dwellers.

Once you have acquired the taste and use of this grain,, it alone can change your life for the better,, in countless ways. As Iilah mentioned,, when the Great One sculptured and created us on earth,, He did not use a mound of dead animal flesh,, nor did he use an acidic substance. He made man an alkaline being, and gave us the necessary foods to maintain this highly calibrated alkalinity. Acid, chemikilled foods bring upon hypertension in children and adults,, along with

52

every other disease known to man,, which later stimulates one's aggression and hostility towards one another,, regardless of age and upbringing.

We have seen rheumatic and arthritic pains, diabetes, allergies, skin disease, piles, etc., etc., all come to an acceptable tolerance level within months,, when these people went to a natural diet, using millet as one of their main staples. As well,, when children are brought up with this grain,, they grow to be far healthier, wiser, and attentive to reality and common sense.

Millet is a multi-seasonal grain, suitable for eating summer and winter.

Before we get down to cooking,, let me fill you in on a few things about millet:

1. Always have the water boiling before you add the washed grain. If added while the water is cold,, the millet is liable to burn because it settles on the bottom of the pot.

2. The method of cooking millet that I am about to explain is designed to achieve a particular texture of grain that is firm and sliceable when cooled. This texture is necessary for a number of the recipes within this book and is much more suitable to the palate of newcomers to this type of food, because it has much more body. This method makes it easier to cook the grain completely and avoids the problem of sticking.

3. Millet that is fully cooked on a stove top burner is very prone to sticking. Also,, the texture of the finished product is porridge-like when cooled. It is soft textured and watery.

MILLET

To cook millet, we use a stainless steel pot which has no handles so it can go from the stove top into the oven. It is simpler and saves dishes.

Bring to a boil in a 2 qt. pot:

    6 c. water
    ½ tsp. salt

Wash and drain:

    2 c. hulled millet

When the water is boiling,, add the millet. Reduce the heat and simmer with a lid for 20 min. Stir occasionally. (Use a flame tamer).

Preheat your oven to 350°.

After about 20 min., you will notice that the grain begins to 'crack open'. (It is no longer in smooth, round balls). This is the point at which millet starts to stick. Stir well and cover. Place in the oven and bake for 30 minutes.

When the grain is slightly crusted and firm to the touch, it is cooked enough. Remove from the oven and let cool, then refrigerate.

It is best to prepare this grain while doing your morning food preparation or the night before so it is properly cooled by the time you need to use it.

When cooled, millet can be sliced for millet steaks, (page 261), diced as in 'millet cubes a'la veggies', (page 263), or crumbled and spiced to be used in numerous other ways.

Never pressure cook millet.

For breakfast ideas, check 'millet porridge' in the cereal section.

BOILED MILLET

Millet may be cooked on the stove top till it is completely cooked, yet, as I mentioned, you must be careful it doesn't burn. The amount of water you use will give two completely different textures.

Soft Texture:

Boil in the same proportions as you would for baked millet ,, 3 to 1 and use the same procedure. Rather than removing the millet from the heat when the 'millet balls' open ,, continue cooking on a very low heat using a flame tamer. Stir often and remove from the heat as soon as the majority of the water is gone.

Millet is quite good this way ,, however it is like a very thick porridge. To put a "plop" of this on a supper plate will not have as much appeal as a 'millet steak', unless you have acquired a taste for it.

Crumbly Texture:

Cook as you would for the above texture using a proportion of 2 parts water, 1 part millet.

Cook till the water is gone.

This is less likely to stick with the smaller quantity of water ,, because the millet doesn't develop as much cream. When cooked, this will have a fluffier texture of well opened yet individual millet balls. This may have a slightly chalky taste depending on the type of millet.

Eat as is or cool and reheat later by steam frying or in a casserole with other cooked ingredients.

A Bit About Rice

Rice, which is a balanced, acidic grain, is invaluable when used in harmony with an alkaline diet. It is primarily a southern hemisphere grain and should be second or third on your list of basic foods. It other words,, in the winter months it should be eaten no more than three or four times a week,, yet during the summer months,, you could quite easily double the weekly intake, without reprocussions.

There are many kinds of rice available which should be taken into account. Never use any kind of commercial quick cook or converted rice products. They are not only valueless,, they are detrimental to your health. In the natural lines of rice, you have:

> Short grain brown rice
> Long grain brown rice
> Basmati rice
> Wild rice
> Sweet rice

Each of these are very nutritious and healthy. During different seasons of the year, some are better suited than the others.

Short Grain Brown Rice

This is the best rice for the fall and winter months. Because of its compact structure, it adds more vitality to your system and produces more heat energy which is needed at that time of year. This is a hearty tasting rice with a nut-like flavour.

Long Grain Brown Rice

Long grain brown rice is more conducive to warmer spring and summer months. It will give the vitality needed to balance a summer diet which is generally lighter.

Basmati Rice

Basmati rice is a particularly tasty strain of long grain brown rice and is grown in India. Although it is a balanced and nutritious grain, it doesn't have the quality of a short grain brown rice. It can be purchased in brown or white form. Look for the brown. It is an ideal rice for fried rice, paella, etc.

Wild Rice

This is considered the queen of the natural rices. In actuality, it is a seed,, not a rice. However,, taste and texture wise,, it beats them all. Being that it is so expensive, it is generally used only for special occasions,, so regardless of what time of year it is,, bon appétité!

RICE

There are basically two different ways to cook rice. Boiled or pressure cooked. Here is the general method for each.

Boiled Rice

The trick to boiling brown rice properly and not having it stick and burn is to not stir it at all. Stirring disrupts the natural boiling channels which are set up from the beginning.

Combine in a saucepan:

4 c. water   ½ tsp. salt

2 c. washed rice (short or long grain)

Bring to a boil and turn down to a simmer, cover with a lid.

When the water level has cooked down below the level of the top of the rice, lower the flame more and put a flame tamer under the pot to prevent scorching.

Simmer with a lid till all the water is gone. To see when the water is gone, slide a wooden paddle down thru the middle to the bottom. Push gently to one side to observe just how much water remains. When the bottom is dry, remove from the heat.

The above proportions will make a well cooked rice which has a slightly sticky texture. This rice is ideal for serving fresh, re-steamed or in a casserole.

To have a less sticky rice, remove the lid and aerate the rice to allow the steam to escape or turn the rice into a large bowl.

Depending on what you want to prepare with the rice will determine what alterations you make in the water proportions.

To make a rice which is fluffy and is less starchy, cook:

    3½ c. water   ½ tsp. salt
    2 c. washed rice

This will produce a rice which has a better texture for making fried rice or for eating fresh if you enjoy the chewier texture of brown rice.

To produce a creamier rice which is well suited to making rice balls, rice pudding and sauces, use:

    4½ c. water   ½ tsp. salt
    2 c. washed rice

The extra water allows the rice granules to open more, producing a creamier consistency.

This will hold together better for rice balls, will blend to a smoother sauce and taste sweeter as well.

PRESSURE COOKED RICE

The advantage to pressure cooking rice is it "cracks" the grain and does a more thorough job of cooking it. This does not mean boiled rice is not well cooked, just to a different degree.

Most pressure cookers are large and you will have better results if you use a double batch of any of the above types of rice.

Add washed rice, water and the salt to the pressure cooker. Bring to a boil uncovered and simmer for 2~3 minutes. Seal pressure cooker and put steam nozzle on. When the pressure is up, set your timer for 40 minutes.

Let the pot 'shoosh' strongly for 5 minutes. Then place a flame tamer under the pot and adjust the flame to where the pressure is 'shooshing' gently. Allow to cook till the timer goes off. Then remove from the heat and let the pressure subdue before loosening the top.

Pressure cooking grain is a little tricky as you can't look to see when all the water is gone. As you get accustomed to it, you may find 5 minutes more,, or less, is better,, or that the flame should be a little higher or lower.

With practice, your nose can tell you what your eyes can't see. Try this experiment. Within the last 10 minutes of cooking, lift the steam nozzle fractionally so you get a wiff of the steam. Note the aroma and repeat once or twice more till the timer goes off. When you open the pot, take note of the degree to which the grain is cooked. If still watery cook a little longer the next time and notice the change in smell that the extra 5 or 6 minutes of cooking produces. Using this method,, you will know if the rice has run out of water in less than 40 minutes. One whiff can save you from scorching a pot of grain.

STEAMED RICE

As an alternative to cooking fresh rice every time ,, we often cook enough for a few meals and have some steamed rice and vegetables a day or two later.

Steam heating rice keeps it moist and soft, plus it makes it fluffy. The best way to steam heat rice is in a bamboo or stainless steel steamer. Both are readily available through numerous types of stores.

Since our taste buds have become accustomed to the more subtle flavors of plain grain ,, we are often quite content to have a nice, simple meal of steamed grain and vegetables , accompanied with a sauce (hot or cold), salad and some interesting condiments.

This is also a quick , easy way to prepare a meal from leftovers. Simply put precooked rice (or even rice balls) on the bottom of the steamer. Arrange leftover vegetables and/or sauce on top of the rice and steam together.

WILD RICE

Considered to be the "queen of rice", wild rice is actually from the seed family. Because of this, it needs to be cooked differently.

The proportion for cooking should be:

4 parts water   a little salt
1 part rice (washed)

It should be boiled on a flame tamer with a cover till all of the water is gone. The rice should be fluffy and each granule should be split.

Rice, From the Outside In

Iilah has assisted many people by using cooked short grain brown rice and/or chew'd, raw short grain brown rice as a healing agent for both internal and external applications, with great success. Mind you,, this should not be attempted without masterful guidance. To relieve agonizing back pains due to kidney or infectious liver ailments,, we applied steaming hot ginger compresses. Afterwards, we put a well cooked, mushy rice and ginger powder back-pack on the lower area and wrapped the patient up in cotton and plastic for the night. Come morning,, the improvement was miraculous.

By properly applying these methods, we have cured the worst cases of infectious hepatitis within 24 to 48 hours, as opposed to the customary procedure of a two to three month quarantine.

Another example of this grain's ample medicinal properties was demonstrated when we cured the worst case of jungle staff infection ever seen,, after all else had failed,, both organic and chemical. This was done by applying a cream made of soaked, but raw, short grain brown rice and almonds. Each mouthful was chewed with one's own saliva till it formed a smooth, thick cream. This was then applied to the infection, and bandaged in place.

The combination of the well chewed rice masticated with the saliva creates a mixture that combats the infection by neutralizing, then drawing it out. Overnight, this cured what weeks of other efforts had not. Iilah has used this raw brown rice as an internal cleansing agent for various different reasons.

People who have eaten a processed, chemikilled diet for 15 to 30 or 40 years of their lives, have accumulated quite a stockpile of toxins and substances which the body cannot rid itself of because of the constant input of more.

When these people switch to a natural,, organic diet with a proper balance of foods,,, the body is then allowed to clean house. If the change of food is handled wisely and in proper balance, these toxins are released through the elimination channels. However,, due to the extent of the build-up,, sometimes the toxins need to be released more rapidly. This is where people sometimes develop rashes or open sores,, usually in the extremities, like your feet, hands, or around the armpits or groin. Some people assume this is a reaction to eating these different foods, rather than realizing it is the new foods which are allowing the old foods to be released. This condition of elimination is not critical,, however it does need to be taken care of.

Iilah has assisted many people with this exact condition. Zabro, Iilah's father, was faced with this about 7 or 8 months after he and Shanola had changed their diets. Both his hands broke out in a condition which assimilated the same texture that W.C. Fields' nose used to look like. Iilah had him soak his hands in a hot ginger bath for 1 hour. Iilah then sprinkled some ginger powder and cayenne pepper on each hand, front and back. Then, he packed brown rice completely around each hand. (The rice was cooked till quite soft and creamy,, then cooled to where it was hot, yet cool enough to leave a finger knuckle deep, without it being uncomfortable.) The rice was held in place by cloths and was then wrapped in plastic. It was really quite humourous, as Zabro looked like he was ready to box with someone. Plus,, when he had to go to the bathroom,, it presented a bit of a predicament when Shanola kiddingly refused to help (she finally did, though).

This was applied in the evening and was left on all night. When it was removed in the morning,, the change was phenomenal. By that evening, his hands were less inflamed and healing. The process was repeated, and by the next day, it was gone.

The hot ginger bath opens all the pores to allow the toxins out, and the rice acts as a drawing and healing agent.

BUCKWHEAT
(A NORTHERN GRAIN)

Buckwheat is a nutritious grain high in fibre and vitamins.

It is an excellent winter food with a unique flavor all its own.

Buckwheat can be bought whole or cracked, raw or roasted. It is considered an acidic grain.

Here are two methods of cooking buckwheat which will give you completely different textures to work with.

SOLID TEXTURE

This method uses whole buckwheat, either raw or roasted.

Bring to a boil:

    6 c. water
    1 tsp. salt

Wash and add:

    2½ c. whole buckwheat

Simmer on a low heat using a flame tamer and stir frequently. Cook till the kernels are soft and all the water is gone.

This is tasty served fresh as a hot gruel, with tahini - miso, cream sauce, etc., or you can let it cool and slice it as you would 'millet steaks' (page 261).

BUCKWHEAT
CRUMBLY TEXTURE

This method uses raw buckwheat (unroasted) in whole groats or cracked form.

Cooking buckwheat in this way will create a crumbly grain which is slightly chewy. The ideal texture for Kasha and Bow Ties.

Bring to a boil:	small	large
6 c. water	4	8
1 tsp. salt	2/3	1½

Meanwhile, beat and set aside.

3 eggs	2	4

In a dry skillet or wok, roast:

3 c. buckwheat	2	4

Stir constantly with a steel spatula till grain is slightly roasted and quite hot. Pour egg mixture onto the grain while stirring. Keep stirring. At first it will be very lumpy,, but as you continue stirring, making sure to scrape the bottom well, each grain becomes more separate.

When the whole mixture is crumbly, pour the grain into the boiling water.

Reduce the heat to a low simmer, cover and cook till the grain is dry.

Remove the lid, stir up the grain slightly and let cool.

Check the breakfast cereal section for other delicious uses of buckwheat in its whole and ground forms.

3 Grain Blend

Lilah has shown where this hearty grain mixture has endless possibilities,, from hearty snack foods on down to gourmet heart throbs fit for the family banquet.

When cooked properly, the texture of this grain can be made into everything from hamburgers to meatloaf onto a finely-grained sandwich loaf.

This makes a medium sized batch, approximately 8 cups,, however, when you have mastered this texture, you may want to make a double batch as it keeps well in the fridge for 4~6 days and can be used to make numerous dishes.

Using a pot which goes from stove to the oven, boil:

> 6 c. water   1 tsp. salt

Wash and add to the boiling water:

> 1 c. millet (washed)

Turn grain down to a rolling boil. Stir occasionally. Preheat oven to 350°.

When the millet granules appear to be well open and the liquid creamy (approx 20~30 minutes of cooking). Turn off the heat and add:

> 1 c. bulghur (medium grit)
> 1 c. cracked buckwheat (whole will
>   suffice if you don't have cracked)

Stir till well mixed. The texture should be like a thick, coarse porridge.

Add a lid and place in the oven, and bake for 30~40 minutes. The grain should feel firm to the touch when cooked enough. Remove from the oven, let cool to room temperature and then refrigerate.

2 Grain Blend
(makes approx. 8 cups)

This grain mixture is similar to our 3 grain blend, yet it is lighter in color and flavor. It is more suitable to such delicately flavored dishes as paté, habitant tourtier, zausages, etc.

The method used for this recipe is the same as the 3 grain blend.

Bring to a boil:

    6 c. water   1 tsp. salt

Wash and add to the boiling water:

    1¼ c. millet (washed)

Preheat the oven to 350°.

Simmer on a low heat, with a cover. Stir the millet occasionally. Cook till the millet balls are well opened. (approx. 20~30 minutes).

When cooked, remove from the heat and add:

    1½ c. bulghur

Stir well, cover and bake for 30~40 minutes.

Remove from the oven, cool and then chill.

In some recipes, it calls for this 2 grain to be made with cracked buckwheat in place of bulghur. This makes a darker, heartier flavored grain.

BULGHUR

(makes approx. 5 cups)

Bulghur is a quick and easy grain to prepare as it is already cooked.

Bulghur is made by pressure cooking whole wheat kernels. It is then dried and cracked to various sizes.

Bulghur is not the most nutritious or valuable grain compared to most, however it is a good mixing grain and is ideal for tabouli.

For most purposes, medium grit bulghur is fine.

When cooked, this grain has a crumbly, individual texture.

Bring to a boil:

    4 c. water   ½ tsp. salt

When boiling, add:

    2 c. bulghur

Simmer with a lid till the grain is dry and fluffy. As with rice, do not stir it,, just check through the center to see when the water is gone.

Barley

Pressure Cooked:

Wash and soak (if possible)

    2 c. whole barley groats
    5 c. water

Add to the pressure cooker:

    barley and water
    1 tsp. salt

Bring to a boil. Add the lid and pressure nozzle. When the pressure comes up, place on a flame tamer, turn down to a simmer and cook for approx. 40 minutes.

Remove from the heat and let the pressure go down on its own. Remove the lid and stir the grain. Serve or let cool and refrigerate.

Boiled Barley

Wash and soak (if possible) :

    2 c. whole barley groats
    6 c. water

Place in a pot :

    barley and water
    1 tsp. salt

Bring to a boil. Place on a flame tamer and turn down to a simmer. Cover and cook till all of the water is gone. Do not stir. Test to see if the water is gone as you would for boiled rice.

To reheat barley, it may be steamed, or fried in a skillet with a little oil and water.

BARLEY AND RICE

One of our favorite ways to cook and eat barley.

This may be boiled or pressure cooked (Reduce the water volume slightly if pressure cooking.)

SPRING AND SUMMER MIX:
Wash and bring to a boil in a pot:

    1½ c. rice (long grain brown or basmati)
    1 c. barley groats
    6 c. water

Simmer on a flame tamer with a cover.

Cook till all the water is gone.

FALL AND WINTER MIX:

Cook as above, yet change the proportions to:

    1½ c. rice (short grain brown rice)
    ½ c. barley groats
    4½ c. water
    ¾ tsp. salt

Each of these mixtures should be soaked for 4 hours or more, if possible. This allows the life~energy within the grain to be re-activated.

Barley also makes an excellent breakfast grain, especially if freshly ground. Check the cereal chapter for its use with other grains. Likewise, finely ground barley mixed with other flours makes very good bread. Check the bread chapter.

BARLEY AND MILLET

This mixture is very nice served freshly cooked or baked to a firm textured loaf.

The barley adds a chewiness to the millet.

This grain mixture should not be pressure cooked.

Wash and soak:

 1 c. barley
 3 c. water

Place in a pot and bring to a boil:

 barley and water
 ½ tsp. salt

Simmer with a cover for 30 minutes.

Then, add to the pot:

 4½ c. water
 1½ c. washed millet
 ½ tsp. salt

Preheat oven to 350° if you are going to bake the millet and barley into a loaf.

Place on a flame tamer and continue cooking on a low flame until the millet balls are well opened (approx. 20 ~ 30 minutes).

Pour into an oiled loaf pan and cover. Bake for 40 minutes.

Serve as is, hot from the oven ,, or chill and reheat in slices.

Tofu

Tofu is a food product that was developed by the Chinese in 160 B.C. It is the most popular soy protein food throughout East Asia,, and is quickly becoming popular in most first world countries. It is a low cost food product that supplies high quality protein. Tofu is also cholesterol free, low in calories and saturated fats. It is high in phospherous, and contains Vitamins B1, B2, and B3.

Besides being healthy for you,, tofu can be made into numerous everyday favourites,, ranging from hors d'oeuvres,, omelettes, and main courses, to spreads, dips, sauces, dressings, and even beverages. It can be used to replace egg, cream, and cheese texture in many recipes, such as mayonnaise, whipped cream, cheese cake, omelettes, etc.

Tofu can be eaten in its raw state and is delicious this way when freshly made,, altho this is an acquired taste. When brought up with tofu,, young children will just as soon eat a chunk of raw tofu than any other kind of snack food or treat most children would ask for. To a newcomer's taste,, tofu can seem rather "blah" and tasteless. It is this quality that allows tofu to be used so easily in replacing other substances.

Most high protein foods require a lot of digestion, whereas tofu is very easily digested. It is the most digestible of all natural soybean foods, thus it is excellent food for babies, elderly people,, or those with digestive problems. It is ideal for dieters or very active people who want a light meal which offers high protein, good nutrition, and is low in calories (only 164 per 8 ounce serving).

Tofu contains some linoelic acid and also lecithin which aids in metabolizing, breaking down, and eliminating saturated fats and cholesterol which collect in the bloodstream and vital organs,, especially the heart. Soybeans are the only legume which is a complete protein,, thus it contains all of the eight essential amino acids.

I will not attempt to tell you how to make tofu,, as there are many good books available on this,, and seeing as it is a timely operation, you may prefer to simply buy your tofu which is available throughout many outlets today. It is wise to enquire about the tofu you buy,, as some producers use better quality ingredients than others. Ideally,, look for tofu that is made from organic soybeans and spring water, and is activated with nigari.

Each producer of tofu has its own recipes and methods,, therefore, textures vary depending on this. These are the three basic types available on the market:

1.   Regular - has a moderate firmness, yet crumbles easily. Is ideal for most recipes.

2.   Firm - is more dense than the regular, as it has had more water pressed from it. Is more suited to cutting in cubes and is better for making "Frozen Tofu" (page 78) (has a more granular texture,, almost gritty.)

3.   Silky - is very soft and creamy. Falls into pieces easily and has a texture similar to a thick pudding. This is ideal for sauces, whipped cream, and dips, as it blends to a very fine cream and has no grit. If this is available to you and you use it,, you may have to reduce the water in the recipe a little, as this type of tofu has more liquid in it.

At this point, I would like to go over some of the basic cooking methods that will be called for throughout the book:

Baked tofu
Blended tofu
Scrambled tofu
Mock tofu beef
Mock tofu chicken

Baked Tofu

Slabs:

One of the simplest and easy ways to serve tofu is to bake it. It is quick, tasty and can be used in conjunction with many other dishes depending on how you slice it.

First, preheat the oven to 350°.

Remove tofu chunks from the water and gently dry on a clean dish towel.

Slice into ¼"~½" thick slabs and place on a lightly oiled tray.

Tamari each piece and spread it with your finger to cover evenly. You may also sprinkle each slab with cayenne, garlic pwd., basil, tarragon, etc.

Bake for the length of time which gives the desired texture you like. A short baking of approx. 20 min. will give a soft, pipin' hot morsel. Now, if you let it bake for 30~40 min., it will get crispy and well browned, even down right chewy if you leave it long enough.

Tofu baked in this fashion is quite tasty to use in cold sandwiches. Do not cook it too much as it becomes chewier when cooled.

Cubes:

Likewise this can be done by cutting the tofu into ¼" to 1½" cubes. Prepare as above, but cut into cubes. Bake, turning once or twice so they cook evenly. Tamari each time.

Similarily, either of these methods of cooking tofu can be done in a frying pan, deep fryer or by broiling. Either is very good, yet we usually bake em' as it is less oily.

SCRAMBLED TOFU

This method gives a texture similar to scrambled eggs.

Remove the tofu from the water, rinse and dry lightly on a towel.

Crumble the tofu between your fingers into a bowl making sure there are no large lumps.

Heat a skillet with a little oil in it.

Add the tofu and stir frequently while cooking. Do not cover.

Continue cooking till the tofu has a 'scrambled egg' texture which occurs once some of the water has cooked off.

At this point you should add some salt of a sort. We generally use tamari, although if I want the tofu to stay white for a particular recipe, I use salt. I have even used umebosi vinegar at times. (This makes it pinky).

BLENDED TOFU

There are several recipes which call for blended tofu, such as mayonnaise, sauces, dips, etc. Each of these recipes are self explanatory, however, in most cases a food processor is easier to use and will make a thicker mixture than a blender.
If all you have is a blender, it will work fine, but in order for some of these mixtures to blend easily, you may have to blend them in half batches.
Also, to assist the mixture to blend, run a chop stick around the lower edge of the blender, tight to the sides, in the same direction as the blender rotates.

FROZEN TOFU

Treating tofu in this fashion gives you a whole new texture to work your imagination with. This technique of freezing the tofu and thawing it, gives a chewier texture and when marinated, it allows the tofu to absorb much more flavor.

Do not use soft tofu, regular or firm is best.

To achieve the texture we desire, the tofu should be rinsed well, then towel dried and set on a plate or tray. Arrange the chunks so they don't touch each other and place in the freezer. After 12~24 hours, bag the frozen tofu in plastic so they don't pick up any undesirable flavors or suffer from freezer burn. Tofu may be kept like this for several months. Use the freshest tofu available.

Preparation of tofu in this fashion should be done the day before you want to use it in a meal.

Remove from the freezer early in the day:

   4 ~ 9 oz. chunks of frozen tofu

When thawed, marinate in one of the two following broths.

MOCK BEEF MARINADE

Combine in a saucepan and bring to a boil:

3 c. water	2 tbls. garlic
1 c. tomato juice	2 tsp. whole black
1 c. grated beet	pepper balls
4 cloves	½ tsp. carraway pwd.
½ c. tamari	2 bay leaves

Add the thawed tofu chunks to the broth and reheat till it boils.

Tofu Beef Marinade,

You may also cut the chunks in half, into slices or into smaller cubes.

Cover and simmer for 40 min. Remove from the heat and let cool to room temp. Refrigerate in the broth till ready to use. Marinate for a minimum of 12 hrs. Can be kept in the broth for up to 4~5 days.

When ready to use the tofu, remove from the broth and let drain. Reheat the broth to just below the boiling point, cool and then freeze in a container. This broth can be used 2 or 3 more times. Add a little more water and grated beet to enhance the color.

Mock Chicken Marinade

Follow the same method as above, substituting this broth.

Combine in a saucepan:

  4 c. water
  ½ c. light, barley miso or 1 tbls. salt
  2 tbls. chopped garlic
  2 tbls. ground corriander
  1 tsp. sage
  1 tsp. oregano
  1 tsp. basil
  1 tsp. paprika

Beans

Throughout the world,, beans are a main staple in many countries. Beans and legumes are a most nutritious and tasty food. Legumes are rich in B vitamins (thiamin, niacin, B6, folacin). They are rich in iron,, however, the iron is more assimilable if eaten with Vitamin C rich food,, i.e. broccoli, peppers, tomatoes, peas, lettuce, etc.

Beans are an excellent source of plant food protein. Although beans are not a complete protein and lack some essential amino acids,, this can be overcome by eating them in conjunction with other grains and seeds.

Beans and legumes are low in fat and high in fibre.

We ate beans quite frequently when we were first changing from a devitalized and processed diet to one which consisted of whole grains and vegetables,,, yet as the years passed and our diets became more refined in a lot of respects,, we found that beans were no longer needed or acceptable in their whole state. We still eat some bean products such as tempeh, tofu, soymilk, falafel, and humus,, as we find these more easily digestible because of the process of preparation they go through.

I heard Iilah explain it once to some folks in a cute analogy. He said, "When you're creating a new building, you have to pour in lots and lots of cement, but once it's finished, you only need to supply enough energy and maintenance to sustain it". That's very true with the human body. When we first changed our diet,, we used to eat three times what we eat now,, lots of beans, a good amount of dairy products, and much more sweets, pounds of nuts and nut butters,, and foods prepared with oil. That was our cement which rebuilt our bodies,,, but now, the type of food we eat as a general rule consists of our main grains, plus tofu and tempeh,, numerous vegetables, very little dairy, some nuts and nut butters, and fruits in season.

If whole cooked beans and legumes agree with you,, by all means eat them. Throughout this book, I have included all our good old bean recipes we used to make, plus all the ones we still use that incorporate tempeh and tofu.

Iilah showed us in some ancient writing which dated back to the early Egyptians to the times of Horus and Osiris,, which stated how they would not eat meat or animal products, and few even ate beans. It stated that beans hindered their divinity. Their diets consisted of whole grains, cooked and raw vegetables, unleavened breads that contained flower pollen,, plus fresh fruits and nuts.

All beans should be washed well and soaked for at least 6 hours, or overnight. If possible,, it is good to change the water once or twice during their soaking time. Some beans are renowned for having small stones in em. It's easiest to look for these before they are washed,, so do this when the beans are dry.

If you soak and cook beans with a strip of Kombu, it alleviates some of the gasious effects that beans can have.

Aside from using tempeh and tofu regularly,, the primary beans you should cook the most with are adzuki beans, chick peas, lentils, lima beans, and some kidney beans now and then.

All other beans and dried peas should only be eaten occasionally and in moderation.

Listed on the next page are the basic preparation and cooking times needed for the many different types of beans,, and some points of interest.

BEAN	DESCRIPTION	SOAK?	COOKING TIME	CALORIES (1½ cups per serving)
ADZUKI BEANS	Traditionally a Japanese bean with a delicious, delicate flavour. They cook well in conjunction with millet or rice.	Yes	1 hour	146
CHICK PEAS	Typically a middle eastern or Indian bean. Has a nutty flavour. Are good in sauces, dips, salads, soups, patés, and main dishes.	Yes	1-2 hours	187
LENTILS	Have a mild, yet distinctive taste. Good in soups, salads, and main dishes with or without other grains.	No	30-45 minutes	106
SOYBEANS	They are bland and are not great on their own. Best in casseroles or loafs. Soybeans are more easily digested in the form of tempeh or tofu.	Yes	3 hours plus	127
LIMA BEANS	Tasty on their own, in casseroles, chili, and soups.	Yes	45 mins. (baby) 1½ hours (reg.)	95
KIDNEY BEANS	Great in chili, soup, stews, and salads. Best cooked spicy,, otherwise they are bland.	Yes	1½-2 hours	109
BLACK & PINTO BEANS	Popular in Mexican and South American cooking. Tasty, earthy flavour.	Yes	1½-2 hours	145
RED BEANS	Distinctive and savory. Very good with rice, in soups, stews, and salads.	Yes	1½-2 hours	145
SPLIT PEAS	They have a specific flavour that is great in soups.	No	30-40 minutes	115

Aduki Beans

These are one of the healthiest beans there are aside from products made of soybeans, like tofu and tempeh. They have a high vitamin C content, as well as many other essential minerals.

Pick through and wash:

> 1½ c. aduki beans

Soak overnight:

> wash beans
> 2 - 10" strips of kombu
> ample water

In the morning, rinse the beans 2 ~ 3 times.

Combine in a saucepan:

> rinsed beans and kombu
> 4 ½ c. water
> 1 tbls. honey
> 1 tsp. salt

Add to the pot in a spice ball.

> 2 small or 1 large bay leaf
> 5 chillies
> 1 tsp. carraway pwd.

Either pressure cook for 40 minutes or boil for 1 ~ 1¼ hours, or until all the water is gone.

In either case,, cook on a flame tamer.

If you like beans slow simmered and saucey, cook on a low flame for as long as possible. Top up with water and continue cooking till the beans are well opened and creamy.

Tempeh

Tempeh is originally the national food of Indonesia. It has a chewy texture which is often missing in meatless foods. Fresh tempeh has a nutty flavour and smells similar to mushrooms. Being very versatile, it can be used in casseroles, sandwiches, stews, soups, salads, or on its own as the main course.

Tempeh is a cultured product made from soybeans or from a mixture of soybeans and other grains such as millet, rice, and/or barley. It is produced by mixing cooked soybeans (or soybeans and grains) with a mushroom-like culture. This is then pressed into thin layers (3/4 inch) and allowed to incubate at a specific temperature. The benefit of this process is it enhances the flavour, binds all the ingredients together, and breaks down the composition of the beans so they are more readily digested. People who find beans very hard to assimilate will find that tempeh digests very well.

Tempeh can be made at home, but considering that it is readily available in the freezer of most health food stores at a reasonable cost, it hardly seems worth the bother. Tempeh is best stored frozen. Being a cultured product, it continues to age (or grow) even when refrigerated. This aging does not spoil the tempeh,, however it develops a stronger aroma and small black spores. It should be eaten within a few days after being thawed.

Tempeh should always be steamed 15 to 20 minutes. It can then be mashed, cubed, or sliced,,, sautééd, deep-fried, baked, or marinated.

Seitan

Seitan is a uniquely textured, grain-based food which has the texture of beef, and lends itself to a variety of different spices and flavourings. Seitan is made from the gluten part of the whole wheat flour. Although wheat gluten is an incomplete food,, it is easily digested and rich in protein. It can be eaten year round,, although it should be used moderately in comparison to other grains (one to seven times per month).

We use seitan in our restaurant to make dishes like Steak au Pouive Flambe,, Veal Fettuccine,, Shish Ka Bobs, Cabbage Rolls,, and our Vegetable/Meat Pies,, plus many other dishes. The fact that these recipes assimilate meat dishes is intentional,, however, it is not designed to be an exact duplication,, but it does satisfy a food taste which many of us were brought up on.

Any dishes made with seitan are ideal for the real "meat and potato" type guests,, or those who are vegetarian connoisseurs. Seitan is made from wheat gluten,, so let's make the gluten first. Seitan should be made a day or two ahead of when you plan to use it.

WHEAT GLUTEN

There are two methods by which to make gluten. One is a high yielding, easy way and the other is a small yielding, hard way.

Let's go over the hard way first so you will have an appreciation for the easy method. Both result in the same finished product.

Combine in a bowl:

   12 c. whole wheat flour
   1 tbls. salt

Stir in:

   6 c. cold water

Knead to make a smooth dough. Continue kneading for about 20 minutes. The kneading develops the gluten out of the flour. Place in a bowl and cover with cold water. Refrigerate for 1 hour.

The next step is to wash all of the starch and most of the bran out of the dough. This can be done by two different methods:

1) ~ tear off 2"~3" ball of dough at a time. Rinse and knead the dough under a slow running tap with as cool a water as is comfortable for your hands. (Put a strainer underneath because sometimes a piece falls off). Continue rinsing till the dough feels 'rubbery' and looks like most of the bran is gone. This takes 2~4 minutes per handful. Repeat till all of the dough is finished. When completed, knead the pieces together and press into a loaf pan. Refrigerate for at least 4 hours or even overnight. Yields approx. 4 cups.

2) ~ put the dough in a large bowl or pot and cover with cold water. Knead the dough.

Wheat Gluten, cont.,

till the water is very milky and thickened. Pour off the water and cover again. Repeat this 5~7 times. Each time, the water will get clearer. When the water gets only slightly cloudy and the dough feels quite elastic, it is done.

This will yield about 4 cups of gluten.

The easier method of making gluten uses half whole wheat flour and half "gluten flour." Buy what is called "80% gluten flour." Proceed with the previous directions using the following flour proportions.

> 2 c. whole wheat flour
> 2 c. 80% gluten flour
> 1 tsp. salt

Form into a dough using:

> 2 c. cold water

This dough only has to be kneaded for about 10 minutes. Let the dough set for 1 hr. Rinse using either of the previously described methods.

This dough will rinse clear much quicker and will yield about 4 c. of gluten.

SEITAN

Seitan is the oriental name used for gluten which has been cooked in a flavored broth. The gluten can be cut and shaped into a variety of shapes and sizes, depending on what you are making. In general, we cut the dough into 1"~1½" pieces. If planning to make something similar to steak, cut or shape the dough into ½" thick slabs.

The finished product will be slightly larger than the original cut as it swells once cooked.

Seitan, cont.,

For each 4 cup batch of gluten, combine in a large pot and bring to a boil:

    8 c. water
    4 - 6" pieces of kombu
    1 c. tamari
    ½ c. ginger (wash ginger and remove
         any bad spots. Slice into ⅛" thick
         pieces)

When the broth is boiling, drop the seitan pieces into the pot. Bring back to a boil and turn down to a simmer. Cover and stir occasionally. If cooking 'steak pieces', stir gently as they are fragile while cooking. While boiling, the seitan expands greatly but it contracts when cooled.

Simmer the seitan for 2-3 hours till most of the broth is gone. Cool to room temperature, then refrigerate. Seitan will keep in the fridge for 7-10 days or it can be frozen on a tray and then stored in bags.

Spiced Seitan:

An alternative batch with a little more spice to it. (Only use this with the '80% gluten flour' mix.

Measure these ingredients twice, into separate bowls:

¼ c. grated beet (as for lemon rind)	1 tsp. carraway
	1 tsp. celery sd.
2 tbls. tarragon	1 tsp. paprika
2 tsp. thyme	1 tsp. black pepper
2 tsp. garlic pwd.	¼ tsp. cayenne

Add 1 batch of spicing to the flour mixture before adding the water. Add water and knead the dough. Let it set, go through the rinsing process and chill.

When you prepare the broth, add the second bowl of spicing to the regular mixture.

Global Prathology

Having been lucky enough to have visited and lived with many of the remote native peoples of the world,,, I have found those who have been left alone in their remote and untouched environment, to be most healthy, happy, and definitely the most enlightened of all, relative to the energies and vibrations of kreashon. Then there are the poor natives, who are subsedised by their governments. They live amidst the palms, by the sea and rice fields, in their little grass shacks. They get their quarterly rations of unhulled unbleached rice, some beans, corn, and they raise a few chickens, catch their daily fish, use wild herbs, drink lots of coconut milk. Boy,,, I tell yah,,, talk about a healthy, good lookin', peace lovin' people, who walk around smiling all the time. ii,,, their minds are at peace as well,,, because each day,,, they are still free to play at work,, while making an honest living doing it as a family together with a tribe who's still free to enjoy each other.

When these tribes get too big,,, three or four different denominashonal religions move in,, small businesses,,,, taxes skyrocket, soda pops, white sugar, white rice, white drugs, white flour, lots of meat,,, coolers,,, ice creams,,, synthetic clothes,,, and before you know it,,, they all have tooth, heart, stomach, ego, diabetic, and cancer problems to contend with as well. Soon,, policing becomes necessary, and more crime, and then,, yawl know of the poor souls who stand up in their church and parliaments saying, "We are making civilized people out of these heathens". Imagine,,, people are literally killing themselves playing this game of economics which is camouflaged to look like it's a God-sent life saver. Well,,, one thing is for sure,,, it's a lesson to be well learnt.

Boy, I tell yah,,, yawl would cry if you had seen how the conscientious natives lived 500 years ago on the Hawaii Islands, before religion and the white man's ways came to

their lands. Knowin' the Great One as I do,,, I can assure
you, He would rather live with them, then and there with His
family, than with the present day fightin' and snipin'
Christian families living over there in the Nors of
Irelands... Tsk, Tsk,,, Tsk.

        Throughout my world travels,,, I have seen where
80% or more of the people living in the cities are sick and
out of shape,,, while on the other hand,,, the natives who
are still able to lead a simple life, are really healthy and
happy, etc., etc. Now I'm not talkin' about them who have no
fertile land left and are being starved off the face of the
Earth. Wherever there are jobs for money,,, there are mounds
of toxic waste, and criminal negligence, and political abuse,
all being done for the love of God and the Good of Man...
True,,, it all was supposed to happen in order to complete
what had to get done,,, yet don't forget,,, it's allowed to
stop and change for the good of man, as well. I do believe
it's what's being awaited for, before the Divine Intervenshon
can manifest equally for all.

        Well,,, times are a'changin',,, because many more posi-
tive scenes are being repeated throughout. There I was, over
in the Napanee of the Kanadas, when I was witness to a cute
story,,, Standin' there in the food line of one of these
great feed stores, I see this young fellow in his mid 40s
unloadin' his basket of produce onto the cashier's table.
Without meanin' to do so, he be gather'n lots of attention,
because here he was, emptyin' his basket which had been
filled with sale items of greens, legumes, and fruit from the
produce department. It looked so out of place next to the
baskets filled with white bread, cases of soda, chips, dips,
cake mixes, whippy stuffs, canned veggies, roast beefs,
deodorants, hot dogs,,, and The Enquirer. Well, I could see
what was goin' through a lot of people's minds,,, and I actually heard one sweet 'lil ol' lady say to her husband,,,
"Charley,,, do you think if we ate what that guy's got in his
basket, we would get to look and feel like him?" In other
words,,, all these people are pickin' up something special

from this young man,, and the question and answer of why it be so, sat right there in his basket.

Good folks everywhere are seein' it,, and doin' it themselves, more and more. It's about time,,,, and, with the same breath,, please beware of stagnation, both on a physical and spirited plane. ii,,, you have to really do it with consistency in order to maintain konkshus equilibrium.

BREAKFASTS

CHAPTER 2

Breakfast

Breakfasts and Cereals

Throughout our years of learning about diet and nutrition, what we have become accustomed to eating in the morning has reflected a growing understanding of ourselves and of what is required to give our spirited monastic day a proper kick-off.

Our diet has evolved to where we eat basically two meals a day. Our breakfast meal is generally eaten about 10:00 to 11:00, and consists of a whole grain, freshly ground porridge,, a fresh miso soup, and some sour dough bread lightly toasted. Ideally,, this is the most wholesome, balanced, nutritional morning meal one can eat, and I will elaborate on this later.

Many people new to healthful eating realize the deficient, degenerative effects that a modern day breakfast has. A processed, sugared cereal served with cow's milk, white toast, and jam, or some bacon and eggs,, all washed down with orange juice or coffee, sure isn't what God's finest creation deserves first thing in the day.

Upon realizing this and making certain changes,, beware that you don't substitute more natural, yet unbalanced, partially whole foods. As a transition, these are okay for a short while,, but any whole, puffed cereal served with soy milk and honey is still acid-forming. Plus, many people conceive whole wheat, or whole grain bread and granolas as being a good source of grains. This is not true. Bread has a minimal nutrition level unless made with freshly ground, whole organic flours. Granolas are only partially cooked and very hard to digest. Eating yogurt and fresh fruit is also very unharmonious to a balanced diet, especially if you live in a northern climate.

Any of these transitory foods can be eaten on occasion, varied with whole grain porridges.

Contrary to most people's preconceived tastes,, cereals and porridges should not be eaten with milk or sweetener. Sweets, mixed with grains, creates fermentation in the stomach and intestine. When we eat porridge, we have it in a savory style,, garnished with any variety of condiments such as gomasio, nutritional yeast, lecithin, tekka, flax seed, etc. In combining the live vegetable value within the miso soup, we have a well balanced,, very nutritious breakfast.

For those who have to eat very early,, porridge or a whole grain will do,, with a lunch of fresh soup,, some other grain, a sandwich, vegetables and/or salad,, and then later, a light meal. I realize this is not feasible or practical for everyone right off,, however, it gives you an objective to work towards in reshaping your daily intake.

The following recipes are listed in the order of those which are most nutritious and healthful, on to the ones which should be eaten occasionally in moderation.

BREAKFAST

The word "breakfast", as well as what properly constitutes break-fast, has lost its common-sensed understanding for most people.

The first meal of your day was so called because it is with this food that you break- (your daily 12-hour) fast. Ideally,, the human system is designed to be fed nourishing foods only from day break to just before sunset. The bulk of a person's daily food intake should be eaten before 1 or 2 o'clock in the afternoon, because it is during this time that the digestive system does most of its work. A third meal of the day should be a light one.

Unfortunately, this type of an eating schedule does not fit into most economic time schedules. People wind up eating a fast breakfast, or none at all. The reason their bodies don't crave a nourishing meal in the mornings is because they eat a very filling, late supper the night before, which their digestive system is still working on. This type of eating schedule leads to lethargy, obesity, and debilitation of general health, as the body is working over-time to digest a full meal which is usually totally imbalanced and acidic,, rather than allowing the digestive system to be resting.

WHOLE GRAIN PORRIDGES

There are many ground and cracked whole grain porridges available on the market. Seven grain, twelve grain, Red River Cereal, etc. In comparison to commercial cereal, they are very nutritious and flavourful. However, any grain or seed which has been ground or cracked loses valuable nutrients.

For a minimal expense of $25 or less, you can purchase a hand grain grinder or an electric coffee mill. Either will grind a sufficient amount of cereal for each day's use in a matter of 1 or 2 minutes.

This allows you to mix and combine your own grains and seeds according to the time of year and your own preference.

Before giving you our numerous favorite grain blend, I would like to outline the basic procedure and similarities they all share.

- Almost all grain should be cooked in a proportion of 3 parts water to 1 part grain, unless otherwise stated.

- Do not add grain to the water until it is boiling. Stir in with a wisk to prevent lumps.

- Add a small amount of salt at the beginning.

- Place the pot on a flame tamer as soon as the porridge has been added, to minimize sticking. Reduce flame to a slow simmer.

- The finer the grind, the quicker the cereal will cook. Most cereal should simmer for a minimum of 30 minutes. (We grind ours coarsely and let it cook for 2 to 3 hours.)

  (If you put porridge on when you first get up, it will be cooked by the time you wash, do some morning exercises, and get ready to go to work.)

- Keep covered while cooking, and stir occasionally.

- In the last 5 minutes of cooking, add a dash or two of Tamari. Stir in and simmer briefly.

- Buy a variety of whole, organic grains and seeds. Place them in clear glass jars where they are readily available,, preferably near your grinder.

PORRIDGE

The grains and seeds which are best suited for porridge are:

oat groats	buckwheat groats
millet (hulled)	brown rice cream
corn (cracked)	soy flakes
barley groats	durham semolina
rye berries	pumpkin seeds
sunflower sds.	sesame seeds
almonds	flax seeds

For the nutritional value of each of these grains, check in the grain section.

PHEYLONIAN 3 GRAIN

This is our favorite blend because of its delicate flavor and natural sweetness.

Mix a jar of this combination, 'cause once you try it, you'll want it often.

Combine in a jar:

9 c. oat groats	1 c. whole almonds
6 c. barley groats	1 c. sunflower sds.
3 c. rye berries	1 c. pumpkin sds. (pepitas)

Grind only as much grain as you need for each morning.

Boil 1½~2 cup of water for each adult serving. Add 1 part grain (ground) for every 3 parts of water.

Add ground grain to boiling water. Cook on a flame tamer with a cover for a minimum of 30 minutes, up to 2 hrs. Stir occasionally.

Pheylonian 3 Grain, cont.,

For a uniquely different porridge ,, cook this mixture whole.

Use a proportion of 4 to 1 and cook overnight. This can be done in a heavy pot inside a wood burning oven at a low temperature ,, in an oven at 225°, or in a crock pot on a fairly low temperature. Cook each with a lid.

In the morning, the grains will be soft and well opened. The whole almonds have the texture of soft beans and the whole mixture is bathed in a naturally sweet cream.

Try it ,, you'll really enjoy it.

There are numerous other grain mixtures we enjoy as porridge. I will list them in proportions so you can either mix what you need for the day or combine a batch and store it in a jar.

* 1 prt. oat groats
  1 " cornmeal

* 2 prts. oat groats
  1 " buckwheat
  ½ " almonds

* 2 prts. millet
  1 " rye
  ½ " pumpkin
           seeds

* 1 prt. durham
           semolina
  1 " cornmeal

* 1 prt. millet
  1 " barley
  ½ " sunflower
           seeds

* 1 prt. rice cream
  1 " soy flakes
  ¼ " flax seeds

* 2 prts. rice cream
  1 " buckwheat
  ½ " sesame sds.

~ try your own
   combinations

MILLET PORRIDGE

One of the healthiest porridges ,, especially for children and older folks , as it is easily digested and very alkaline.

Combine in a saucepan :

    3½ c. water
    3/4 c. washed millet
    pinch of salt
    ¼ c. raisins or currants

Bring to a boil and simmer on a flame tamer with a lid. Cook for 20~30 minutes, until the millet balls are well opened and the grain is creamy and soft to chew.

Serve with nut or soy milk and a little bit of sweetener or serve in a savory fashion with a dash of tamari, a little margarine ,, some gomasio or whatever condiments you enjoy.

Other variations :

    Add to the grain from the beginning.

    ★ ¼ c. coconut   ★ substitute 1½ c. of
    1 tsp. vanilla   water with apple j.
                     ½ tsp. cinnamon

    ★ ½ c. sunflower sds.
    ¼ c. almond butter

                    ★ ¼ c. sesame sds.
    ★ ½ c. raisins   (freshly ground)
    ½ tsp. nutmeg   2 tbls. tahine

As a quick breakfast alternative ,, you can use some precooked millet. Reheat by using a little water. Simmer on a flame tamer till hot and creamy.

OATMEAL
(FROM ROLLED OATS)

An age old standard of the western world which is abundant in most of the elements needed to build general health. It is particularily healthy for children as it contains a high quantity of silicon which is important to the development of healthy bones, teeth, hair, eyes, nails and a good complextion. Oats are also rich in phosphorus which is required for formation of brain cells and for the nervous system. It is excellent for building body tone and resistance to disease.

Oats are one of the few grains which do not suffer noticably from being steel cut or rolled, as it retains the bran, middlings, endosperm and germ.

When rolled, they certainly cook much faster.

Bring to a boil:

    6 c. water
    1/2 tsp. salt

When boiling, add:

    2 c. rolled oats

Turn down the heat and place on a flame tamer. Watch closely till it comes back to a boil as oatmeal is renowned for boiling over.

Simmer for 10 minutes, then cover. Cook for 20~30 minutes more, stirring occasionally.

Serve with soy or nut milk, some sweetener or soaked raisins, currants or fresh fruit.

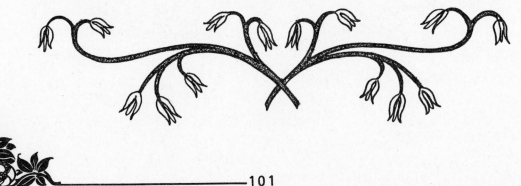

CORNMEAL PORRIDGE

A quick, enjoyable cereal when you are in a hurry. It only takes 20 min. from start to finish.

Cornmeal is listed in many blends at the beginning of this chapter, however, it is very nice on its own occasionally.

Bring to a boil:
    3 c. water
    ½ tsp. salt

When the water is boiling, stir in with a wisk or spoon:

    1 c. cornmeal

Turn the heat to low, place on a flame tamer, cover and cook till thickened. Stir occasionally.

Finely ground cornmeal cooks very quickly, yet some organic cornmeals are quite coarse. They should be cooked longer or be ground finer before cooking.

Serve in a savory fashion with condiments or garnish with dried fruit, some sweetening and soy or nut milk.

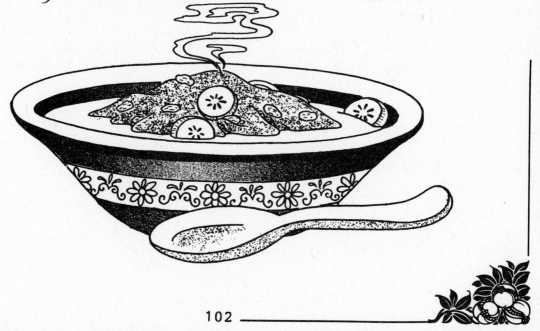

KUZUME

A very nutritious breakfast meal with a unique flavor and texture. It is also an excellent meal for anyone who is convalescing or retoning a sensitive system. The ingredients in this dish are very easily assimilated and is quite soothing on the intestinal tract and the stomach.

It is also very alkaline and tasty.

The three main ingredients in this dish are:

Umebosi plum: it is a Japanese plum which has been pickled in a salt brine.

It is helpful in stimulating proper digestive juices and has an anti-putrefying effect which can eliminate mild stomach problems, intestinal fermentation or lung problems.

Kuzu: is a starch similar to arrowroot, but of a more medicinal, nutritious variety.

Kuzu thickens when cooked, is very alkalining and soothing to the stomach as it strengthens and regulates the digestion. It is easily digested and quickly assimilated by the intestines.

Nori Seaweed: this is a tasty seaweed high in vitamins and minerals, particularily calcium. Calcium is important for neutralizing toxic acid and steadying the nerves, plus it gives strength and durability.

This can be eaten at any time of the day; however, it is a well balanced, nutritious start to any day.

For each serving, combine in a saucepan:

1 c. cold water
1 heaped tbls. kuzu (stir till dissolved)
1 umebosi plum or ½ tsp. of paste
1 sheet of nori (torn into small pieces)

Kuzume, cont.,

Bring to a boil, stirring constantly till the mixture is thickened and the liquid is clear, not milky.

Add: precooked rice or millet (the quantity is up to you).

Simmer for 10~20 minutes. Just before it is finished cooking, add a dash of tamari. Simmer 1 minute more.

Serve garnished with tahini~miso, gomasio, nutritional yeast, etc. A slice or two of some whole grain, sour dough bread will round this out nicely.

OMELETS

Occasionally we make omelets for breakfast if we have family or friends staying overnight.

They can be made very simply, using a variety of bases from egg and tofu, to millet or corn-meal. You can incorporate vegetables into them and make them very fancy, with cheese or with-out.

Here are some of the versions of omelets which we have made.

Rice Porridge

Rice cream is made by grinding short grain brown rice. You may buy this or grind it yourself. It should be fairly fine but not as fine as flour.

Bring to a boil:
  3½ c. water
  ½ tsp. salt

When boiling, add:
  1 c. cream of brown rice

Simmer on a flame tamer with a cover for 20~30 minutes. Stir occasionally.

As with the millet porridge, you may add a variety of seeds, nuts, fruits, flavorings, etc. to the rice porridge. Get creative and come up with your own blends.

Steamed Rice

For those new to a vegetarian diet, this would no doubt seem bland, but we've learned as we get older, the simpler things in life are often the best for us.

As you improve the foods you eat, your taste buds change. You may find you lose your cravings for so many sweets, plus your taste buds become heightened to flavors which you never noticed before.

With this in mind,, and due time, have some freshly cooked or steamed rice for breakfast. You can add 1 or more of any number of tasty condiments listed in Chapter 9.

GRANOLA

Tastewise "Granola" is a very satisfying food which most have eaten at one time or another.

Granola should only be eaten for breakfast once in a while (if at all), or as a munchable treat occasionally. It should not be served to children till they are old enough to chew it properly. People with intestinal or stomach problems should avoid granola.

There are numerous tasty granolas available on the market. This is the house blend we make.

CRUNCHY GRANOLA

Combine in a large bowl:

> 6 c. rolled oats
> ½ c. raisins or currants
> (washed and soaked 1 hour or more)
> ½ c. sunflower sds. (washed and soaked)
> ½ c. chopped almonds ("   "   ")

Heat in a saucepan till liquid:

> ½ c. sunflower oil
> ½ c. barley malt
> ½ c. soy milk powder

Pour the liquid mixture over the dry ingred. Work with your hands till crumbly.

Layer granola ½" thick on an oven tray and bake at 300°. Check and turn every 5~7 minutes. Remove when it is evenly browned and crispy.

Granola has the capacity of being a nutritious food, however, due to the fact that most of the ingredients are essentially raw and un-soaked, regular granola is very hard to digest and therefore most of the nutrition can not be assimilated.

Granola, cont.,

Fancy Granola

Combine in a bowl:

        6 c. rolled oats
        ⅓ c. currants   (washed and soaked)
        ⅓ c. raisins   ("   "   "   )
        ⅓ c. dates (washed, soaked and chopped)
        ½ c. almonds
        ½ c. pine nuts
        1 tsp. salt.

Heat in a saucepan:

        ½ c. oil
        ½ c. barley malt or rice syrup
        ½ c. soy milk pwd.

Mix liquid into the dry ingredients and bake as described in the previous version.

Scrambled Tofu Eggs

A tasty, spiced scrambled egg version using very little egg.

Combine in a blender:

        2 eggs   1 tsp. tarragon
        1 c. tofu   ½ tsp. garlic pwd.
        1 tbls. good tasting   ¼ - ½ tsp. salt or
           nutritional yeast   tamari

Blend till smooth and then fry as you would scrambled eggs. Serve hot.

BUCKWHEAT ~ APPLE PANCAKES

Peel, pare and cut into 1/8" slices:

    2 c. apple

Combine in a bowl:

    2 c. durham or whole wheat pastry flour
    1/2 c. buckwheat fl.
    2 tsp. baking pwd.
    1/4 tsp. salt

In another bowl, beat till fluffy:

    2 eggs

Add to the eggs and beat till well mixed:

    2 c. soy milk   1 tsp. cinnamon
    1/2 c. honey   or 1 tbls. vanilla

Pour liquid into the flour and stir till mixed.

Heat a cast iron frying pan or grill.

Butter or oil the surface and pour 1/3 ~ 1/2 of a cup at a time into the pan or onto the grill. Let run to a circle. (Sometimes the texture may need an adjustment. Batter should flow to about 1/4 ~ 1/3" thick. Either add more milk or a little more flour).

As the bubbles pop threw evenly in each pancake, flip and brown the other side. Remove from the grill and keep warm till all are cooked.

Most people love pancakes smothered in butter and maple syrup. As a less sweet alternative, mix:

    1/2 c. maple syrup   2/3 c. tahine
    1/2 c. apple juice   2 tbls. margarine
                            (melted)

A Honey of a Bee Story

There be these little bee stories I've bin wantin' to share with people for a long time,, and to be able to sit and chat with yawl in your home while doin' so. Well,,, what a treat.

Many times I be hearin' people ask these Pheylonian friends of mine,,, "While on your travels south, did you ever have any encounters with them there killer beez?" Well,,, that they did, but not with those tiny little amazon swarms yawl hear so much about. Ever so rarely have people had the time to hear the whole of one of these stories,,, never mind what's worthwhile about all of 'em!

I've no other way to put it. From all the fascinating stories they be holdin' about their exciting journeys throughout,,, many a fine adventurous movie could be produced,,, for they have seen and experienced much of that which is known to modern man as being the mythologies of old.

Anyway,,,, let us start from the greatest bee story I ever heard someone live to tell in this lifetime. ii,,, it bee the one closest to their hearts, and other sensitive spots, as you'll see when I finally get around to tellin' it.

Here they were,, brought to the base of the "Sacred Volcano", as it is called by the 12 tribes who live in the mountainous jungles surrounding this bottomless lake. They arrived in their homemade mobile home called "Mohtar",,, as in come onnnnn, motor,, don't give up now! Why this particular volcano be called the Sacred Mountain and not one of the other three, is explained with more detail in their "Alpha, Mu, and Omega" book.

Meanwhile,,, after camp was set up at the base of the Great Mountain,,, it didn't take them long to realize that this was really some place very special,,, because their first night was a shocker,, without any damaging jolts. You might say it was more like an enlightening array of cosmic voltons what befell them.

Imagine landing at an 11,000-foot altitude, looking up at a volcano yet a mile higher, beginning right at the tip of your toes. Here, it's early evening, and because of the cumulative clouds movin',,, one could faintly see the dense, tropical growth cresting this ancient sleeping giant. Two native brothers of the Navichuk family were visiting with these loving strangers, and when asked if there were any guides who were available to take the Philoxians within the crater, an immediate look of fright came upon their faces,,, and they said there were no paths, nor would anyone take them to the ridge,, never mind inside the crater. Soon after, they left, shaking their heads in such a manner as saying, "Crazy gringos!" They had agreed to return on the morrow.

From such an altitude,, the stars glistened like huge diamonds, just a'sparklin' within reach,,, and the moon, grayshus me,,, it looked like a huge day glow beach ball comin' right at'cha. ii,,, what a picture. Within these few frames is where Nantika, Awanota, Isan, Sesuwa, Tawlia, and Iilah came to realize that this here mountain wasn't your every day, run of the mill volcano,,, ii,, noh way.

Suddenly,,, here they were, engulfed in an ecstatic outburst of silent lightning emanating from the ground up. ii,,, its density equated that of the Aurora Borealis,, and tremendous flashes of purple, green, white, gold, and pink lightning intertwined, cauzing one to think they had just landed on some strange, distant planet. Well, they might as well have,,, for their experiences to follow were not of this time,,, yet in reality,, it wasn't just 20 years ago when all of this took place for real.

Within two days,, after intense dialogue between themselves and the Navichuk brothers,,, they had finally convinced them to take them up part of the way,,, but it was well agreed upon that they would not crest the ridge,, nor would they remain on the mountain as the sun began to set. So, with immediate plans made before the brothers could change their minds,,, an early departure on the morrow was arranged for their ascent onto this mystifying mountain which held so many secrets of the ancient times long forgotten.

Finally,,, after a restless night and early breakfast,,, they began their arduous climb. From the bottom, it looked easy enough,, yet it took several hours to just get through the corn fields on the western base side. Already,, deep signs of fatigue were beginning to set in,,, and it seemed as though the whole mountain was still ahead.

Folks,,, now I'm briefin' the story some,,, because, here again, many a novel could be writ about this intriguing adventure.

Soon after the corn fields, came a small tree'd, tropical jungle, and the mountain got steeper. Having forgotten they began this mile-high climb at an 11,000-foot altitude, made the carrying of all their equipment and their breathing painfully difficult. By nightfall, they were exhausted, alone, and already well into the third section of a giant tree'd, tropical rain forest. That evening and night were not without incident. They were engulfed in clouds, and in order to set up their tents in a lean-to fashion,, they had to dig into the steep edge, with their legs partially dangling over. Food had to be prepared,,, and to top it off,,, the sounds emanating from this ancient jungle were phenomenal. Several hours into the night is when they experienced their first encounter with a U.F.O. (again,,, more details can be found in their "Alpha, Mu, and Omega" book).

Late into the next afternoon,, they be goin' over the ridge, toppin' this mighty mount. ii,,, imagine turnin' your head to the left, envisioning the youthful Atlantian Caribbean,,, then to the right, instantly absorbing the magnemosity of the pulsatin' Mother Pacific. I tell you,,,

it's so easy to get carried away, because each minute represented an inflow of accumulative vishons and timeless gran-
deurs of man's earlier advent upon the Earth. Myyyyyy goodness,,, it was like goin' back and standin' there as we all
did nine thousand years ago. The ridge was but only 15 to 30
feet wide in spots, and the crater's mouth not more than a
quarter-mile across.

   Camp was set in a sandy rock crevasse, neatly tucked
away on the high side, above the tree line. Corn flats and
fresh picked, garlic flavoured helevah (a hard wood tree
mushroom) were a'sizzlin' over their small camp fire. Soon
after supper,, they were safely tucked away in their tents
and were asleep before the count of 10. ii,,, exhausted
they were. Here again,, their slumber wasn't without incident,, for once more our extra-terrestrial compadrés returned
to pay them a visit.

      Having survived such an inspection from our galac-
tic friends for a second time,,, a deep realization befell
them of why <u>this</u> was the sacred mountain, and not the
others. I remember Iilah laying awake for a spell, contem-
plating the silent mysteries of what might lie in store for
them upon their early descent into the deeps of this shadowed
crater. Having already observed many of the hidden revelations within the untouched, tropical jungles of this mountain
left everyone activated with a touch of awesome anxiety.

   In rising with the sun and affirming their position upon
the ridge of this energized monstrosity,, the grains for the
day were made, nori rolls put together, and rigging checked
for their dangerous descent into the unknown. After proper
nourishment, do-in, and a quick meditation,,, they went over
the ridge. Having brought 300 feet of rope left them short a
hundred or so,,, yet they reached bottom with only minor
mishaps. From this new position, looking upwards to the
ridge,, it was made obvious that they had not entered shrub
jungle,,, instead, they were standing at the base of giant,

lady-like banyans, extending their limbs and vines hundreds
of feet upwards.

Unable to cut through the 12-foot tall, wire-meshed
undergrowth,, they had little choice but to take the devine
pathway,,, ii,, dee vines. So up they went some 20 to 30
feet, then out onto the appropriate limb, securing just the
right vines. Then, with a gasp and a gulp, and the adrenalin
stirred,,, up, up, and away. Gads,,, talk about a thrill-
ing experience. Some swings covered at least 60 to
80 feet,, and only once did they come crashing down, landing
unhurt atop this springy undergrowth, where their laughter
could be heard echoing throughout the crater. Finally, by
late morning,, they reached the centre of this ancient,
virgin-forested paradise.

To their amazement, the tree line stopped abruptly, and
here they were, standing in the middle of a huge, circular
burn ring which had been charred from the top down, rather
than from the bottom up, as would do a typical grass fire.
Because of the previous nights' encounters,, it was obvious,
without question, about just what had cauzed such a perfect
burn ring to be. While standing there, somewhat awestruck by
the grandeur of the whole experience, Iilah began to feel a
certain uneasiness, because till now, all had gone too well.
Had they bin guided to the kohr of this forbidden land, only
to reach an oracle of surmise being tended by the spirits of
the Holy Ancients?

For some unknown reason,,, Iilah's instincts were
stirred to where chills ran up and down his spine, and his
heart thumped out a beat to match the growl of his stomach.
Suddenly,, there it was,,, a sound like no other ever
heard,,, and the four who had dared to trespass onto these
sacred lands, were now being confronted with a fate far worse
than death itself. ii,,, at first glimpse,, Iilah thought
they might be one of the ever so curious species of humming
birds,,, but when one hovered at eye level, 7 inches from his
nose,,, Iilah's heart almost exploded. Here were the

extinct, hierogliphic, giant killer beez which had survived
the perils of Atantis by having bin raised with the mountains
to such heights within the protective walls of this enormous, 7,000 year old greenhouse.

Obviously,, this inactive volcano had already procured
its tropical growth while being at sea level, after the sink-
ing of the Great Motherland of Mu. Then,,, a few thousand
years later when Atlantis met with a similar fate and the
continental plates shifted and rammed into each other once
again, cauzing the mountains to rise to such great heights,,,
this sacred, extinct volcano rose up atop it all, with all of
its inhabitants and growth intact. Thus explaining why the
other volcanos and mountains around it had so little or no
growth at all,, for they were active at either level,,, and
nothing, the sorts of what was in and around this mount, ever
grew at these heights elsewhere.

Immediately, Iilah whispers to his colleagues,,
"Stand ever so still,, don't swat,, and think only sweet
things". What they were confronted with here was a scouting
party from the main swarm,,, perhaps some 12 or 13 beez. As
described by Iilah, having had eye to eye contact with the
leader of the pack,,, it had a brilliant golden velvet body,
bigger than the average thumb,, and wings like a humming
bird. Its head was the size of a full marble, and it would
rotate from side to side, up and down,, conducting a full
analysis of the intruders. Iilah could recall the sweat just
a'gushing out all over. Then slowly,, this pulsatin' module
left eye contact and ventured lower, 'round to Iilah's back-
side,,, and at this point is where Iilah realized that God's
got one heck of a sense of humour, although it wasn't all
that funny at the time. Remember that old joke about someone
being bit by a poisonous snake in the mounded, remote areas
of the gluteus maximus,, and only a good friend could suck
out the poison? Well,,, wearing short sarongs has its benefits at times,, but this wasn't one of them. Iilah could
feel the wind from its wings centered equally onto each

cheek,, and he don't mean the ones on his face, either! Talk about wincing the smile of death!

What seemed to be an eternity of time soon passed,, and this one particular bee in question resurfaced to make eye to eye contact once more with Iilah,,, and soon,, reassuring calm overwhelmed him. The vibrations experienced now were those of new found friendship,,, and before taking leave,, these curious beez reflected a playful ayre and flew several circles around my Pheylonian friends. Then, off they went,,, not being seen or heard of again, until that evening when supper was being eaten around a small campfire. The same few came by to observe, smell, play, and even taste some of the honey which had been put out for them to sample. I remember Isan commenting on the expression one bee gave while sampling this Canadian honey,,, it was as though he were sayin',, "Man,,, this ain't nothing compared to what we got stashed".

As their adventures went on,, so must this fine cookbook,,, and of exactly why this story was condensed and immortalized accordingly like the other stories incorporated into this superb amalgamy of gastronomic pleasures,, was to show yawl one thing. Be it that their vibrashons, smells, and activities reflected that of the unnatural disharmonious way of life, and the stench of dead, decaying flesh was picked up, rather than the essence of nature's natural nectars,,, they'd all bin goners. As was put by the Alcaldi of the Mayan Tribe they lived with at the base of the mountain,,, no one has ever lived to tell such a story,,, and it had bin witnessed where those who were bit by these giant, venomous beez would roll and scream in agonizing pain for several hours before their heart would contract into seizure.

Well,,, all I could say is thank God,,, and bear in mind,,, who ever heard tell of a bee biting a flower?

Chaum,,,

Kjo Dindee

VEGETABLES

CHAPTER 3

Vegetables

STEAMED VEGETABLES

When preparing any vegetable for a meal, rather than boiling it, you are far better off, nutritionally and tastewise, to steam them.

Boiling vegetables robs much of the nutrition from them, while steaming retains all the goodness and makes it easier to prevent over cooking.

The taste and color is also much nicer when steamed, especially broccoli, brussel sprouts, fresh greens, carrots, etc.

Use either a metal or a bamboo steamer.

Here is a list of the vegetables which are best steamed:

Broccoli	Carrots
Cauliflower	Corn
Green Beans	Cabbage
Brussel Sprouts	Jerusalem Artichokes
Kale	Chard
Beet Greens	Squash
Peas	Asparagus

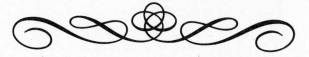

Vegetables are quite nice steamed on their own, however, we have created some very tasty and attractive dishes by combining certain vegetables to be steamed together.

The order in which they are listed is the order in which they should go into the steamer.

Steamed Vegetables, cont.

Here are some of the variations we have tried. I'm sure you will come up with some very good ones yourself.

Cauliflower (flowerettes)
Broccoli (cut lengthwise)
and/or Brussel Sprouts(halved)

Onions (½" wedges)
Carrots (¼" diagonals)
Zucchini (½" half-rounds)

De-cobbed Corn
Swiss Chard (chopped coarsely)
Chives (chopped coarsely)

Leeks (1" diagonal pcs.)
Celery (½" " " ")
Snow peas (whole)

Onion (½" dice)
Carrots (" ")
Potato (" ")

Shallots (sliced fine)
Beet Greens (whole)
Spinach (whole)

Purple Cabbage (1" chunks)
Kale (chopped coarse)

Green Beans (cut in 1"~1½" pcs.)
Cauliflower (flowerettes)

Carrots (½" diagonals)
Green Cabbage (1" chunks)

Broccoli Casserole

Wash:

    2 bunches of broccoli

Trim bottom ends and peel bottom inch or two of the stems if they seem tough.

Slice broccoli lengthwise so the bottom of the stalks are no thicker than ½".

Arrange in an oiled casserole dish. The broccoli should not be more than 2 layers thick.

Slice and singe fry:

    2 med. onions
    ½ lb. mushrooms (washed and squeezed)

Peel and sliver:

    6 ~ 8 cloves of garlic

Arrange mushrooms, onions and garlic evenly on top of the broccoli.

Add a ½" of water to casserole and sprinkle liberally with tamari.
Dot with marg. (optional)

Cover and bake for 25-35 min., depending on how well you like broccoli cooked.

This may be served as is,, or the remaining broth can be poured off,, thickened with a little arrow~root fl. and poured back over the broccoli.

This same basic recipe can be applied to a number of different vegetables, singly or combined:

    ~cauliflower (in flowerettes)
    ~carrots (quartered lengthwise)
        and brussel sprouts (halved)
    ~potatoes (1" cubes) and snow peas (whole).

VEGGIE-BLISS

A delightful and colorful side dish.

To prepare the carrots and zucs, use a grater with a ½" wide grate hole (large grate size). This gives a nice size chunk which is very thin, thus it cooks well with a light frying.

Wash and grate:

>   2 c. carrots
>   2 c. zucchini

Peel and dice:

>   2 med. onions

Fry in a large skillet or wok:

>   diced onion   1 tbls. oil

When onions are half cooked, add carrots and zucchini. Add a little water, cover and simmer.

Meantime, boil:

>   2 c. peas   (drain when tender)

When carrots are tender, add the cooked peas. Sprinkle with tamari, raise heat and singe fry for a minute or two.

Serve pipin' hot.

A variation of the above dish for summer meals.
Prepare above dish using ½ quantities of all ingred.

Boil: 3 c. water   ½ tsp. salt

Add: 1 c. elbow noodles

When cooked, drain noodles. Add cooked veggies and dress with mayonnaise,, or ½ c. of Isabel's Coleslaw Dressing. (page 302)

SCALLOPED POTATOES

A delicious way to serve potatoes for guests,,and easy, as they can be prepared ahead of time and reheated.

Peel, wash and slice into ¼" thick rounds:

    5~6 med. potatoes
    2 med. onions (in rounds)

Preheat oven to 375°.

Make a sauce by blending:

    2 c. water
    1 c. cooked millet

Repeat sauce again, adding following ingredients and blend well:

    4 tbls. marg.   1 tsp. garlic pwd.
    1 tsp. bl. pepper   1 tsp. salt
    or ¼ tsp. cayenne ½ tsp. thyme

Combine the 2 batches of sauce.

Break the onion slices into separate rings. They are more flavorful this way.
In an oiled casserole dish, layer onions and potatoes starting with onions and ending with potatoes.
Pour sauce over onions and potatoes.
Sprinkle with paprika, cover and bake for 45 min. at 375°,, then uncover and bake till golden brown.

SWEET N' SOUR-KRAUT

Wash: ½ c. raisins
Scald raisins with: 1 c. boiling water
Let set for 5 min., then drain.

In skillet, heat: 1 tbls. oil

Add: 2 c. sauerkraut   1 tbls. carraway sds.
      raisins   1 tbls. apple cider
                          vinegar

Sauté,, tamari and serve when hot.

BAKED CAULIFLOWER

Wash and break into 2" flowerettes:

   1 lrg. cauliflower

Steam until almost cooked, yet still firm.

Make a mixture of:

   2 c. bread crumbs   1 c. grated cheese
   1/4 c. gomasio   or 1 c. Soy Cheese

Blend a sauce of:

   1 1/2 c. water   2 tbls. marg.
   1/2 c. cooked millet   1/2 tsp. salt

Margarine or oil a casserole dish.
Spread 1/2 of bread crumb mix on bottom.
Arrange cauliflower pieces.
Pour sauce evenly over cauliflower pieces.
   (you can make and use more sauce if you want.)
Sprinkle with remaining crumb mix.
Bake uncovered for 20 min. at 375°

MEXICORN

Mexicorn can be made from fresh de-cobbed corn
or from that which has been stored frozen.

Prepare and dice, very fine:

   1 green or red pepper   2 cl. garlic
   1 onion

Sauté in a skillet with a little oil.

Meantime, boil:

   4 c. corn

When cooked, drain well and add to sautéed veggies.

Tamari and sauté for 5 mins. more. Serve.

Kahpusta Royale

This is one of Zabro's favorite meals, and altho it is known by many other names throughout the different European countries ,, this is how he calls it.

The quantities being called for do seem large, but this will cook down a lot.

Prepare and slice very thin:

    6 c. green cabbage
    2 c. onions
    6~8 cloves of garlic

In a large wok or heavy steel pot, heat:

    3 tbls. of oil

Add cabbage, onion and garlic.

Fry on medium heat and stir as needed so it doesn't stick. Cook for about 30~40 min.

In the last 5 min., add :

    cayenne pepper (to taste)
    tamari or salt ("   ")
    1 tsp. carraway pwd.

Serve this as a side dish or create a main course meal by adding Kubusah Sausages Slices (page 245) with a bean dish on the side.

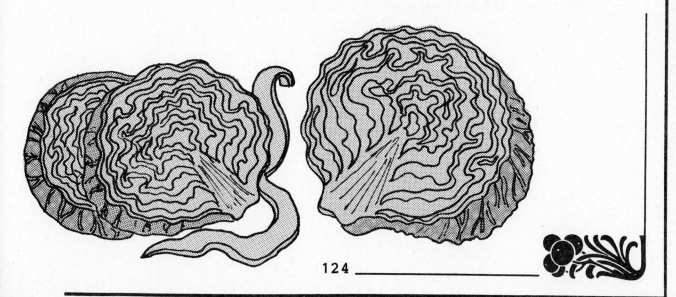

GLAZED CARROTS

Prepare:

    4 c. carrots (wash and cut into ¼" diagonals)
    1 med. onion (diced small)

Sauté vegetables in a covered skillet with:

    2 tbls. marg   or   1 tbls. oil
    1 tbls. water   2 tbls. water

Stir and tamari lightly while frying.
Combine:

    ½ c. water   1 tsp. arrowroot fl.
    1 tbls. umebosi vinegar

When carrots are tender, add arrowroot mixture and stir till thickened.

Simmer 1 minute, then serve.

SAUTÉED GREEN BEANS

When serving guests, this is an attractive and very tasty way to serve green beans.

Trim and wash:

    1 handful of fresh green beans per person.

Leave whole and steam till just barely cooked.
Remove from steaming pot to retain crispness.
Heat a large skillet and melt:

    1 tsp. marg. per serving

Add beans, stir well and fry on a medium heat.
Sprinkle with garlic pwd. and tamari.
Raise flame and fry, stirring frequently till they have a singe to 'em.

Remove to a dish and serve immediately.
So's to not overcook the green beans, fry them for only 5~7 min.

MOULDED SPINACH CASSEROLE

Boil: 4 c. water

Clean and wash:

    2 pkg. spinach (approx. 8 cups)

Pour boiling water over spinach „ let set for 2 min.
Drain spinach and chop coarsely.

Preheat oven to 325°.

Peel, slice and sauté:

    2 onions

Blend a mixture of :

    2 c. water   6 tbls. flour
    ½ c. cooked millet   ½ tsp. salt
    6 egg yolks   4 tbls. marg.
    ⅛ tsp. nutmeg   (optional)

Slowly add blended mixture to the onions.
Simmer, stirring constantly till thickened.

Add the chopped spinach.

Beat egg whites till stiff.
Fold hot mixture into egg whites.

Turn into oiled, 1 qt. ring mold and set into pan
of hot water.

Bake at 325° for 30 min, or until well set.
Chill.

Remove from mold and serve reheated with a
mushroom cream sauce (page 283).

Unlike other recipes in this book where you can
omit the use of eggs „ this one will not work
properly without them.

EGGPLANT PARMESAN

Wash (and peel if desired)

    2 or 3 eggplants

Slice into 1" thick rounds (you should have 2 or 3 slices per person).

Combine:

    2 eggs (well beaten)   2 tbls. tamari
    ½ c. water

Mix separately:

    2 c. bread crumbs   ⅛ tsp. cayenne
    ½ c. parmesan cheese

Oil a large oven tray or two small ones.
Dip eggplant in egg mixture, then in crumb mixture.
Place on oiled tray and top with grated cheese (opt.)
Bake at 350° for 25-30 min.

EGGPLANT PARMESAN CASSEROLE

Prepare, dip and bread eggplant as in previous recipe.

Oil the sides and bottom of a casserole dish.

Place a layer of breaded eggplant slices (use ⅓ of 'em)

Open a: 14 oz. can of tomato sauce

Add to sauce and mix well:

    1 tsp. oregano   ½ tsp. salt
    1 tsp. garlic pwd.   1 tsp. basil

Add ⅓ of sauce on top of eggplant slices.

Sprinkle with grated cheese. (opt.)

Repeat twice more.

Bake uncovered at 375° for 30 min.

POTATOES A'LA ONIONS

A delightful and fancy way of serving potatoes. It's one of our favorites when company visits.

The flavor of potato and onion become steamed together with the margarine and seasoning.

You will need 1 large or 2 small potatoes per person.

Peel 'em, or just scrub well if skins are good for eating.

Cut across the width of each potato into 1/4" slices (only cut 3/4 of the way thru so the slices are attached).

Peel 1 onion for every 2 lrg., or 3 small potatoes. Slice onion into 1/4" thick half rounds. Place onion slices in between potato slices.

Arrange the potatoes in an oiled casserole dish and garnish with:

salt	fresh gr. black pepper
dabs of marg.	or paprika
tarragon or parsley flakes	

Add 1/4" of water and cover with a lid, or foil. Bake at 375° till done (approx. 50~60 min.)

POTATO LATKES

These are very tasty, especially hot from the pan, but they are very oily,, so eat them only a few times a year.

Grate:

6 potatoes	1 onion

Add:

3 eggs (beaten)	1/4 c. flour
1 tsp. salt	2 tsp. baking pwd.
1 tbls. oil	pinch of cayenne

Mix well and drop by spoonfulls into 1/4" of hot oil. Brown on one side,, turn and brown again.

HIZIKI DELIGHT
(serves 4~6)

Soak for 1 hr. or more:

   ½ c. hiziki (seaweed)

Prepare and cut:

   2 onions (sliced in ¼" pieces)

   2 carrots (cut in matchsticks)

Drain and rinse seaweed. Place in a pot.

Add onions on top of seaweed, then the carrots.

Fill with water to just cover the seaweed.

Bring to a boil without a lid and cook for 1 minute. Reduce the heat and simmer till all of the water is gone. (approx. 40 min.)

Just before serving,, sprinkle with tamari, stir well, and simmer for 1 minute more without the lid.

Serve.

HIZIKI STRUDEL

These are ideal to serve to family or guests for lunch, supper or at parties.

They can be made in small single serving size turnovers ,, or made and baked in a long strudel and cut into single servings.

Prepare a batch of Hiziki Delight (above) and drain off any excess liquid.

Add to taste:

   tahini-miso   cayenne
   tamari

Stuff pastry (rolled to 5" circle or a 12" oval) with the filling and seal the edges well. Bake on an oiled tray at 350° till the pastry is cooked. Tasty served hot or cold.

CREAMED VEGETABLES

Everyone's family gets tired of plain vegetables now and then, so, for an alternative you can cream 'em.

Use any one vegetable alone, or create a combination of vegetables to add color and texture.

Quantities for this recipe are up to you, however, as a guide, 1 cup of cream sauce is sufficient for every 3~4 adult size servings of vegetables.

Prepare a batch of : Cream Sauce (page 283)

Let the sauce cook while you prepare the vegetables for steaming. Start vegetables steaming when sauce is ready to blend. Blend sauce.

Return blended sauce to pot, add steamed veggies and simmer till hot. Serve as a side dish, over noodles or on top of rice.

Vegetables that are best for creaming:

Carrots	Jerusalem Artichokes
Broccoli	Cauliflower
Corn	Peas (podded or snow)
Zucchini	Brussel Sprouts
Onions	Green Beans

Or any combination of vegetables from the 'Steamed Vegetable' recipe (page 118).

KOMBU AND VEGETABLE NISHIME
(serves 4~6)

Early in the day soak:

    3 6" pieces of kombu

Later,, drain and rinse the kombu. Cut it width-wise into ½" pieces. Place in a pot with 1" of water. Add a lid and cook for ½ an hour.

Meanwhile, prepare:

    3 c. diakon (lohbok) (quartered in 2"pcs.)
    2 c. onion (wedges)
    2 c. carrot (quartered in 2" pieces)

When the kombu has cooked ½ an hour,, add the vegetables. Replace the lid and simmer till the vegetables are almost cooked. Sprinkle with tamari and cook without a lid till the vegetables are tender and most of the water is gone.

We make this same dish utilizing a variety of other vegetable combinations.

    3 6" pieces of kombu
    3 c. parsnip (cut diagonally in 1" thick pieces)
    2 c. carrot ("   "   " " "   ")
    1 c. burdock ("   "   " ¼" "   ")

    3 6" pieces of kombu
    3 c. diakon (quartered and cut in 2" pieces)
    2 c. onion (wedges)
    2 c. brussel sprouts (halved)

    3 6" pieces of kombu
    3 c. cauliflower (cut into flowerettes)
    2 c. zucchini (1" thick diagonal slices)
    2 c. leeks (halved and cut in 1" pieces)

CORN IN UME SAUCE

Prepare and cook till tender:

   2 c. corn

   (boil whole corn (shucked) and then cut it from the cob, or use frozen corn (steamed).

Combine in a saucepan:

   1 c. soy milk or millet milk
   1 tbls. umebosi paste
   1 tbls. marg.
   1 tsp. arrowroot flour.

Stir well till dissolved, then place on a burner and bring to a boil, stirring constantly. When thickened, add the cooked corn and simmer on a flame tamer for 5 minutes.

Serve as a side dish or on top of noodles.

CORN-ON-THE-COB SAUCE

Admittedly, corn on the cob is a hit with people of all ages and what always comes to mind with corn is melted butter and salt.

As you know though, neither is particularily healthy, especially if you're watching your salt and dairy intake. Regardess of all this, here is an alternative spread for corn on the cob which will give a nice zip.

Cream together:

   1 tbls. ume paste   1 tbls. tahine
   1 tbls. soy marg.   1~2 tbls. water

Spread on hot corn as you would butter. Kept in the fridge, this is good for a week or so.

BAKED ENDIVES

The first time I had the opportunity to taste this dish, lilah was using fresh, imported Belgium Endives. Well, I tell you, I'd never tasted anything like it, they just melted in my mouth. They grow endives in Ontario now and they are available in most places,, at certain times of the year.

Assuming you're cooking for six, you will need 18~24 endives. (The white and yellow ones are sweet, the white and green ones can be bitter.)

Trim ⅛" of the bottom of each endive plus remove any brown or bruised leaves. Rinse each one and place in a margarined oven dish. They should not be more than 2 layers thick (cut large ones in half).

Dot evenly with margarine on top of endives (use 4~8 tbls.). Sprinkle with:

    20~30 whole bl. pepper balls
    1 whole hd. of garlic (peeled and sliced
        lengthwise in ⅛" slivers).
    2~3 tbls. maple syrup
    a liberal amount of tamari

Add water till there is ¾ of an inch in the dish. (For a special occasion, use 1 c. of white wine as part of the liquid, or give a sprinkle of Armagnac over the endives.

Cover and bake for 45~50 min. at 350°. You'll know when they're done by the smell and by how they pull apart easily into bite size strands.

This dish can be made in a less rich fashion by using leeks instead of endives, ½ the marg. and no sweetener.

133

BAKED ONIONS AND CARROTS

An easy to make, delicious side dish.

Prepare, per person:

  2 onions   (peeled, yet left whole)
  2 carrots   (peeled and halved lengthwise)

Arrange in a glass or enamel casserole dish. (Preferably one with a good fitting lid.)

Dot with margarine and sprinkle with black pepper and tamari.

Add: ½" water

Cover and bake at 375° for 45~50 min. (Till tender).

While baking, baste the vegetables with their own broth once or twice.

ESCARGOT AU GRATINÉ

Once or twice a year when you are having some special friends for supper and you'd like to please 'em with something very special, this will never fail.

First off, you must choose your mushrooms „ that's right „ mushrooms, not snails „ nice, big, firm mushrooms. Go to a market which sells mush-rooms loose and pick 'em about 1½" wide. Pick hard, firm ones which won't crumble when the stem is removed from the vulva. You will need 7~9 mushrooms per person „ plus a few for samplers. (for this recipe, about 50 mushrooms.)

Wash each mushroom carefully and then remove the stem. Set each cap to dry, right side up on a cloth or paper towel. This is best if done at least 1 hour before they are fried.

Meantime, prepare and chop:

　　3 c. fresh parsley
　　10 ~12 good sized cloves of garlic
　　stems of mushrooms (¼" pieces)

In a wide bottom skillet, melt:

　　2 tbls. margarine

Bring to a sizzle and add as many mushroom tops as will fit into the bottom of the pan in 1 layer, stem side up. Fry until they are singed brown, dash with tamari and Armagnac and frazzle 'em for another 2 or 3 min., making sure they don't burn. Turn and singe lightly, then remove from the pan. Give one a taste „ then repeat till all the mushrooms are done. Be careful not to over-cook them as they will shrink a lot. They will cook more when stuffed and baked.

Escargot au Gratiné, cont.,

When all the tops are cooked, add to the pan :

    4 tbls. of margarine
    chopped parsley, mushroom stems
        and garlic
    1 tsp. tarragon

Sauté on a med. heat, stirring occasionally to prevent burning. When almost cooked, sprinkle with pernod and tamari. Ingredients should be browned and sauc

While this is frying ,,, place the mushroom tops upside down in the escargot dishes, or on an oven platter. Arrange in groups of 7 or 8.

Preheat oven to 350°

Fill each mushroom with the fried parsley mixture and pour any remaining sauce over them evenly. With thumb over the pernod spout,, sprinkle a wee bit more pernod over each dish.

Top with some grated Canadian Cheddar Cheese, You can use a more expensive gruyere cheese, yet it's not really necessary.

For a final touch, open up a bottle of fine burgundy wine, a dry one. Have a sip and put these little delicacies into the oven. Simmer till golden brown. (approx. 20~30 min.)

Now, pour your guests each a glass, have a seat,, relax and wait till the smell drives you mad.

Serve with hot garlic bread to soak up all the delicious sauce.

ARTICHOKE DE PAPA LEON

This is a rich entreé which should be served before,, or with a carefully planned lighter meal. (The large ones, size of grapefruits, should be served halved, as they are a meal in themselves. Small to medium sized ones are ideal.

Iilah first learned of this recipe from a very fine master Chef, Pa Pa Leon, who used to own a refined little hotel in Brussels, which was famous for it's cuizine and hospitality.

This recipe is basically the same as Pa Pa Leon taught, yet since becoming vegetarian, Iilah has modified the sauce to suit our more sensitive stomachs.

The artichokes should be cooked early in the day.

Scrub each one well and remove any blemishes or bad leaves. Cut the stem to about 1" long.

There are two methods of cooking artichokes:

1) Place stem down in a pot (it's best not to double layer them) and add water till they float. Add a bit of salt and cover. Simmer for 30~40 minutes. Midway thru cooking, turn each one so the opposite side is emersed. The artichokes are cooked when a leaf pulls easily from the center and the 'meat' on the inner side is tender.

2) Place stem down in a pressure cooker. Add 1" of water, a sprinkle of salt and seal cooker. Once the pressure has come up, cook for 15~20 minutes, depending on their size. Remove from the heat and release the pressure slowly.

Remove artichokes from the pot and set in a strainer, bottom side up. (If you boiled 'em, give them a little squeeze to remove excess water, being careful not to crush them.

Now,,, for la Salsa,,,,

Artichoke De Papa Leon, cont.,

Truly it is this sauce which makes the meal special.
Say we're cooking for 6, measure:

2 c. mayonnaise ('real' or tofu)

The speciality of this sauce is the delicate flavor of onion. Grate half of an onion on the fine side of a grater, so what you get is a thick juice.

Add to the mayonnaise:

1~2 tbls. of onion juice
1 tbls. tahine
1/4 tsp. finely gr. black pepper
1 tsp. maple syrup or liquid honey

For those who enjoy a moderate liquor habit, you may add:

1~2 tbls. of Mediera or Grand Marnier

Cream together and refrigerate in a covered dish.

Serve artichokes at room temperature with the chilled sauce.

If you're not familiar with eating artichokes,, it is done by removing one leaf at a time. Hold it by the pointed end, dip the wide end into the sauce and draw the bottom half of the leaf through your teeth, scraping off the tender meat on the inner edge. Repeat this with each leaf. When you come to the 'heart', remove the prickly stuff at the very center and eat the whole heart.

edible part of
the leaf

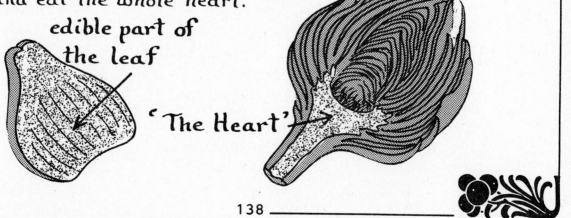

'The Heart'

STUFFED MUSHROOMS
AU GRAND MARNIER

This recipe requires 24 large headed mushrooms. Buy them where they are sold loose so you can pick ones with big, wide caps.

Early in the afternoon wash the mushrooms, yet do not squeeze them. Remove stems and place mushroom caps stem down on a paper towel or cloth. Let drain for a couple of hours.

In a wide skillet, melt:

   2 tbls. margarine

Sauté half the caps, bottom side up, till well browned. Sprinkle with tamari, sauté a little more, then turn and brown lightly. Remove and place on an oiled tray. Do likewise with the other half.

Chop finely:

   the mushroom stems
   1 med. onion
   4 cloves garlic

In the same skillet as you cooked the mushrooms, melt:

   4 tbls. of margarine

Add the chopped mushroom stems, onion and garlic. Sauté till lightly browned, tamari, sauté a little and remove from the heat.

Into the pan with the fried mushrooms, add:

   1 c. bread crumbs
      or cooked grain (bulghur, rice, millet)
   ½ c. grated cheese
      or ½ c. soy cheese
   ¼ c. finely chopped parsley
   ½ tsp. tarragon pwd.
   1 tbls. Grand Marnier

Stuffed Mushrooms au Grand Marnier, cont.,

Stuff each cap by spoonful. Heap each one a little if needed to use up all of the stuffing.

Place stuffed caps on an oiled serving platter. Bake at 350° till good and hot and browned lightly.

As a finishing touch of serving flare, pour 1 ounce of heated Grand Marnier over the mushrooms and flame them. Let burn till the flame goes out on its own. This evaporates the alcohol and leaves only the aromatic flavor.

SPICED HOME FRIES

We took to making potatoes this way as a less oily alternative to french fries.

For best results, boil the potatoes in the morning.

Scrub and pare 1 lrg. or 2 sm. potatoes per person. Cut in halves or quarter and boil with a little salt till cooked.

The most important thing in this recipe is to not overcook the potatoes. Knife test them till barely cooked. If overcooked, they fall apart while frying.

Drain and let cool as soon as they are cooked. When cool, cut into 1" pieces.

The potatoes can be skillet fried, grilled or baked. Melt an appropriate amount of marg. (or oil) into a skillet, or onto a grill or tray. Stir in potatoes.

Sprinkle with salt, garlic pwd. and black pepper or cayenne, to taste.

Cook, stirring as needed till well browned. Serve.

Seaweeds

Seaweeds have been scientifically proven to contain an abundance of organic substances and mineral elements which are so important for overall good health. Most of these substances are lost daily and need to be replaced regularly. Eating a variety of the many types of seaweeds available throughout the week will supply you with an ample supply of minerals such as iodine, zinc, sulphur, iron, copper, phosphorus, potassium, sodium, silicon, calcium, nitrogen, and more.

Besides being nutritionally sound to eat,, seaweeds are very tasty and offer a variety of textures and flavours. They can be incorporated into soups, salads, casseroles, vegetable dishes, grains, etc.

Because of the high mineral content of seaweeds, they are a wise food to eat daily to allay environmental radioactivity and pollutants which are becoming increasingly prevalent in our food, water, and air. It is an accepted fact that radioactive isotopes exist in some food products. Whether a food product is grown organically or not,, there are various free radioactive isotopes added to our environment from daily power plant emmissions and fallout,, not to mention those administered directly through radiotherapy and nuclear medicine.

Different radioactive substances share common atomic structural characteristics with certain natural minerals. Iodine resembles iodine 131 and 125,, potassium to Cesium 137,, iron to plutonium,, calcium to Strontium 90,, Vitamin B12 to Cobalt 60,, etc. Each of these false minerals collect in different internal organs or in our bone and muscle structure. They cause havoc and disrupt the proper bodily functions of the thyroid, the reproductive organs, kidneys, liver, and lungs.

When a pure source of these necessary elements is not present in one's diet,, the body will accept and absorb these radioactive substitutes. Alternatively,, when the body is supplied with the proper minerals and vitamins,, it will choose the natural elements and reject the inferior quality substances. A balanced whole grain diet, including seaweeds, acts as a preventive measure against environmental radiation and pollutants.

Sodium Alginate is an element found with sea vegetables such as kombu, wakame, hizuki, arame, and even agar agar. This element has the capacity to bond with radioactive isotopes deposited within any organs, muscles, or bones,, and eliminates them through waste matter. It has similar effects on other environmental pollutants such as lead, cadmium, iron, barium, etc.

In summary,, a wholesome, balanced diet, including seaweeds, strengthens your immune system and acts as a preventive measure against environmental pollutants and radioactivity.

A half-ounce serving of seaweed four to five times weekly, in conjunction with a proper diet, will supplement many necessary elements. When you get to really enjoy eating seaweeds,, be careful not to over use them, as too much of a good thing is not healthy either. Eat no more than half an ounce per day.

An Analogy of Cancer
It's cauze, It's Cure

I'd like to elaborate, if I may, about some of the horrific facts of life which might shock you into realization, as well as convince you to establish a more personal, positive reaction towards caring for yourselves and your families a little more. Sure, you love them,,, yet what you're feedin' 'em might just be the reason they're all gettin' so sick. Billions of wasted dollars could be better put to use if the world's stubborn economists, scientists, and governmental heads would simply accept the true cauze of cancer,, as well as that of most every other fatal disease. Many children aged three and four are getting different forms of cancer,,, and if you look at the diet their families are on,,, no wonder,, these damaging cells are passed on through the birth cycle,,, and the children don't have a chance to reconstitute their cellular structure because they are fed the same toxic, acidic diet their parents were brought up with. No one is to blame but availability itself.

Be ye believin' in it or not,, everyone is born with cancerous cells within their metabolism. They were originally put there with the intent of being a positive source needed to combat anything really negative which might have entered the humane system. As man's bloodstream becomes more and more polluted over the ages, with the same intoxicants and emulgeons which are killing our lands, forests, creeks, rivers, lakes, and oceans,,, the humane cells become overworked and literally change sides from good to evil.

Allow me to explain. Let's take the lymph, fallopian, breast, and pituitary glands for starters. When these emulgeon'd petrolium products, found in most processed foods, settle to a scum, and pool into these low lying, slow moving viaducts,,, the inner pores immediately secrete a strong mucous solution in order to remove this klinging glob. Now, due to the peculiar nature of this emulsion, it remains intact, and after some time,,, the pores close once again.

Now, one has a layer of scum, and under it,, a strong, mucous-like substance which the body produced,, and soon, it turns rancid after it has no place to go. Soon, the inner pores open again,,, and out comes more secretion, hoping to combat two wrongs, instead of just one. Now, after this procedure repeats itself over and over for some three to seven years, a tumour has formed,, and the universal body has no alternative but to produce the worst combatin' it can muster up. ii,,, the cancer cells come into power, and like an organic acid,,, they begin to eat up the rancid mucous, along with the emulgeon'd scum which cauzed the trouble to begin with. Now the problem is,,, most who have these cancerous spots growing within, generally maintain a very acidic system, as well as taking very acidic drugs,,, so, these cancer cells thrive and feel quite at home. As a matter of fact,,, they generally go on to absorb one's digestive tract, and filter organs as well.

When the Good Lord kreated the humane form to the likeness and imagery of His own,,, He made man from the alkaline soils and minerals, and not from the acid earth it's become. After the great upheavals when conscious man had begun to kill for his food and pollute the Earth with his alchemies, did man's kind change from the easy going, alkaline way of life, to the hyperactive, acidic life of deception for sake of economic rule. Once a person returns to a natural, alkaline lifestyle of common sense,,, his energy, along with all else to do with life's values, falls into a more conducive and harmonious situation. When the bloodstream becomes the doctor it was meant to be, it retains its capabilities to revitalize a hurting system, as well as to rejuvenate it. This includes the logical balancing and transformation of one's nervous system, cauzing man's outlook of why he's really here to come to light, deed, and activity.

Yes, folks,, it has been proven many times over that cancer can be beaten, providing it is caught while the patient still has the energy to help himself. If only people could be brought to realize that the finest medicine of all is presently available to everyone equally, and can be easily adopted through a tasty, healthful, preventive diet. Sure,,, it's an embarrassment to the medical profession,,, yet, when their hearts click in, instead of their egos and pocket books,,, maybe then they too will stop dying of this dreaded, economic killer.

Some time ago a dear friend be telling me, "Kjo,,, for 40 years of my life, I was a real macho meat eater and steel worker,,,, I was rough and tough,, and feared only one thing,,, and that was of ever becoming a living vegetable. Then, 20 years ago, I was given half a year to live, if that. That's when my son changed my diet of the unnatural to a macrobiotic one,,, and my wife was pleased to make the necessary adjustments, and now,,, I've finally realized what it means to blossom as a flower of kreashon,,, and my only remaining fear is of ever having to become a meathead once again".

Ah,,, the sweet pains of wizdom. ii,, unless one pays the proper dues and actually works toward a konkshus fulfill-ment, one will never know of it until it is too late to do anything for the self, or one's loving family. To dine own self ye must be true,, no matter what you say or know.

If only people would take the time to analyze common sense for a change, instead of chemical, chemical, chemical. Remember,,, modern medical science teaches a false pasifica-tion through toxic drugs, until the diseased organ is put to the knife,,, rather than a healing organic diet, which not only cures and rebuilds the molecular organ, but also cures the reason why it became diseased to begin with.

SOUPS

CHAPTER 4

Soups

Home Made Soups

Homemade soups are as traditional as Grandma's Apple Pie, whether it's a simple vegetable variety on to a gourmet french onion soup.

Soup as a general fare is very nutritious as it retains all the goodness in the broth.

To maintain the freshness of each vegetable in any soup,, boil the vegetables which require the most cooking time first and add the quicker cooking vegetables in the appropriate order and timing.

Miso Soup

Traditionally, miso soup is basically a miso broth with a small amount of sautéed vegetables, ie,, onion, carrot, etc. This is our version of miso soup which has seaweed and more vegetables.

Soak for 10 minutes:

6" piece of wakame seaweed

Prepare and sauté in a little oil in a soup pot:

1 c. onion (thin slices)
3/4 c. carrot (shaved in small slivers)
3/4 c. diakon radish (1/4" thick half moons)

When the onions are tender, add to the pot:

4 c. water   the seaweed (chopped)

Bring to a boil and simmer for 15~20 minutes.

Prepare: 1 c. of greens (kale, chard, collards, etc.)

Add greens to the soup and simmer 5 min. more.

Mix together:

1/2 c. water   1/4 ~ 1/3 c. miso

Turn the soup off and add the miso. Stir well and serve.

VEGETABLE ~ SEAWEED SOUP

Soak: 10" piece of wakame seaweed

Boil: 8 c. water

Prepare and add to the water:

1 onion (diced)	4 cl. garlic (chopped)
1 st. celery (sliced)	1 c. parsley (" ")
1 potato (½"dice)	1 tsp. basil
½ c. broccoli (sliced)	wakame
4 oz. soba noodles (break into 1" pcs.)	

Simmer till cooked (approx. 20 min.)

Add miso, tamari or salt to taste.

MINESTRONI

Soak overnight:

½ c. chick peas	½ c. kidney beans

Boil: 10 c. water   1 tsp. salt

Add drained beans and simmer with a lid till they are cooked. (45~60 min.)

Meantime, prepare and cut:

1 c. onion (diced)	½ c. celery (sliced)
½ c. carrot (" ")	½ c. cabbage (chopped)

Add chopped vegetables to soup, plus:

½ c. tubettini ndls. (or other sm. tubular pasta)
14 oz. can of whole tomatoes
3 cl. garlic
½ tsp. black pepper

Simmer till the vegetables are cooked.

Serve with a sprinkle of parmesan cheese and a good crusty bread.

CREAM OF CELERY SOUP

This is a deliciously, creamy and savory soup which is great on cold days.   This soup will have the best flavor if you use crisp, green celery.

It's the kind of soup you will want to make enough of so you have leftovers, cuz it's better the next day.

Peel, chop and sauté in a heavy bottom soup pot:

    2 onions   2 tbls. marg (or oil)

Add: 7 cups water   1 tsp. salt

Bring to a boil, meantime prepare and add to soup:

    6 st. celery (¼" slices)   1 tsp. basil
    3 med. potatoes (1" pcs.)   1 tbls of dried
    sautéd onions   parsley

Simmer till potatoes are fully cooked.
Let cool for 20 min.

Blend soup, 3 cups at a time.
Return to the pot,, bring back to a boil.

Serve garnished with croutons, chopped parsley, and grated or parmesan cheese (opt.).

CREAM OF MUSHROOM SOUP

Boil: 6 c. water   1 tsp. salt
    ½ c. millet (washed)

Add: 1 c. diced onion   ½ tsp. savory
    ½ tsp. thyme   ½ tsp. chevril

Wash, squeeze, dice and sauté:

    1 lb. mushrooms

When soup has cooked, blend. Return to the pot and add mushroom, reheat.

Serve with croutons or swieback.

ROSY RED SOUP

Bring to a boil in a saucepan:

    6 c. water   1 tbls. salt
    1 ~ 14 oz. can wh. tomatoes (or 2 c. fresh)

Prepare, cut and add to the pot:

    1 st. celery (diced)   1 tbls. chevril
    2 med. leeks (sliced)   ½ tsp. sage
    ½ c. beets (¼" dice)   2 bay leaves
    1 c. parsley (chopped)   4 cl. garlic (diced)
    ½ lb. mushrooms (¼" slice)

Simmer till vegetables are cooked. Remove bay lvs.

Can be served as is or with the addition of 1 cup of cooked rice.

BARLEY ~ KOMBU SOUP

Soak: 8" piece of kombu (soak a minimum of 1 hr.)

Bring to a boil:

    8 c. water   ½ c. barley (washed)
    kombu (cut in ¼" pcs.) 1 tsp. salt

Simmer on low, with a lid for 1 hr. (Barley should be well cooked or it will not be easily digested.)

Meantime, prepare and dice:

    1 c. carrots   1 c. celery
    1 c. onion

After soup has boiled for 1 hour, add:

    cut vegetables   1 tsp. basil
    1 tsp. savory   1 tbls. oil

Top up with a little water if the soup is too thick and add tamari or miso to taste.

Heat till good and hot. Serve.

EGG DROP SOUP

Boil: 8 c. water

Prepare and add to the water:

    1 onion (diced)   1 st. celery (sliced thin)

Simmer for 15 minutes.
Prepare and add:

    2 c. ch. spinach, chard or chinese cabbage
    2 tsp. grt. ginger rt. (in a tea ball)
    ¼ c. tamari   3 cl. garlic (slivered)

Simmer for 10 minutes.

Blend: 4 eggs   ¼ c. flour
    or ½ c. tofu   ¼ c. water

Pour slowly into boiling soup while stirring steadily.
Simmer 5 min. more. Serve with hot bread.

CELERY SOUP AU GRATIN

Make this using 'Cream of Celery Soup' (page 150)
Such a fine soup is well deserving of being served
in this fashion.

For each person you will need:

    1 french onion soup bowl
    1½ c. of cream of celery soup
    1 slice of durham or whole wheat bread
    2 cl. of garlic (finely chopped)

Place sliced bread on tray and spread with garlic.
Bake at 350° till golden brown.

Bring soup to a heat and add: (per serving)

    pinch of finely ground black pepper
    1 tsp. Armagnac cognac (opt.)

Celery Soup au Gratin, cont.,

Fill each bowl no more then 4/5's full of soup.

Cut each toast slightly smaller then the opening of the hole in the bowl. Add cut off pieces of the toast first, then add the whole piece of toast on top.

Top with grated cheese, mochi or soy cheese and bake for 25~30 minutes at 350°.

This soup is essentially a meal in itself and only needs to be accompanied by fresh garlic bread and salad.

ADUKI~BEAN SOUP

Combine in a pot and bring to a boil:

    5 c. water
    1~1½ c. cooked aduki beans
    ½ c. cooked kombu (chopped fine)
    3 cl. garlic
    1 tsp. dill

Prepare and sauté in a little oil:

    ½ c. onion (½" dice)
    ½ c. carrot (¼" dice)
    ½ c. celery (¼" dice)

When fried ,, add to the soup.

Simmer for 30 minutes.

Add: 1 c. chopped greens
        (kale, collards, spinach or chard)

Cook till the greens are done.

Tamari or miso to taste. Serve.

CREAM OF PARSLEY SOUP

Bring to a boil:

8 c. water   1 tsp. salt
3/4 c. millet (washed)

Prepare and add to the water:

2 med. size onions (diced)
1 st. celery (1/4" slices)

Simmer for 15 min.

Prepare and add:

2 c. chopped parsley
4 cl. garlic (chopped)

Simmer for 5~10 min., then cool for 20 minutes.

Add: 2 tbls. margarine (optional)

Blend then reheat. Serve garnished with croutons and a sprinkle of chopped parsley.

GREEN GARDEN SOUP

Boil: 8 c. water

Prepare and add to water:

2 leeks (sliced)   4 oz noodles (buckwheat,
1 lrg. carrot (1/4" sl.)   spin. fettucini or egg
                              ndls.)

Simmer for 15 mins.

Prepare and add to soup:

1/2 c. chopped parsley
1 1/2 ~2 c. chopped greens (swiss chard,
          kale, ripini, collards or spinach)
1 tbls. grated ginger rt. (in a tea ball)

Simmer for 1 min. more.

Add miso, tamari or salt to taste.

CREAM OF ASPARAGUS SOUP

Peel, slice and sauté in a soup pot:

    1 med. onion   2 tbls. soy marg.

Sauté till well browned and syrupy. (10 min.)

Wash: 2 bunches asparagus (approx. 24 stalks)

Remove 1½" tip from each stalk. Cut remaining stalks into 1" pieces.

Add to the soup pot and bring to a boil:

    3 c. water
    chopped asparagus stems
    ⅓ c. millet (washed)
    1 tsp. salt

Simmer with a lid for 25 min.
Remove from the heat and cool for 10 min.

Meanwhile, use a little of the stock from the soup to boil the asparagus tips. Do not over cook them. Drain the stock back into the soup as soon as they are cooked.

Add to the soup:

    1 c. soy milk   2 tbls. soy marg.

Blend half the soup and strain through a metal sieve. Repeat, then return all of the soup back to the pot. Add the asparagus tips and reheat.

Serve as is or top with a spoonful of tofu sour cream and a sprinkle of paprika.

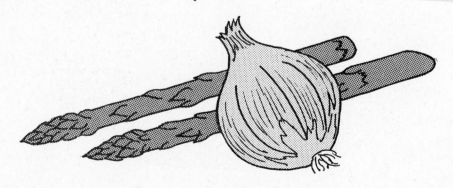

BORSCH SOUP

The night before, soak:

    1. c. of aduki beans or kidney beans

Bring to a boil:

10 c. water *	1 tsp. salt
soaked beans	1 tbls. oil

Boil for 1 hour or pressure cook for 30 min.

Meantime, prepare and dice:

1 c. beets	1 cup onion
1 c. carrots	1 cup cabbage

When the beans have cooked, add:

diced vegetables	⅛ tsp. cayenne
4 bay leaves	1 tsp. tarragon
1 tsp. basil	

Simmer with a cover for 30 minutes.
Garnish with croutons, finely chopped parsley, and some natural sour cream or 'Tofu sour cream'.

*As a tasty alternative, you may substitute 2~3 cups of stewed or fresh tomatoes in place of the same amount of water. (If using fresh tomatoes, they should be scalded to remove the skins and pared to remove the core.

PHEYLONIAN GARLIC SOUP

A gourmet soup with a remarkably delicate flavor.

Once when we were serving this to some guests who were well acquainted with gourmet cuisine, the overall response was one of great pleasure. Upon asking for a little more, one man commented, "This is very good,, but, it needs a little garlic. Well, when Lilah told everyone what the soup was made of, we all had a good laugh and a little more soup.

Peel and chop finely:

> ½ lb. garlic

Melt in a thick-bottomed soup pot:

> 2 tbls. soy marg.

Add: ¼ of the chopped garlic
⅛TH tsp. ground black pepper

Sauté till well browned (not burnt). Dash with a little tamari and sauté another minute.

Add to the pot:

8 c. water	2 tbls. tamari
remainder of garlic	1 tsp. saffron
1½ c. potato	1 tsp. black pepper
1 tbls. tarragon	balls (in a tea ball).

Bring to a boil and simmer with a lid for 30 minutes.

Add: 4 c. chopped parsley
¼ c. medium sweet, quality sherry
2 tbls. soy marg.
2 ~ 4 tbls. light miso (to taste)

Simmer for another 20 min. Remove from the stove and let cool slightly. Blend till smooth in 3 c. batches. Return to the pot and reheat.

Serve with croutons, grated cheese (opt.) and a sprig of parsley.

Island Madness

Once upon a time, not too long ago, back in the '70s, a team of knowledgeable persons came upon this untouched and unchartered ocean island. It had a particular ayre of gentleness to its panoramic landscape, and once ashore,, these scientific people were astonished at the many different species of animals which inhabited this pure and beautiful island. After a brief study,, they were amazed to see that half of the animals living here were of a carniverous species, and lived elsewhere in the world,,, yet here,,, these animals would play and feed next to the other animals they would normally kill and eat in other places on Earth. No animals were eating each other here,,, and all ate different forms of vegetation. Some,, who were afraid of water everywhere else on the Earth,, would wade and swim to eat sea weeds and shell fish.

Well,,, what en ecological study this would make. Sure enough,,, a year and a grant later,,, comes the troops. There's the biologist, the anthropologist, the zoologist, the doctor, lawyer and Indian Chief,,, rabbi, priest, and reverent one. ii,,,, and the choice spot amidst it all is set up for camp. I hope yawl don't mind me funnin' a bit,,, because like every other story in this fine book of cookin',, this is a true one, as well,,, and it's best to be able to laugh some along with a tear and a smile over it all.

With camp set up and stores in place,,, they wave goodbye to their sailing comrades who are to pick them up nine months from time of their departure,,, and all other communications and supply trains would be communed by air and radio. It didn't take long for them to start their research. After $100,000 and three months of extensive study, their astonishments were unanimous over one thing: This island was ecologically unstable,,, because for a definite fact,,, half the animals who were supposed to be killing and eating the other half, weren't. As bewildered as they were over it all,,, the intensive research went on. Animals were caged, shot, pinned, tagged, operated on, injected, rejected, and injested. Before you know it,, there was a garbage problem on this adorable little island,,, and wouldn't you know it,,, from it alone came the scientific solution to their mind boggling misinterpretashons. ii,,, from all the remains of their canned meats, lab carcasses, and hot barbecues dumped onto this site,,, these friendly animals began to munch on the remains.

After a few months noticeable changes were taking place with the island's inhabitants, and all focuses were centred on the dump. Many animals were getting lazy, and did not want to dig, root, pick, or grapple for sea weed and shell fish. They preferred the fast food junk line at the dump site. Soon, they began to argue and bicker over territorial rights,, then the inevitable took place,,,, they began to fight and kill each other,,, and, you guessed it,,, it wasn't long after that they began eating each other. They grouped, and the larger ate the smaller, etc., etc.,,, and folks,,, so help me,,, nine months after this scientific team set foot onto this amazing island, along with quite a few hundred thousand wasted,, did they pack up their gear and leave. Their reports were well documented, and the ultimate revelation to it all went as so: "The island and its animal inhabitants are now in ecological balance with the rest of their brothers and sisters around the world".

They are killing and eating each other for survival.

Deja Vu of Astral Demise

Dreams are timeless voyages, and into these time zones forbidden to life's consciousness, flow man and woman for the better part of their lives. As a matter of fact,,, so many are unaware of the realities to reality,, their integrated circuitries remain dormant, even while awake, unless they are stimulated to some degree now and then by a drug, junk food, ritual, sex, or booze.

From youth,,, most children are being misguided by the System, rather than taught how to develop their natural and psychic abilities. Of course, the System revolves around economics,, and yawl know where that's a'headin' to,,, while on the other hand,,, the Eternal Universe revolves around common sense and consciousness. As mentioned throughout the Introduction, diet plays a tremendous role relative to one's true psychic developments and spiritual expanshons. When diet, spirituality, and one's psyche are developed toge- ther,,, 'astrality' and 'déjà vu's' unify into a present day, to the hour, to a now type thing, as well.

This chapter is designed to help all those who can't or won't go to zen or a swami guru etc., to enhance their reali- zation about what's bin missed. Life is not easy for these grandfolks who had to fight wars, go through depressions, and raise arrogant children, all at the same time. Like them,, many of today's modern new-wave'rs, etc., are having to face the same unkanny reality,, only it's illusioned to look real different. Quicksand always has the same resulting effect,, yet its basic appearance on the surface differs from place to place and time to time.

When will the salt of the earth come to realize all the grounds they have lost, physically and spiritually, by allowing the youth to make the same mistakes they were not allowed to make. Because people can't always get what they want to fulfill their basic needs,,, they often pretend it doesn't exist, and in turn, make it awful hard for those who should have it, to get it. It, of course, being a full, simple, and happy life.

Shure, all worth having exists, and is there for the taking,,, yet in truth,, it's wired up in such a way where no one gets anything for real, unless they put in for real. False activity has always equated the reactshunists modee de aporendi, relative to all things.

In as much as we're all goin' to Heaven,,, all is not yet as it should be,,, for as long as the monies and chips of the world govern man's intellect,, there will continue to be crack pots and jack pots put in power. Of course, there are always those who really would like to honestly help all their people come to experience life's truer meaning with the same dignity and pleasure they and their families would like to experience it as being,,, yet they too get caught, and lose some of the basic simplicities relative to our real purpose for being here.

I've heard it said,,, "Ahhhh,, what's going to happen is going to happen, no matter what,,, so what the heck,,, might as well party". Well,,, what I saw was an enlightened person being blinded by her own glowing ego. ii,,, ya'r what you eat, and she failed to see, where sitting on top of quicksand with a real majik karpet under you, is worth far more than just throwing any old karpet onto the sludge, and jumping into it.

Real majiks aren't under people's control,,, yet,, because all of the Astral Powers have been abused in the times of Once, Long Ago, in the Kingdoms of Equal Allotments,,, all along, there have bin those who had to sell out for the exabishun of power, rather then bestowin' the proper bejewelments onto them not so fortunate. The sharing of time and happiness by those who know better, must complete a full circle of reprokushon,,, otherwize,, terrorism and wars will always break out. When the ultimate enactment of it comes to a calming sense about it all at grit levels,,, why, I do declare,,, everyone will be astral-bound one day,,, once and for all. Till then,, if you don't believe in it,,, try not eating for a spell, and see how light-headed you get,,,, better yet,, try eating proper and see how light you get. If you are skeptical, or don't believe in that astral part of you,,, try going to sleep with a scale next to your bed, and weigh yourself just before you go to sleep, and write it down. Now,,, no going to the bathroom, unless you weigh it,,, and when you awake come early morn', weigh yourself immediately before the deep breath,,, and see for yourself the noticeable loss. Then,,, walk around for a bit, taking in nothing or letting out nothing but air,,, and you will see how your weight comes back to normal. In other words,,, something you didn't know about was there,,, it left,,, and it came back. What it is, and where did it go, and what did it do, are all worthwhile questions which remain unanswered each day and night of people's lives.

Man's full astral kauzmik self is always within himself,,, yet look at the limited reflections being imposed. No wonder, hardly anybody's happy with each other anymore,,, because in fact,,, they are unhappy with themselves. Obviously, the wrong game is being reflected to everyone,,, and it's time the politishuns and their mentors should want to help the ailing social structure, rather than worry about economics so much,,, if all is to react accordingly. Before it's too late for anyone,, those in power must adhere to common sense. Then,,, only with the positive reactshons,, can the story of Kreashon get on with the more elloquenchall kah-mohds in dee kauzmos.

The Great One be telling me His Self,,, "Kjo,,,, the simplest of my children are most ready to accept and fulfill common sense,,, they just need a break".

Along with the relevancies of space, time, and dimenshonal travel, there should be more of the proper schools,,, just teaming with students who qualify to learn the such.

Problem is,,, there isn't, is there,,, because there aren't enough qualified teachers yet. ii,,, imagine, through the basic diet of gritts alone (meaning basic whole grains and veggies), how every individual can teach himself how to partake in the present dance of konkshus atoms. Having knowledge and doin' tricks,,, be they religious, physic, or not,, will not qualify one to enter soyt'n universal classrooms until the proper forms are filled out with substanance of value. Of course, I be talkin' about your personal form, because one must go beyond the paper of it all, in order to become a real reflector of peace loving truth. The diplomas being given today are not for the good of man,,, but for the good of economics alone.

There is so much more joy to be had when people actually fulfill the dimenshons of their own kauzmik self,,, rather than just pretending to know all about it, or, be one of those to say,, "Man, I don't believe in all that shtuff". I've always had to smile when I hear about those monks in remote monasteries who can levitate, and are then burdened to wearing a heavy chain so they don't get too high for their own good. Kinda reminds me 'bout them who could bend a spoon with their minds,, and then they spend the rest of their lives trying to bend something else. The true mystic shows no tricks to no one, until all have learned and are ready to walk together with both feet planted firmly on the ground, being able to honestly handle having their heads above the clouds.

By eating well, for real,, this will activate that atomized character within the subconscious you,,, then you qualify to learn the how to's for real. Only a real peace lovin', walkin', talkin', eatin' proper person, who has proven care for themselves at grit levels, has access to the Universal Files about man's atomic potential. Matters not of what religion or beliefs ye bee holdin' either. Enlightenment means to be as an accepted child of the Great Family, where ye shall reap accordingly.

When your spiritual dream body is allowed to inter-
mesh with your hard-headed egocentric one,,, then you will
function as a God-Headed Basic Unit, enjoying the full illu-
sionary dimenshons of the now. And believe me,,, now is not
as Heaven's to be,,, yet, from here,, and with what yawl get
to work with,,, one must find a reality worth living for. To
experience all dimenshonal perspectives simultaneously,
means to have done the groundwork first. Char what chew
eat,,, and the astral inward reflectshons reflect the same
story as the reflection on the outside of your bod. You've
all seen some mighty fine, good lookin' people not know or
reflect half as much as some real lovin' ugly folk who had
contact with the spirit form within, and vice-versa. This
outer shell we all wear means nothing, unless it's connected
to the inner you,, together qualifying to connect with the
One God.

Look at yourself as being within a tiny bubble nestled
next to seven billion other bubbles, all just a'brewin' within the genteel confines of one big bubble. Some of the
little bubbles have dim lights on, while others got their
brights on, blindin' them what's really tryin' to look out,,,
and, of course, there always has to be someone tryin' to
prick someone else's. And there are those who are just
sittin' there in a blank space,, a'waitin' to be zapped into
some form of recognition.

Let's venture, for a spell, beyond this massive,
translucent module,,, and see who's just a'sittin' back
there, a'blowin' this bubble. ii,,, will you look at
that,,,, thank God He don't boip without konkshusness.

Soh,,, you still want to astral travel,,, if so,,, begin
from within. Know thyself inside and out,,, and then, stand
ready, keen, alert, and peaceful,,, and one day,,, one way or
the other,,, yawl are in for a treat. Just remember the
ground rules,,,, otherwize, nothing of value comes from nothing of value,,, and anything of real value is coming from

those who are honestly sharing peace and good will amongst man's kind,,, regardless of status quo.

Meanwhile,,, people have to stop killin' and dyin' believin' in just this,,, cauzing so many others to die, believin' in that,,,, and then there's those who be killin' and dyin', believin' in nothing. So where does this leave all those who have needs and want to learn,, and are not able to. Well,,, how you say,,, "God bless 'em",,, and let's get on with dee cookin'.

The game is not over yet,,, and look,,, another hundred or so dim lights just came on!

So keep eatin' your grains and veggies, fruits and nuts in harmony with the seasons,,, and it won't be long till your light be shining right there along with the rest who come to know and do better for real.

SALADS

CHAPTER 5

Salads

TOSSED SALADS

In choosing ingredients for your salads, you should look out for and beware of a few interesting points.

Any vegetables that are glossy, waxy or have an oiled sheen to them have been sprayed with an emulsifier to 'preserve' and 'beautify' them. This is most often done to peppers, cucumbers, egg-plant and tomatoes. Avoid buying these or peel them and wash well.

When choosing lettuce never buy iceberg or head lettuce. It is the most chemically grown of them all and is worthless nutritionally.

There are an assortment of other types of lettuce available which are nutritious and very tasty:

romaine   chinese cabbage   endives

boston   escarole   watercress

spinach   belgium endives   leaf

Always wash lettuce well, especially at the base of each leaf, as this is where grit and other unfavorable residues can collect.

You can create delicious tossed salads by com-bining any of these following ingredients, cut to your own desired sizes.

lettuce of your choice (from above list)

carrot   jerusalem artichokes   avocado

celery   alfalfa sprouts   peppers

radish   mung sprouts   snow peas

parsley   fresh mushrooms   broccoli

tomato   purple cabbage   shallots

young beet greens, chard or dandelion

SALAD COMBOS

Here are a number of salad combinations we enjoy with suggested dressings.
Adjust the quantities to your own needs.

CHINESE DELUXE

½ chinese cabbage   diakon radish
¼ mung sprouts   snow peas
¼ watercress   water chestnuts
Use a 'Creamy Parsley' dressing.

IILAH'S CEASAR SALAD

⅔ romaine lettuce   croutons
⅓ boston lettuce   parmesan cheese
finely sliced red onion   'tofu weiner bits'
                        (page 316)
Dress with 'Iilah's Caesar Salad' sauce.

WATERCRESS~ENDIVE SALAD

1 bunch watercress (wash and drain. Only
      cut each sprig into 2 or 3 pieces).
2~3 endives (trim bottom ends and remove
      any bad leaves. Separate all the leaves,
      then wash and drain them. Cut leaves
      in half widthwise.
Use 'Iilah's French Dressing'.

HOUSE SALAD

⅓ romaine lettuce   cucumber slices
⅓ leaf lettuce   grated carrot
⅓ spinach   tomato chunks
Try our 'Pheylonian House' dressing.

COLESLAW

In preparing a good coleslaw,, the cabbage should be either grated or sliced very thin. (Do not grate or cut any of the thick core parts, as they are difficult to chew and do not marinate well.

In choosing cabbage, look for one which is still green. Those which are white are less tasty and not as nutritious.

Coleslaw is best made a few hours before mealtime and allowed to marinate in the dressing while being refrigerated. Any leftovers are even tastier the next day.

Here are a few of our most favorite coleslaw combinations:

Use either of the two coleslaw dressings listed on page 302.

'Regular'
4 c. cabbage
1 c. carrot (grated)

'Deluxe'
4 c. cabbage
1 c. parsley (chopped)
½ c. carrot (grated)
½ c. sweet red pepper
(diced)
½ c. celery (diced)
½ c. currants
½ c. sunflower sds.

Marinate in Isabel's dressing for 1 hour. Turn occasionally. Drain well and add mayonnaise.

'Coleslaw Especiál'
3 c. green cabbage
1 c. purple " "
1 c. carrot (grated)
½ c. green pepper (diced)
½ c. shallots (sliced)

'Hawaian Style'
1 c. cabbage
1 c. carrot (grated)
1 c. crushed pineapple
(drained well)
½ c. raisins
½ c. almond slivers

Isabel's Dressing is very good on this recipe. Replace vinegar with half pineapple juice.

Noodle Salads

We have made numerous versions of these cold noodle salads for many occasions.

They are excellent side dishes for parties or family get-togethers and they make a refreshing meal in the summer when you want to eat something cool.

Each of these recipes would serve as a main course for 4, or as a side dish for 6-8 people.

Each recipe simply calls for mayonnaise, cheese sauce, cream sauce or whatever. The amount and particular variation from the "Dips, Dressings and Sauces" section is up to you.

All of these salads improve in flavor if they are allowed to marinate at least 1 hour before serving.

Here are a number of our favorite combinations.

1) 4 c. cooked rotini (spiral) noodles
   1 c. finely chopped parsley
   ¼ c. " " " " chives (or shallots)
   ½ c. carrot (grated)
   1 tbls. vinegar   mayonnaise
   salt to taste   pinch of mustard pwd.

Mix well and refrigerate.

2) 4 c. cooked spinach fettuccine noodles

Prepare: 1 c. mushroom slices (use crisp, white ones)
         1 c. carrot slivers (large grate)
         ½ c. celery (thin slices)

Prepare and heat a batch of "Isabel's Coleslaw Dressing". Pour over vegetables and marinate for 1 hour.

Drain vegetables and save the dressing.
Combine the noodles and vegetables.
Add mayonnaise to taste and refrigerate.

3) 4 c. cooked elbow noodles
  ½ c. cooked peas
  ½ c.   "   "   carrots (large grate)
  ½ c.   "   "   beets (cook the beet whole,
    with skin, top and tail. When cooked, peel
    and grate)
  ½ c. grated cheddar cheese
  ½ tsp. pwd. tarragon

Make a sauce using:
  ½ c. cheese sauce (or cream sauce)
  ½ c. mayonnaise

Tamari or salt to taste.

Mix well and refrigerate.

4) 4 c. cooked egg noodles (fine)
  1 c. broccoli tops (cut small)
  ½ c. red pepper (diced)
  ¼ c. purple onion
  1 tbls. lemon juice
  1 tsp. paprika
  salt to taste
  mayonnaise or Parsley-Garlic Dip
                        (page 293)

5) 4 c. cooked egg noodles (broad)
  ½ c. ripe tomato (diced)
  ½ c. parsley (chopped)
  ¼ c. green pepper
  ¼ c. celery (diced)
  ¼ c. red radish (diced)

Make a sauce by combining:
  2 parts mayonnaise
  1 part tahine
  1 part tomato sauce (or ketchup)

Add to the vegetables and noodles. Mix well
and salt to taste. Refrigerate.

6) 4 c. cooked vegetable shell noodles
   ½ c.   "   "   green beans (cut in ½" pcs.)
   ½ c.   "   "   broccoli (cut in ½" pcs.)
   1 c. tomato (diced)
   ¼ c. shallots (sliced thin)

Add: sour cream
     or tofu sour cream
Mix well, salt to taste and refrigerate.

7) 4 c. soba (buckwheat) noodles (1" pcs.)
   2 c. finely sliced fresh spinach
   1 c. ripe tomato (diced)
   ¼ c. chives (chopped)

Add enough tahina sauce to bind everything together.
Refrigerate.

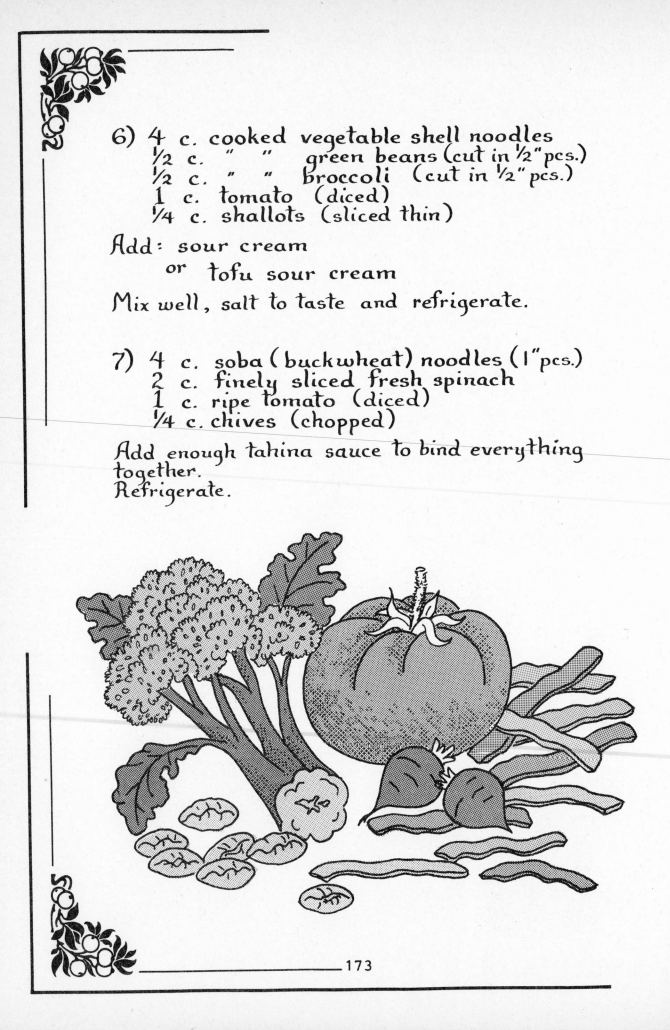

Barley and Cucumber Salad
(Marinated Salad)

Barley is a cooling, warm weather food. This is a delightful way to serve leftover barley as a cold, main dish during the summer.

Combine in a bowl and mix well:

    2 c. cooked barley
    2 c. finely diced cucumber
    ½ c. finely chopped parsley
    ½ c. "   "   " red onion

Add: 1 tbls. apple cider vinegar
     2 tbls. umebosi vinegar
     1 tbls. oil
     ½ tsp. garlic pwd.

Mix well and marinate for 1~4 hours in the fridge. Stir occasionally.

Just before serving, add:

    ½ c. tofunnaise

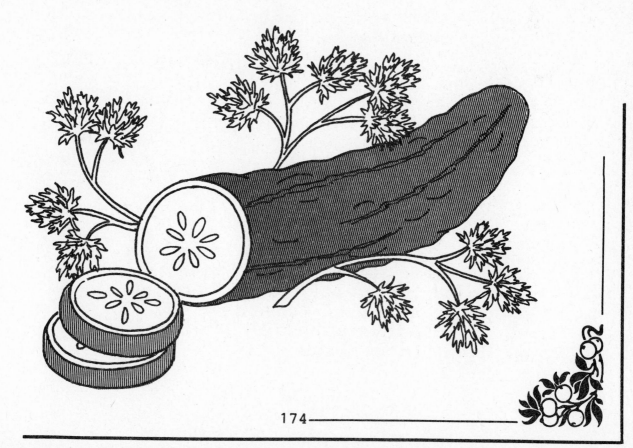

QUICK CUCUMBER PICKLE

Very refreshing in the summertime. An ideal way to utilize an abundance of cucumbers from the garden, as they disappear fast when prepared this way.

English cucs are the nicest for this as the seeds are negligible. If using regular cucumbers, cut in half widthwise and spoon out the seeds before slicing. Peel if the skins are tough.

Slice into ⅛" thick rounds:

   6" of cucumber

Separate slices and layer in a straight sided container or cup.

Pour over the cucs:

   2 tbls. vinegar (apple cider or ume)
   1 tbls. oil
   1~2 tsp. tamari
   1 tsp. lemon juice

Stir till each slice is coated well. Place in the refrigerator. Stir every ½ hr.

These are best if they marinate for 1~2 hrs. before being served.

Pour off liquid before serving. This can be used as is for salad dressing, or add a few tbls. of mayonnaise to make a creamy dressing.

VEGETABLE SEEDS

As a general rule, we always remove tomato or cucumber seeds before using either of these vegetables. lilah explains it thus,, "Why put something which is undigestable into your system only to have it come out the other end,. or worse, get lodged in your appendix."

TABBOULI SALAD

Boil: 1 c. water   ½ c. bulghur
     ¼ tsp. salt

Simmer with a cover till all the water is gone.

Prepare and chop or dice finely:

     3 c. parsley   ½ c. green pepper
     1 c. tomato

Combine in a saucepan:

     2 tbls. olive oil   2 tbls. lemon juice
     1 tsp. honey   2 tbls. apple cider
     salt to taste   vinegar

Bring to a boil and pour over the vegetables.
Let marinate for 1 hour. Stir occasionally.

Add bulghur, mix well and refrigerate.

TABBOULI

This is an improvised version which can be enjoyed as a main part of your meal ,,, or served as a side dish.

It is also good for lunch, served in a pita bread.

Boil: 2 c. water   1 c. bulghur
     ½ tsp. salt

Simmer with a cover till all the water is gone. Cool.

Dice finely and add to the cooled grain:

     1 c. parsley   ¼ c. lemon juice
     ¼ c. cucumber   2 tbls. tahine
     ¼ c. celery   ⅛ tsp. cayenne
     ¼ c. red pepper   salt or tamari to taste

Mix thoroughly and refrigerate for an hour or two. Turn occasionally.

GUACAMOLE

The most essential ingredient needed for this recipe are properly ripened avocados. They should be soft to the touch. The inside should be creamy and a yellow~green color. (Remove brown spots).

Whilst we were in Guatemala, we enjoyed this dish often as an afternoon snack on tortillas or toast. We were able to get huge, tree ripened avocados for a penny a piece. They were sweet and as smooth as butter inside.

The quantity of the ingredients can vary according to your own taste. Here is how we prefer it.

Cut in half, remove pit and spoon out the insides of:
> 3 avocados

Mash till creamy.

Prepare and dice finely:
> 1 st. celery   1 sweet red pepper
> 6 radishes   2 cl. garlic
> 3~4 shallots

Add diced ingredients to mashed avocado, plus
> 2~3 tbls. mayo   tamari or salt to taste

Mix well and chill till served. (Keep covered). The flavor improves if allowed to marinate for 2~3 hrs. before being served.

GUACAMOLE DIP

This is a great dip at parties for crackers or chips.

Combine in a blender:
> 1 c. guacamole   ¼ c. mayonnaise

Blend till smooth.

Repeat till you have enough.

Marinated Salad

Refreshing as part of a summer time meal and ideal for luncheon get-togethers.

A few hours of marinating time is sufficient, however, overnight is better.

Wash and prepare:

- 6" of english cucumber (cut into ⅛" rounds - peel if skin is tough)
- 1½ c. carrot (⅛" diagonal slices)
- 2 med. tomatoes (deseeded, cored and cut into ¼" thick rounds)
- 1 onion (cut into ⅛" rounds. Separate the rings of each slice)

Layer in a casserole dish:

- ⅓ RD onions
- ⅓ RD carrots
- ⅓ RD cucumbers
- ⅓ RD tomatoes

Repeat twice more.

In a saucepan, combine:

- ¼ c. ume vinegar
- ¼ c. apple cider vinegar
- ¼ c. oil
- 1 tsp. maple syrup
- 1 tsp. tarragon
- ¼ tsp. minced garlic
- ¼ tsp. black pepper
  or ⅛ tsp. cayenne pepper

Simmer for 5 min. Pour over the vegetables while hot. Place a plate on top to act as a weight. Cover and refrigerate.

Remaining sauce can be blended with some tofu to make a very nice salad dressing.

Bean Salad

Combine in a bowl :

    1 c. cooked kidney beans
    1 c. " " chick peas
    1 c. " "   green beans
           (cut in ½" diagonals)
    1 c. diced tomatoes
    ½ c. diced spanish onions
    ½ c. diced sweet or hot pepper

Combine in a saucepan :

    ½ c. tomato juice
    4 tbsp. vinegar
    3 tbsp. oil   1 tbsp. arrowroot fl.
    1 tbsp. basil   ⅛ tsp. cayenne
    1 tsp. salt

Bring to a boil and simmer till thickened. (Stirring constantly). Add to the vegetables and the beans and chill till ready to serve.

The longer this sits and marinates for,,, the better it will taste.

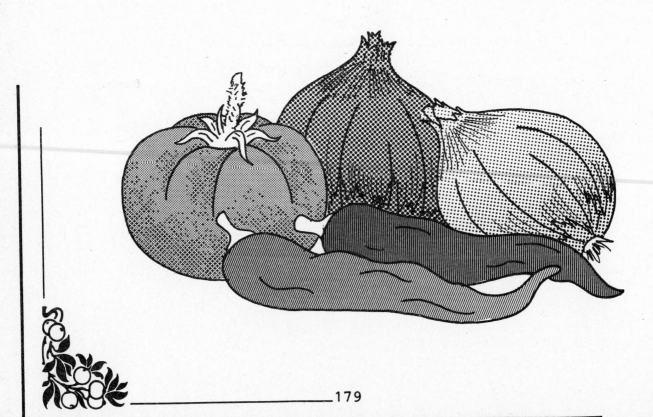

To Bee or Not to Bee

As it were destined for them to do several times before,, here again, the Philoxians were forced to leave all their hard work, possessions, and comforts of their jungle home behind, to hightail it out of there without anything but their rapidly aging caravan and the shirts on their backs. After experiencing four enormous earthquakes where the lands came at them in 12-foot waves,,, volcanos erupting all around,,, platoons of hyped soldiers comin' at 'em each week, shooting their guns,,, typhoid fever, jaundice, heart attacks, and the death of one so dear to them,, all within a two-week period,, it was unanimously decided to get out, just before the monsoons came.

Getting through Mexico non-stop, and without incident, was again, only a dream. For twice more,, were they attacked by three car loads of yokelish bandidos who would cut your throat for a quarter and laugh while doing it. Without exaggeration, if all was to be written about what these Pheylonian friends of mine have had to go through in order to finally settle in this little hamlet, tucked away in a calming, protective fen of Ontario,, it would surely make the "Raiders of the Lost Ark" movie look like a Bambi picture.

ii,,,, finally on their way home to the Kanadas,,, the inevitable major breakdown occurred, right smack dab in the middle of one of the toughest, most exciting hillbilly towns in Georgia. ii,,, Kennesaw, as it be called,, also known to be the only town in the U.S. of A., where it it compulsory to carry a gun at all times. Well,,, with their axle burnt clean through, and it being a Friday afternoon,, time had it to where they could only procure a fix-it shop, and if all went well,, they would be able to leave on the following Monday. As it turned out,, every last cent between them was needed to cover the cost of such a repair,,, so here they

were, with nothing left but their intuitiveness and jungle
instincts.

In wanderin' about,, there seemed to be a festive
air about the town folk,, and after meeting some of the
town's proprietors and the notorious General,,, well, things
started to get brighter.

Here again, yawl are going to have to excuse my modee de
aperendee, because I could go on to write volumes of exciting
tales relating to their stay here,, yet I must condense this
down to two very special stories worth sharin' about Georgia
beez.

Oddly enough,,, for the past 20 years,, the
Philoxians are still the only people in all of North America
to work as they do with pure beez wax,, and are still the
only ones to produce the only pure beez wax candles, derived
from an old Gypsy natural wick'd recipe,, which burns with a
golden halo,, and actually lasts 40 times longer than paraffin.

Being invited by the General, the Mayor, and Police
Chief to partake in Kennesaw's Trade Day Fair, which happened
to be on this very weekend, was a blessing in disguise,,,
because afterwards, they were invited to stay and literally
paint the town from one end to the other. ii,,, I remember
the Mayor and Police Chief standin' there, towering over
Iilah, sayin' to him,,, "Yawl ain't gonna leave till you
paint the town",, and, folks, that's just what they did.
Store fronts, signs, murals, homes,,, why they even painted
a mural for the President's personal pilot who flew Airforce
#1.

While all this was goin' on,,, several dear friends
had invited the Philoxians to camp on their land, giving them
access to their wells and power. Talk about Southern hospitality at its best. Because of it,, this one weekend turned
out to be a year. Once, while camped in the foothills just

out of town,, they be workin' on some signs and peach blossom beez wax candles,, when another remarkable bee incident took place.

It was getting on up to supper time when, without warning,, they were visited by a flashing black knight crested with golden armour. Would you believe, a huge black bumblebee buzzed right into their camp site, and was flying with irratic outbursts, goin' this way, then that way,, zoomin' in, zoomin' out,,, and after doing this for a dozen or more times,, what seemed to be a little frightening at first,,, turned out to be another very rewarding episode worth sharing with yawl. This huge bumblebee soon came to a calm amidst us,, and acted as though it wanted to communicate with Tawlia, who was busily at work, finishing a sign for a gift shop in town. He hovered right in front of her, between her nose and paint brush. At first, she looked a little worried, when suddenly he made a strange VVTT-VVTT sound,, and off he went like a bullet, and we could see this big horsefly knocked to the ground. Then, back he came, just a'hoverin' by Tawlia, as he had done. Seconds didn't go by until VVTT-VVTT again,, and off he went, this time taking out a huge greeny-black housefly, some 12 feet away,,, then back again to Tawlia. Well, by this time, we're all gathering around, and again and again, time after time, he would dart off, knocking some pestilent bug out of our perimeter.

We all sat spellbound,, because never before had such a thing bin experienced. At times, it would sit suspended 2 or 3 inches from her paint brush,, then it would go close to the sign, then back on up right in front of her nose,,, and that's when she remarked, "Hey guys,,, look at this,,, he's got a little golden heart painted right smack dab in the middle of his forehead". I remember Iilah asking,,, "Tawlia,, did you put that there"? Well,, never had we seen the likes of it. It didn't take long before every one of us felt at a full comfort havin' this little guy buzzin' all around us, watchin' every move we made. What a treat,,, then, as quick as he had appeared to us,, off he went,, and it wasn't until the next day that he reappeared at exactly 9 a.m.,,, and so help me God,,, for the next five days, without fail,, 9 till five each day,,, this little dashing black knight would come on the job,, and absolutely bedazzled us all with his antiks.

He befriended each one of us,,, and at times would even sit on our shoulders or paint brushes. As relaxed as he would seem,, no bug, hornet, other beez, flies, or anything was allowed to come within 20 feet of where we were,,, otherwise, he flew direct to them, literally knocking them right out of bounds. Now this is what is most amazing: Never once did he chase a butterfly away,,, he just watched them as we did. At this point, we began to realize that there will be some bugs comin' home to Heaven forever after,,, and for sure,, our brave little knight was to be one of them.

Could you imagine,,, he seemed to take enjoyment in making us laugh. We were saddened somewhat in leaving this spot,,, because never again have we seen such a bee with a heart on its head,, nor one with such a character.

GLOBAL ENTRÉES

CHAPTER 6

Global Entrées

Lovable Meatheads

A lot of people have asked about our Pheylonian Menu, wondering why do we call our Steak au Poivre Flambé, Veal Fettucini, Hamburgers, Meatloafs, etc., etc., as we do,,, especially when there's absolutely no meat in them. To some who haven't wizened yet,, it was even appalling! Well, allow me to elaborate. To those who have been brought up in our Great Western Society, and have reached certain maturities and expanding awareness levels, and have naught else to do but to strive for more enlightenment,,, well, a hamburger is still a hamburger, as is a meatloaf a meatloaf, etc. For example,, my Father, now 70, who went through a few wars, depressions, and a real hard life breaking his back to put meat on the table for his family,, would not go and change all he believed in, and liked, to suit some Eastern Teaching and strange tasting diet, with names and tastes he couldn't even pronounce or identify with.

When it became time for my parents to change their diet, or die for sure of incurable diseases,, I moved in with them, and showed my Mom how to make real good meatloafs and hamburgers etc., which had the right flavour, colour, and texture, enabling my Father to continue taking this food to the steel plant for his lunch, without his co-workers laughing and teasing him. The switch-over wasn't too hard to take,, and within a short time he began to feel much better, and felt quite comfortable in sharing his lunch and his story with others. Soon after, he had to give them the recipes, and they too began their expanshon into new realms of common sense.

Dead, decaying flesh was no longer required, as long as they could still enjoy a good boiger, spaghetti and a meat-a-sauce, etc., etc., etc. Before you knew it,, privately they were eating brown rice, sea weeds, soba noodles, whole grains, etc.,, yet when it came time to have friends or family over for supper,, they would feel quite comfortable in preparing nicely spiced, meatless dishes, made to look and taste familiar to them all. And when it was enjoyed,, then it was said, "You see,, you don't have to eat meat to enjoy a good hamburger". And on it went from there,, snowballin', until some 49 million people have stopped eating meat in North America within the last 20 years. It would be different if this was the Orient,,, but it isn't.

Freezability of Foods

Many of our main course recipes within our cookbook lend themselves very well to being prepared in triple and quadruple sized batches and can be frozen in single or multiple size portions. Especially for the meals which require a little more preparation time, this is an ideal way to enjoy them more often. To mention just a few, there is: Pheylonian Burgers, Meatloaf, Pizza, Escargot, Seitan, Spaghetti, French Onion Soup, Cabbage Rolls, Lasagna, etc. etc.

I will list the recipes which freeze well, but first, let's go over a few general rules:

- In each case, the food should be completely cooked with the exception of any dishes which have dough, such as pizza, meat pies, etc. These should be cooked three-quarters finished so that the dough can be browned in the reheating.

- Freeze the finished product in the size of portions suitable to your needs (single, double, quadruple, etc.).

- Soups, sauces, spaghetti, etc. should be frozen in plastic containers and then bagged when frozen.

- Some foods such as cabbage rolls, seitan, lasagna, etc., should be frozen on trays (covered) so that they freeze in separate pieces. Then, they can be bagged and you can remove the quantities as needed.

- Breads can be baked and freshly frozen, or you can freeze the risen dough (unbaked) in one or two-loaf batches in plastic bags. When ready to use, remove the dough from the freezer the night before. In the morning it is warm and risen, ready to pan. Do not do this with sour dough.

To reheat frozen food items, use one of these three methods:

A. BAKED

Thaw and then reheat in the oven, with or without a cover, depending on the item.

B. SIMMERED

Place in a skillet or saucepan with a little water and a cover. Cook on a flame tamer to avoid sticking. Simmer till hot throughout. Loosen underneath the food with a flipper occasionally to ensure it doesn't stick, and add more water as needed.

C. STEAMED

Reheat in a pot using a steamer. In most cases it is best if the food is sealed in foil or a heavy freezer bag so it doesn't become soggy.

D. FRIED

Certain foods, when thawed, can be fried as you would when they were fresh, i.e. burgers, Salisbury Steaks.

Here is a list of foods which freeze well, with an indication of which method of reheating is best:

Vegetable Meat Pies (A or C)
Aduki-Squash Kombo (B)
Stuffed Green Peppers (A or C)
Chili (B)
Pheylonian Burgers (D)
Cabbage Rolls (A, B, or C)
Leek-Lima Bean Pie (D)
Pizza (A)
Lasagna (A or B)
Salisbury Steaks (A or D)
Habitant Tourtier (A)
Meatloaf Stew (A, B, or C)
Pate
Boeuf Bourguignon (B or C)
Pheylonian Meatloaf (A, B, or C)
Black Russian Sausages
  (A, B, or C)

Three-Grain Blend
  (see Page 67)
Hiziki Strudels (A or C)
Escargot Au Gratine (A)
Soup (in general) (B)
Sicilian Delights (A or B)
Cream Sauce (B)
Cheese Sauce (B)
Delicious Brown Gravy (B)
Sweet 'n Sour Sauce (B)
Carob Icing
Peach Sauce
Strawberry Shortcake Sauce
Pie Dough (in general)
Tofu (see Page 78)
Seitan - Wheat Gluten
  (A, B, or C)

GLOBAL ENTRÉES

DISH	BUCK-WHEAT	TOFU	MILLET	RICE	NOODLES	TEMPEH	3-GR.	2-GR.	BEANS	SEITAN	BARLEY
Lovable Meatheads											
Vegetable Meat Pies		A								P	
Stish Ficks			P								
Breaded Cutlets										P	
Tofu Fettuccine a la Iilah		P									
Shanola's Sunflower Seed Loaf			P								
Coconut Rice and Beans				P					S		
Slavik Gypsy Delight			P								
Aduki-Squash Kombo									P		
Millet Scuffle			P								
Stuffed Green Peppers			P	P							
Buckwheat Squash	P										
Shepherd's Pie							P				
Chillie									P		
Pheylonian Hamburger							P				

P = Primary Base   S = Secondary Base   A = Alternative Base

GLOBAL ENTRÉES

DISH	BUCK-WHEAT	TOFU	MILLET	RICE	NOODLES	TEMPEH	3-GR.	2-GR.	BEANS	SEITAN	BARLEY
Cornmeal Omelet	corn-meal										
Aduki-Millet Loaf			P						S		
Barley Stew and Dumplings											P
Cabbage Rolls				P						P	
Zausages							P				
Zausages in Blankets							P				
Leek-Lima Bean Pie									P		
Iilah's "Montreal Style" Smoked Meat Sandwich										P	
Smoked Meat and Sauerkraut Casserole										P	
Iilah's Tofu-Egg Omelet		P									
Tempura Gooley Balls		P									
Lasagna							P				
Spaghetti and Meatballs							P				

P = Primary Base   S = Secondary Base   A = Alternative Base

GLOBAL ENTRÉES

DISH	BUCK-WHEAT	TOFU	MILLET	RICE	NOODLES	TEMPEH	3-GR.	2-GR.	BEANS	SEITAN	BARLEY
Stuffed Cannelloni							P				
Fettuccine a la Bologese					S		P				
Winter Tempest						P					
Salisbury Steaks							P				
Mock Chicken Croquettes		P									
Lentil Balls									P		
Habitant Tourtier							P	A			
Buckwheat and Mushrooms with Sauerkraut	P										
Meatloaf Stew							P				
Aduki-Millet Burgers			P						S		
Kasha and Bow Ties	P				S						
Blintzes		P									
Pheylonian Knishes							P				
Paté								P			

P = Primary Base   S = Secondary Base   A = Alternative Base

GLOBAL ENTRÉES

DISH	BUCK-WHEAT	TOFU	MILLET	RICE	NOODLES	TEMPEH	3-GR.	2-GR.	BEANS	SEITAN	BARLEY
Pheylonian Onifoo Pie		P									
Sweet 'N Sour Meatballs							P				
German Meat Balls							P				
Wild Rice a la Iilah				P							
Kubahsah and Beans							P				
Mock Chicken a la King		P									
Grain Puppies							P				
Black Russian Sausages							P				
Shish Kebabs										P	
Me Wild Irish Rose				P							
Mock Chicken Cacciatore		P									
Boeuf Bourguignon										P	
Tempeh-Squash Stew						P					
Steak au Pouivre Flambé										P	

P = Primary Base   S = Secondary Base   A = Alternative Base

VEGETABLE MEAT PIES
(makes 8~10 pies)

These have always been a great hit, as most of us from youth were brought up with meat pies. These are as good as any I ever remember eating.

This is a good size batch, any extra are excellent reheated or can be frozen till another time. Extra pies should be only ¾ cooked to allow for reheating.

This recipe requires either :

or   4 c. of seitan pieces (fresh or frozen)
      5~9 oz. cubes of frozen tofu (thaw early in the day).

Prepare a batch of gravy (page 285)

Cut seitan or tofu into ½" pieces.

Set seitan or tofu pieces to drain, retaining all liquid which should be added to the gravy broth.

Prepare a batch of :

Yeast Raised Oil Crust

While dough is chilling, prepare :

    1½ c. potato (cut in ½" cubes)
    1½ c. carrot ("   " ¼" ")
    1 c. corn
    1 c. peas

Boil potatoes and carrots, then corn and peas. Drain.

Sauté seitan or tofu in a little oil, tamari singe.

Thicken gravy.

Combine boiled vegetables, seitan or tofu and 4~5 cups of the gravy. (Save the rest to serve on top).

Line meat pie tins with crust. Fill each pie with mixture to the rim. Moisten crust edges and top with another crust. Fork edges to seal and fork the tops.

Place pies on a cookie sheet and Bake at 350° till crust is cooked.

STISH FICKS
(serves 6~8)

Start this meal early in the day, as the grain has to set and chill.

Use a saucepan that can go from the burner to oven.

Bring to a boil:

    6 c. water   ½ tsp. salt

Wash and add:

    2 c. millet   ½ c. soaked arame
                            (chopped fine)

Preheat oven to 350°. Simmer millet for 20~25 min.

Singe fry: 2 diced onions

When millet has simmered long enough, add:

    6 oz. can of salmon   1 tsp. savory
    2 tsp. tarragon   ½ tsp. salt
    1 tsp. garlic pwd.   ¼ tsp. cayenne

Mix well and bake for 30 min. Remove and cool.

Later,, when the grain has chilled properly, remove from pan and cut into 1" x 1" x 3" sticks.

Mix in a bowl:

    4 eggs (beaten)   4 tbsp. water
    ¼ c. tamari

Combine in a shallow pan:

    1½ c. durham fl.   1½ c. cornmeal

Dip each 'stish' in egg mixture and then roll in the dry ingredients. Place on an oiled cookie sheet. Bake for 30 min. at 350°.

Serve with lemon wedges and tofu tartar sauce, (page 295) accompanied with a side vegetable and salad.

BREADED CUTLETS

This recipe is quite rich and will please even the most adamant meat connaisseur.

Start this recipe the day before.

Make: a 4 c. batch of seitan (page 87)
    (shape the gluten into ½" thick
      steaks approx. 3" x 5" before boiling)

Prepare the broth for cooking the seitan. When it is boiling, drop in the 'steaks'. Cover and simmer on a low heat for 1½ ~ 2 hrs.

Next day , remove seitan slices from juice 1 hr. before you need to start cooking. Let drain, saving juice.

Mix: 4 eggs (well beaten)
    ¼ c. of liquid from seitan

Combine in a shallow pan :

    1 c. cornmeal
    ½ c. durham fl.
    ½ c. bran

Dip seitan slices in liquid mixture and then roll in the dry ingredients.

These can be cooked in two fashions :

    ~ place on a buttered tray and bake at
      350° for 30 min.

    ~ fry in a buttered skillet for 10~12
      min on each side.

Tofu Fettuccine a la Lilah

(serves 6)

Cut into 3/4" squares :

    5 ~ 9 oz. cubes of tofu

Place on an oiled oven tray and bake at 350° for about 30 min. Turn and tamari once or twice. They should be lightly browned and firm to the touch.

Wash, squeeze, slice and sauté :

    1 lb. mushrooms

in : 1 tbls. oil or marg.

Combine in a blender and liquify :

2 c. water	2 tsp. garlic pwd.
2/3 c. cooked millet	1 tsp. basil
1 tbls. miso	1/2 tsp. oregano
1/4 c. tomato paste	1/4 tsp. savory
2 tbls. marg.	1/8 tsp. cayenne

Pour into a double boiler.

Blend : 2 c. water
       1 onion (cut in 1" chunks.)

Add : 2/3 c. cooked millet

Blend till creamy then add to the other blended mixture. Add tofu squares and mushrooms. Simmer for 30 min.

While sauce is simmering, boil an appropriate amount of fettuccine noodles. Also prepare a vegetable and fresh salad to accompany the meal.

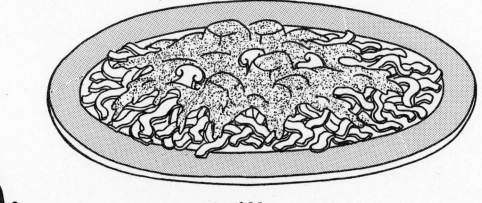

Shanola's Sunflower Seed Loaf

As always, anything which Shanola makes is a hit, and this is no exception.

It's great served fresh made or reheated. Plus it is excellent for lunches and picnics, sliced to go on a sandwich with trimmings (mayo, mustard, etc.)

This recipe calls for:

> 3 c. precooked millet, or lentils

Combine in a bowl:

1½ c. sunflower sds.	2 eggs
¾ c. sesame sds.	1 tbsp. cider vinegar
½ c. walnuts	1 tsp. sage

Prepare and add:

½ c. finely grated beet or carrot
¼ c. diced onion
½ c. diced celery
½ c. chopped parsley

Add grain and mix well. Salt or tamari to taste.

Pass mixture through a meat grinder. Press into an oiled casserole dish or oven pot. (It should be at least 2½" thick.)

Cover and bake at 325° for 1½ hrs.

Coconut Rice and Beans

An adaptation of a traditional Jamaican Dish which has a delicate taste of coconut. We have used basmati rice instead of white, long grain and aduki beans in place of red peas (beans).

Wash and soak overnight:

1 c. aduki beans

The next day, grate the white meat of:

1 med. sized coconut (approx. 3 cups)

The easiest way to get to the meat of a coconut is to first hammer a nail through two of the eyes on the top. Drain the milk into a cup. Now for the tricky part. Place the coconut on a hard surface (stone, concrete, etc.). Give it a good hit with the hammer. Pry it open and remove the meat from the shell with a butter knife.

Boil: 4 c. water

Pour half the boiling water onto the coconut in a bowl. Work with your hands till the water is very milky. Strain the mixture into a pot. Repeat with the remaining water. Discard coconut.

Place the soaked aduki beans in the pot with the coconut milk. Cover the pot and cook the beans till tender. (Do not over cook).

Add to the pot:

3 c. basmati rice (washed)
4 c. water
½ c. chopped scallions or leeks
1 tsp. thyme   1 cl. garlic (chopped)
1 tsp. salt   ¼ tsp. bl. pepper

Simmer on a flame tamer with a cover till the rice is cooked and the water is gone.

Add a little more water if needed to cook the rice properly. Do not stir the rice.

SLAVIK GYPSY DELIGHT

This is a creation of Iilah's in a slavic tradition of taste. It is delicious as either a side dish ,,. or the main course.

For this recipe you need :

    4 c. precooked millet (the baked solid type)

Sauté together :

    1 c. sauerkraut   1 tbsp. oil or marg.

Wash : ½ c. raisins

Pare and slice :

    1 c. apple

Boil : 1 c. corn (fresh or canned)

Crumble cooked millet into a bowl. Add :

    1 tsp. corriander   1 tsp. garlic pwd.
    ½ tsp. carraway pwd.   ¼ tsp. cayenne
    tamari or salt to taste

Add : sauerkraut, raisins, apple and corn.

Mix well and turn into an oiled casserole dish. It is best if it is only about 1~1½" thick.

Even out and top with :

    grated cheese

Bake at 350° for 30 to 40 min.

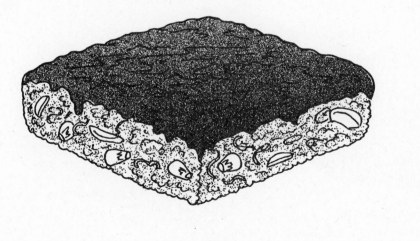

ADUKI - SQUASH KOMBO

Soak overnight :

    1 c. aduki beans
    1 10" piece of kombu

The next day, rinse and drain the beans and kombu.
Cut the kombu into 1/8" strips.

Combine in a pot :

    beans and kombu   2 cl. garlic (chopped)
    4 c. water   1/2 tsp. salt
    1 tbls. tarragon   1/8 tsp. cayenne

Simmer with a cover for 30 minutes.

Meanwhile, prepare :

    2 c. raw squash (butternut, pepper or
      acorn. Peel and cut into 1/2" cubes)
    1 c. onion (1/4" slices)

When the beans have cooked 30 mins. sprinkle
with a little tamari, then layer the onions and
then the squash on top of the beans. (Do not stir
in.) Simmer till the beans and squash are cooked
and the water is gone. (Add a little water if
needed to properly cook the squash).

When cooked, stir in :

    2 tbls. tahine
    tamari to taste

Serve.

MILLET SOUFFLE
(serves 3~4)

Light, fluffy and delicately spiced.

Preheat the oven to 350°.

Wash and slice thinly:

   ¼ lb. mushrooms

Sauté in a little oil till cooked and tamari lightly. Sauté till dry.

Meanwhile, separate the yolks and whites of:

   4 eggs

Whip the egg yolks and add:

   1 c. of cooked millet (crumbled)
      (or tofu if you have no cooked millet)
   ½ tsp. salt
   ½ tsp. maple syrup
   ¼ tsp. tarragon pwd.
   ⅛ tsp. garlic pwd.
   sprinkle of black pepper or cayenne

Combine together:

   ¼ c. durham flour
   2 tsp. baking pwd.

Add the flour mix and the fried mushrooms to the egg mixture and stir well.

Oil a shallow casserole dish.

Whip the egg whites till fluffy and stiff. Fold into the egg mixture and pour into the oiled dish. (It should be no more than 1" thick).

Top with a little cheese if desired and bake for 15~20 minutes at 350°. (Test with a knife to see if it is fully cooked in the middle).

Serve when nicely browned.

STUFFED GREEN PEPPERS
(serves 6)

A combination of millet and rice makes a very good texture for this recipe.

You will need: 6 c. of precooked grain
(½ millet ~ ½ rice)

or, early in the day, boil:

5 c. water	1 c. rice
1 tsp. salt	1 c. millet

Boil grain till it starts to stick, then pop it into the oven and bake at 350° for 30 min.   Cool.

Prepare, dice and singe~fry:

2 med. onions	5~6 cloves garlic
2 stalks celery	

Wash, slice and fry:

1 lb. mushrooms

Crumble cooked grain and add:

fried vegetables	½ tsp. oregano
1 tsp. basil	¼ tsp. cayenne
½ tsp. thyme	

Mix well. Preheat oven to 425°.

Choose good~sized, well rounded, crisp peppers with no blemishes.
Wash 'em and cut the top ½" off, removin' the stem and inner seed core (keep tops and bottoms together.)

Stuff each pepper with the grain mixture.

It is important when preparing these for baking that there be no chance of them falling over as the ingredients will cook out and the peppers fall apart.

To prevent this we use ¼'d or ½'d potatoes to pack inbetween the peppers to prop them up. This is also a delicious way to prepare the side dish.*

Place the peppers and potatoes in a deep casserole dish or roasting pan. (Pack potatoes all around peppers).

Use one of these 3 different sauces :

1) 1 48 oz. can tomato juice
   2 onion, diced fine
   6 - 8 cloves garlic (chopped)

2) a batch of 'gravy' (page 285) add extra garlic and less thickener)

3) blend : 3 c. water   1 c. cooked millet
           ½ c. onion   1 tbls. miso
                               1 tsp. garlic pwd.

   Repeat another batch.

Pour sauce over the peppers and potatoes. Depending on the size of the pan used and the number of potatoes, etc., the amount of liquid recommended,, may not be enough. The sauce should be just below the cut level on the peppers. Add extra water or more sauce if needed.

* to help keep the peppers upright, you can trim the 'nubbs' off the bottom of each pepper so they have a flat surface to balance on.

Do not cut deep enough to break the inside surface.

Cover with a tight fitting lid or tin foil. Bake at 375° for 1¼ hrs., or till a knife slides easily through the side of a pepper and potato.

BUCKWHEAT SQUASH

This dish is an easy-to-make main course or it is a good base to use for making croquettes.

Peel and slice for frying:

　　1 onion

Sauté the onion in a 2 qt. pot with a little oil till it is transparent.

When the onion is cooked, add to the pot and bring to a boil:

　　4 c. water

Peel and cut into ½" cubes:

　　2 c. squash

Add to the boiling water:

　　cut squash　　　　2 c. buckwheat
　　2 tbls. parsley　　1 tsp. salt
　　1 tbls. corriander

Bring the grain back to a boil,, place on a flame tamer, reduce the heat and simmer with a cover. Stir occasionally and cook till all the water is gone.

When the grain is cooked, serve as is with a tahini~miso sauce, a cooked vegetable and salad, or chill the grain for making croquettes.

CROQUETTES

Shape or cut the cooled grain into croquettes.

Mix in a bowl:

　　1 egg　　　　　　　2 tbls. tamari
　　½ c. water

Dip croquettes in egg mix and roll in cornmeal. Bake on an oiled tray till good and hot.

SHEPHERDS PIE
(serves 6)

You will need to have, precooked and cooled:
>   4 c. 3 grain (page 67)

Peel and boil:
>   6~7 good sized potatoes

Peel, dice and sauté:
>   2 med. onions (approx. 1½ cups)
> in   1 tbsp. oil

Prepare: 1 c. cooked corn (use fresh,
>   canned or frozen)

Preheat oven.

Crumble 3 grain into a bowl and add:

2 tbsp. tamari	1 tsp. coriander
1 tsp. garlic pwd.	¼ tsp. carraway pwd.
1 tsp. thyme	¼ tsp. savory

Mix well and press into an oiled 9" x 9" casserole.

Mix corn and fried onions. Layer on top of grain.

Drain potatoes ,, saving ½ a cup of the potato water

Add: 3~4 tbsp. marg.
>   1 c. finely chopped parsley
>   salt to taste

Mash potatoes, adding only enough potato water, (or soy milk) to make them creamy.

Spread potatoes evenly on top of the corn and put some design work to 'em.

Bake at 350° till potatoes are golden brown (approx. 45 min)

While pie is baking, prepare a batch of gravy (p.285) Accompanied with a fresh vegetable, salad and bread, you have a meal fit to please just about anyone.

CHILI

Soak overnight in an ample amount of water:

    1 c. kidney beans
    1 c. lima beans
    1 c. pinto beans
    1 10" piece of kombu (seaweed)

In the morning, rinse the beans and seaweed and add:

    12 c. water   1 tsp. salt

Bring to a boil and simmer for 2~3 hours or pressure cook for 1 hour.

When the beans are well cooked, add:

    2 c. onion (diced)
    1/2 c. tomato paste
    2 tbls. honey
    3~6 chillies } in a tea ball
    2 bay leaves }
    1 tsp. oregano
    1 tsp. basil
    1 tsp. thyme

Continue cooking (unpressured) for 1 hour.

(At this point you may need to add more water to allow the beans to cook properly for the additional hour. The texture should be like stew, not like thick beans. Also, place the pot on a flame tamer to minimize sticking).

When the beans have cooked for a good hour add:

    1/2 c. of bulghur (medium grit)
      or 1 1/2 c. cooked seitan (chopped fine)
    1/4 c. miso (mixed with chili broth)

Simmer for 30~40 minutes till thick and saucey.

PHEYLONIAN HAMBURGER

These are better than any soy burger and are made of 100% pure grain, unlike those 70% chemically processed grain and worst-of-the-meat burgers.

They are delicious and a hit with any age group.

For parties and family gatherings, they can be grilled on the spot,, deli fashion ,,, or made ahead of time. To premake, place cooked burgers in sliced buns,, wrap in tin foil and steam heat when needed.

Make a single batch of " Burger Bun" dough(p. 382) When shaping buns, form dough into 2" balls, roll to about 3½" wide and ½" thick. Moisten top of buns and sprinkle with sesame seeds.
Let rise on an oiled tray. Bake till golden brown.
(Don't over bake as they will become hard.)

Ahead of time you will need to cook and cool a:
4 c. batch of 3 grain, (page 67)

Crumble grain and spice it to "meatloaf recipe". (p. 231) Grind if necessary and make into ½" thick burgers shaped to the size of the buns. (Wet hands will make it easier to shape grain.   When ground, this grain works well in conventional "patti-stackers".

Place burgers on an oiled pan at 350° for 30, mins. Flip after 20 min.

While burgers are baking, prepare trimmings:

thin cheese slices	mayonnaise
tomato slices	dill pickle slices
thin onion rounds	sprouts or lettuce

Also set out: a natural mustard
                    a natural ketchup

We've found these to be very popular served with home fries and coleslaw. Everyone can dress their own burger as they like it.

CORNMEAL OMELET

Bring to a boil in a saucepan:

    4 c. water   1 tsp. basil
    1 tsp. salt   ½ tsp. curry pwd.
    1 tsp. tarragon

When boiling, stir in with a wisk:

    2 c. cornmeal

Place on a flame tamer and reduce the heat to a simmer. Watch that it doesn't "blurp" at you, as it can give you a good blister. Simmer for 20~25 minutes with a cover. Stir occasionally.

Preheat the oven to 350°.

While the cornmeal is cooking, prepare:

    2 onions (¼" slices)
    1 green pepper (½" squares)
    ¼ lb. mushrooms (¼" slices)

Sauté vegetables till tender and singe fry.

When the cornmeal is cooked, stir in the sautéed veggies and add:

    1 tbls. marg.   2 beaten eggs (opt.)

Combine and add to the cornmeal:

    ¼ c. durham flour
    2 tsp. baking pwd. (alum~free)

Mix well and pour into an oiled pan to a 1" thickness. Layer with tomato slices (opt.) and sprinkle with grated cheese or mochi.

Bake for 30 minutes and serve.

This is a hearty, whole grain breakfast alternative in an omelet fashion.

ADUKI~MILLET LOAF

Soak overnight:

    1 c. aduki beans
    8" strip of kombu (broke in 2" pieces)

In the morning, drain and rinse the beans and kombu. Put into a pot with:

    4 c. water   ½ tsp. salt

Simmer with a cover on the pot till all the water is gone. (1~1½ hrs.)

When the beans are cooked, remove the kombu and cut it into ¼" widthwise strips.

Add to the beans:

    4½ c. water
    1½ c. millet (washed)
    1 c. carrot (cut on a large grate size, ½")
    sliced kombu
    ½ c. diced onion
    ¼ c. fresh parsley
    2 tbls. gomasio

Preheat oven to 350°

Cook the millet and beans on a flame tamer with a lid for 30 min.

Pour into an oiled loaf pan, cover with a lid or foil and bake for 40 min.

This loaf can be served fresh from the oven or it can be chilled and reheated in 1" thick slices. Serve either way as is, or with any number of different sauces (gravy,, tahini~miso,, cream sauce, etc.).

If you plan to reheat the loaf in slices, which gives a firmer texture, complete the cooking and baking in the morning so the grain has the time to chill thoroughly.

Barley Stew
and Dumplings

A hearty winter dish to please the whole family.

In a wide pot (10"~12") combine:

    1 c. washed barley groats
    6 c. water
    1 tsp. salt

Bring to a boil. Reduce the heat and simmer with a cover for 1½ hours.

Meanwhile,, prepare:

    2 c. onion (1" wedges)
    2 c. carrots (1" diagonal chunks)
    1 c. celery (¼" diagonals)
    2 c. potato (1" chunks)
    2 c. cabbage (1" chunks)
    4 cl. garlic (thin slices)

When barley has boiled 1½ hours add all of the prepared vegetables, plus:

    1~28 oz. can of whole tomatoes
    3 c. water
    ¼ c. tamari
    1 tsp. marjoram
    1 tsp. oregano
    ½ tsp. thyme
    ⅛ tsp. cayenne

Return lid to the pot and simmer until each of the vegetables are well cooked.

Meantime,,,
    on
        to
            the Dumplings,,,

DUMPLINGS

Measure and sift into a bowl:

    2 c. durham or whole wheat
        pastry flour
    1 tbls. baking pwd.
    1 tsp. salt
    1 tsp. basil

Wash and chop:

    1 c. parsley

Mix together:

    2 eggs (beaten)   3/4 c. soy milk

Add the liquid to the flour. Stir to form a soft dough. This is best if mixed just before you are ready to cook the dumplings.

Sprinkle the parsley evenly over the stew.

Drop the dumpling dough into the simmering stew by spoonfuls. The balls should be 1"- 1½" in diameter. Drop close to each other, but not touching (approx. 16). Cover tightly and simmer for 10 minutes. Turn each ball and cook for 5 minutes more.

This is a good sized batch. Any leftovers are even better reheated the next day.

CABBAGE ROLLS

These are a must at Christmas time here at Philoxia and are a real treat during other times of the year.

To make the stuffing you will need:

- 6 c. cooked short grain brown rice
- 4 c. cooked seitan (chopped very fine or passed through a meat grinder)
- 2 large green cabbage

While preparing the stuffing, it is a good time to steam the cabbage leaves.

The cabbage leaves are easiest to remove if the cabbage is steamed and the core is cut from the center.

Remove any bruised or bad leaves. Make 4 conical cuts around the core. Remove the core and cut away any remaining parts of the core.

Place a steamer in a large pot and add water to the level of the steamer. Place the cabbage head in the steamer, core down. Place a cover on the pot and bring to a boil.

Simmer for 10 minutes, then gently try to remove 4~6 leaves using tonges. Return the lid and continue steaming. This is a lengthy process as only a few leaves come off at a time. Continue till all the useable leaves are off. Repeat with the other head. Top up the water level as needed.

While the cabbage is steaming, prepare and sauté:

- 2 c. onion (diced)
- 2 c. celery (")
- 1 lb. mushrooms (sliced)

Tamari singe and cook till dry.

Mix in a large bowl:

the rice, the seitan, sautéed veggies

Add and mix well:

¼ c. melted marg.	1 tbls. thyme
2 tbls. garlic (diced)	½ tsp cayenne
1 tbls. basil	tamari to taste

Cover and refrigerate till the leaves are ready.

As the cabbage leaves cool, trim the thick core part on each leaf to about ⅛" thick.

Prepare a sauce of:

1½ c. tomato paste	2 tbls. garlic
4 c. water	1 tbls. basil
½ c. miso	1 tbls. oregano
2 tbls. honey	

Oil a large casserole dish and line it with any small or leftover leaves.

Using one leaf at a time, shape a handful of stuffing into a sausage shape. Place it at the base of the leaf, fold in the sides and roll it up.

Place each roll side by side in the pan. When you have a full layer, add ⅓ of the sauce. Continue with another layer of rolls and add more sauce. Make a third layer if needed and top with the remaining sauce.

Cover with any extra cabbage leaves (this prevents the cabbage rolls from burning.) Cover with a lid or foil.

Bake at 350° for 60 minutes. These are excellent reheated.

ZAUSAGES
(serves 6~8)

This recipe requires : 8 c. 3 grain (cooked & cooled)

Crumble cooled grain into a large bowl.
Mix together in a small bowl:

1 tbsp. paprika	2 tsp. thyme
1 tbsp. garlic pwd.	1 tsp. corriander
or fresh garlic	½ tsp. sage
1 tbsp. gr. black pepper	⅛ tsp. clove pwd.

Sprinkle spicing over the grain and mix well.
Pass grain thru a meat grinder.

Form grain into 1"x 4" sausages. (The easiest way to do this is by rolling a 2" ball of grain with wet hands, then roll to the proper length and thickness on a wet counter.

Roll in bread crumbs and place on an oiled oven tray. Bake at 350° for 30 ~ 40 min.

ZAUSAGES IN BLANKETS

Prepare sausages as in above recipe.

Make a batch of pie crust.

Do not roll sausages in bread crumbs.
Bake sausages for only 25 to 30 min., just till they become slightly crusty. Cool for 1 hr.

Roll dough to ⅛" thick and cut it into 3½" wide strips.

Wrap cooled sausages in crust, cut to fit, moisten edge and seal.

Place on an oiled tray.
Bake at 325° till pastry is a golden brown.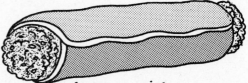
Serve with fresh salad and a vegetable dish.
A sauce of gravy or tahini~miso goes well with these.

LEEK-LIMA BEAN PIE

Rinse and soak overnight in ample water:

    1 c. baby lima beans (check for stones)
    6" strip of kombu seaweed (cut in 4 pcs.)

In the morning, rinse the beans and kombu twice.
Put both in a pot and add:

5 c. water	2 bay leaves
1 tsp. salt	2 chillies

Boil the beans for 20 minutes uncovered. Spoon off any 'foam' or 'scum' that forms on the top.

Cover and place on a flame tamer. Simmer till the beans are well cooked. Stir occasionally. The beans should be creamy yet cooked quite dry. Remove the bay leaves, chillies and kombu. Save the kombu for another dish.

Prepare enough pie dough for 1 full 9" pie.

Clean and prepare:

    4 c. leeks (cut in 1" chunks)
    1 med. onion (cut in 1" wedges)

Saute leeks and onion in a skillet with:

    2 tbls. marg.   1 tbls. water

Cook with a lid till tender. Sprinkle with tamari and cook uncovered till the liquid is gone.

Preheat the oven to 350°. Roll the pie bottom and top. Line the pie shell with bottom crust.

Mix the leeks with the lima beans and add:

    1 tbls. tarragon   salt to taste

Fill pie shell and add the top crust. Seal the edges and bake till golden brown. Bake till cooked. Baste and bake 5 minutes more.

Serve with a complimentary green vegetable and a salad.

Lilah's 'Montreal Style' Smoked Meat Sandwiches

For those of you who have ever visited a Montreal delicatessen, you really know what a smoked meat on rye is all about. This recipe will make you think your eating the real thing again.

The day before you want to serve this, make a:

4 c. batch of 'Spiced Seitan' (page 87)

Spice and prepare the gluten as recommended and refrigerate it in a loaf pan for 2~3 hours.

Prepare the 'spiced seitan broth' and bring it to the boil. Remove the gluten from the loaf pan and cut it into 4 even pieces.

Drop each chunk into the broth and simmer with a cover for 1 hour.

Remove each chunk from the broth and refrigerate for 1 hour. When cooled, slice each chunk into slices, as thinly as possible.

Return the seitan slices to the pot and simmer for 1 hour more. Cool and refrigerate seitan and the broth together, overnight.

The next day:

One hour before meal time, remove the seitan slices from the broth so they may drain.

Meanwhile, prepare any or all of these garnishes.

thin onion slices	cheese slices
tomato slices	dill pickle slices

Also set out:

mayonnaise	sprouts or lettuce
natural mustard	

Smoked Meat, cont.,

When all is prepared and table set, fry the seitan slices in a little oil till hot and singed. Tamari.

Wrap a loaf of sliced rye bread in foil and warm it in the oven.

Remove the seitan from the pan and keep hot while you fry the next batch, if needed.

Serve while hot with the bread and trimmings. Everyone can put 'em together to their own likes.

SMOKED MEAT AND SAUERKRAUT CASSEROLE

Prepare a batch of seitan according to the 'Smoked Meat' recipe or utilize leftovers which were fried for sandwiches.

Drain an appropriate amount of seitan slices for each serving. Sauté in a little marg. and tamari.

Drain: ½ c. sauerkraut per serving

Oil a casserole dish.
Make alternate layers of sauerkraut and seitan.

Sprinkle each layer of sauerkraut lightly with:

    carraway sds.
    finely ground black pepper
    finely chopped garlic

Finish with sauerkraut, sprinkled with paprika.

Add seitan juice to fill the bottom inch of the casserole. Cover and bake for 30 minutes.

Serve with potatoes, a side vegetable and salad.

This recipe can be prepared by wok frying all the ingredients together, using less liquid.

Iilah's Tofu~Egg Omelet
(serves 2~3)

This is the omelet Iilah makes for our guests at Philoxia ,, either for breakfast or as a lunch time meal. It is delightfully spiced and deliciously light, yet filling.

Prepare and sauté :

    ½ c. onion (sliced thin)
    ¼ c. green pepper (½" dice)
    ¼ c. mushrooms (sliced thin)
    1 clove garlic ("   "   ")

While the vegetables are sauteing, crack into a bowl :

    3 eggs

Whip till fluffy. Using soft or regular tofu, crumble it into a measuring cup till you have:

    1 c. of tofu

Whip till creamy and add:

    ¼ tsp. tarragon
    ¼ tsp. maple syrup
    ¼ tsp. salt
    pinch of black pepper

When the veggies are cooked , tamari them and singe slightly. Add the sautéed veggies to the egg mixture. Pour into an oiled pan to a ¼" thickness.

Top with tomato slices and some grated cheese or soy cheese.

This can be either baked in a hot oven (350°) for 15~20 minutes (till firm to the touch) or it can be cooked on top of the stove using a flame tamer for 5 minutes, then broil it till cooked solid and nicely browned.

Tempura Goolie Balls

The name may sound strange but they sure are tasty. We started calling them by this name because with the sweet n' sour sauce on them, they sure are 'gooey'.

Serve with either of the sweet n' sour sauces on page 287 and accompany with rice, an oriental vegetable dish and salad.

An hour or two before meal time, rinse and cut into 1" squares:

> 3 9 oz. blocks of med. or firm tofu

Place the cubes in a bowl and sprinkle with tamari (approx. 2~4 tbls.) Cover and place in the fridge. Stir occasionally.

Prepare a batch of Sweet N' Sour Sauce.

Combine in a bowl:

> 5 c. durham flour   2 tsp. alum free
> 1 c. corn flour   baking pwd.
> 1 tbls. tarragon   1 tsp. salt
> 1 tbls. garlic pwd.   ¼ tsp. cayenne

Mix well and store in a jar.

When ready to cook drain the tofu squares.

Place in a bowl:

> 1 c. of tempura mix

Stir in with a wisk:

> 1 c. cold water   ½ tsp. honey (opt.)

Heat 2"~3" of oil in a deep pot or fryer. When hot (400°) dip the tofu squares in the batter and drop into the oil. Cook till golden. Turn once.

Cook in batches till all are done.
Use similarily with seitan chunks, millet squares, (p. 263) or chunks of zucchini, mushrooms, green pepper, broccoli heads, cauliflower, carrot, etc.

ITALIAN CUISINE

Most Italian dishes are traditionally made of pasta, tomato sauce,, some vegetables and meat. This type of food is quite acidic and should not be eaten regularily,, however as we all know, they sure are tasty dishes , and when eaten occasionally ,, they sure are good moral boosters.

In redesigning each of these dishes, lilah has modified the ingredients with miso and grains to cut the acidity as well as to build up the nutrition value.

When choosing the pasta for each meal, use those made with whole grain flours,, such as whole wheat, buckwheat ,, soy or artichoke flour. Commercially, there are certain pastas made exclusively of durham semolina and salt. These are quite satisfactory and are more traditionally acceptable.

The cheese used in any of these dishes , should be an undyed, natural and unprocessed cheese . If you are able to purchase cheese from a small reputable dairy which uses no emulsifier , chemical additives, coloring, or stabilizers, you are quite fortunate. Worst to worst, avoid any large corporate brand name cheeses as they are tampered with the most.

It is unfortunate what some companies do to food products, especially cheese. We have bought some in the past and upon cooking with these chemical cheeses, found them to give a milky run-off to one side leaving an unmelted glob of emulsified gelatin in the middle.

Never use processed cheese slices, cheese spreads or commercial cottage cheese as they are extremely processed and chemically treated.

PIZZA

Makes approx. 3 ~ 12" or 6 ~ 8" pizza's

Start by preparing a: batch of pizza crust (p. 383)

In a saucepan, combine :

1-28 oz. can whole tomatoes (blended)
8 oz. tin tom. paste   1 tbsp. parsley
1 tbsp. honey   2 tsp. oregano
2 bay leaves   1 tsp. carraway pwd.
2 tsp. basil   1 tsp. salt
¼ c. miso   ¼ tsp. cayenne

Bring to a boil and simmer for ½ an hour.

Wash and prepare vegetables: (slice all ingredients as thin as possible. This allows the vegetables to cook quickly and the flavors to blend better.)

Prepare any or all of these vegetables :

2~3 zucchini   2~3 tomatoes
2~3 peppers   6~8 tofu weiners
2 stems broccoli   (cut in ⅛" diagonals)
1 lb. mushrooms   1½ lb. cheese (approx.)
2~3 onions   (cheddar or mozzarella)

For an added touch, fry the tofu weiner slices in a skillet with a tbsp. of oil. Sprinkle with garlic powder, cayenne and tamari while frying.

Cut dough into 3 or 6 equal pieces. Roll to desired size. Thickness should be ¼" or less. Place on oven trays and form a raised lip all around. Preheat oven to 425°.

Add to sauce: 12 cl. ch. garlic   2 tbsp. flour

Stir sauce well and spread onto pizza crusts.

Layer vegetables in the order they are listed above. This is important to the out come of flavour and appearance.

Bake till crust is cooked and cheese browned (20~30 min) If making enough for a second meal, or for freezing, cook that portion a little less than fully done.

LASAGNA

This is an excellent dish to serve dinner guests as you can make it ahead of time and reheat it when needed. It actually tastes better when reheated.

This recipe requires:

    4 c. of precooked 3 grain (page 67)

In a large saucepan, boil:

    16 c. water   1 tsp. salt
    1 tbsp. oil

When boiling, add:

    1 pkg. of lasagna ndls. (made of durham semolina)

Cook till soft, but not falling apart. Drain and rinse noodles with cold water, so they will not stick together.

While noodles are cooking ,, combine in a saucepan:

    4½ c. water   or   6 c. tomato
    12 oz. can tomato paste   sauce

Add: ½ c. miso   1 tsp. carraway pwd.
    1 tbsp. honey   ½ tsp. celery sd.
    1 tbsp. oregano   ¼ tsp. cayenne
    1 tbsp. basil

Simmer for 30 min.

Grate: 4 c. cheddar cheese

Prepare vegetable ingredients. (These should be each cut as thin as possible).

    2 onions (cut in ½ rounds)
    ½ lb. mushrooms (1/8" slices)
    2 green peppers (lengthwise slices)

cont.,,,

Remove sauce from the heat and add:

    4 c. 3 grain (crumbled)
    6~8 cloves garlic (finely chopped)

Lasagna is best made about 2" thick, so choose a casserole dish or pan that is suitable (approx. 9"x13").

Oil the dish and sprinkle a few onions across the bottom (this keeps the noodles from sticking to the pan.)

Proceed with consecutive layers of:

    ¼ of the noodles
    ⅓ of the vegetables
    ¼ of the sauce and grain
    ⅙ of the cheese

Repeat twice and finish with:

    remainder of the noodles
    remainder of the sauce
    remainder of the cheese

Cover and bake at 375° for 1 hr.

Then, remove cover and bake till the cheese is nicely browned.

Serve with garlic bread,, a side vegetable and salad.

The addition of thinly sliced zucchini or broccoli to each layer is very nice.

To enhance the flavour of the vegetable ingredients, the onions, peppers and mushrooms can be 'singe fried' before being layered into the lasagna.

This dish freezes and reheats with good results. Cut into single or double proportions before freezing.

SPAGHETTI AND MEATBALLS

(This is a good size family batch)

For this recipe you will need:

6 c. precooked 3 grain (page 67)

Use fresh tomatoes when in season, as they will make the nicest tasting sauce.

Wash, core and quarter ripe tomatoes. Blend and strain out seeds and skins. Continue processing till you have:

16 c. tomato puree

or combine:
2 c. tomato paste
6 c. water

Bring to a boil in a saucepan and add:

1 tbsp. oregano	1 tsp. thyme
1 tbsp. sweet basil	1 tsp. celery sd.
2 tbsp. honey	½ tsp. cayenne
2 bay leaves	

If using fresh tomato puree, let simmer with spicing till boiled down to about half. Simmer for about half an hour if using tomato paste proportions.

Prepare vegetable ingredients:

2 c. diced onion
1 c. diced celery
1 c. green pepper (½" sq. chunks)
1 c. zucchini (¼" thick half moons)
1 lb. mushrooms (¼" slices)

We singe fry each of these vegetables before adding them to the sauce. Frying the vegetables enhances the flavour of the sauce, however, simply boiling them in the sauce will make a tasty spaghetti also. If you choose to fry em, singe on a medium ~ high heat,, tamari and remove from pan while still crisp.

Add vegetable ingredients to the sauce and simmer with a cover for 1 hr. (stir occasionally).

.......cont.

Crumble 3 grain and spice according to recipe at the bottom of this page.

Grind grain, if necessary and shape into 1" balls. Place on an oiled oven tray. Bake at 350° for 30 min. Turn once while baking. Chill if time allows.

Prepare:

    2 c. broccoli (top flowerettes, chop stems).
    6~8 cloves garlic (chopped fine).

Half an hour before meal time add broccoli and garlic, plus:

    ½ c. miso   1 c. bulghur

Boil an appropriate amount of:

    spaghetti ndls. (durham or soba)

(usually a 1" handful per serving is sufficient)

Add meat balls to the sauce 10 min. before you are ready to eat.

Grate an appropriate amount of cheddar cheese, unless you plan to use parmessan cheese.

When noodles are cooked, drain and rinse with hot water. Serve with the sauce and salad on the side.

MEATBALLS

Crumble: 6 c. precooked 3 grain
Add: ¼ c. tomato paste
        ¼ c. miso
        1 tbsp. garlic pwd.
        1 tsp. corriander
        1 tsp. tarragon
        1 tsp. basil
        1 tsp. sage

Mix well and proceed to form into 1" balls. Grind if the texture requires it.

STUFFED CANNELLONI

This is definitely one of my most favorite Italian dishes. The first time we had this was when lilah was preparing Tiamma's 25ᵀᴴ birthday meal. You should have seen all the smiling faces.

This recipe requires a :

   250 g. package of Cannelloni Noodles
   (Buy the type that doesn't require pre-boiling.)
Either of these stuffings is equally satisfying.

MEATLOAF GRAIN STUFFING

You will need : 5 c. of cooked 3 grain (p. 67)
Spice to "meatloaf" recipe (page 231, do not grind)

Sauté : 2 onions (diced)

Add to grain : sautéd onions
            2 eggs (beaten)
            ½ c. grated cheddar cheese

Mix well and fill noodles. Place single layered in an oiled 9" x 13" pan.

Cover with the contents of a 48 oz. can of tomato juice. Sprinkle with cheese and cover.
Bake at 350° for 45 min. Remove cover and bake till browned.

TOFU, SPINACH, CHEESE STUFFING

Wash and chop :

      1 pkg. of spinach
Scald spinach with :

      4 c. boiling water
Let set for 5 min., then drain well.

Sauté : 2 onions (diced)

Crumble : 3   9 oz. cubes of tofu

Grate : 2 c. cheddar cheese

Mix spinach, onion, tofu and half of the cheese.
Add :

     1 tsp. tarragon   1 tsp. garlic pwd.
     1 tsp. salt

Mix well and fill noodles.
Continue as for previous stuffing.

These stuffings can be used with manicotti noodles.

MUSHROOM MARINARA SAUCE WITH FETTUCCINI

Wash and slice :

     1 lb. mushrooms

Singe fry in a large skillet with :

     2 tbsp. oil (or marg.)

When mushrooms are cooked, add :

     1 24 oz. can. whole tomatoes
       (or equivalent of fresh, deskined ones)
     3 4 cl. garlic (chopped fine)
     1/4 c. fresh parsley (chopped)
     salt and pepper to taste.

Simmer on a low heat for 20~30 min.

Meantime, cook enough fettuccine noodles for the number of people being served.

Mix: 4 tbsp. arrowroot fl.   1/2 c. water

Add to the tomatoes and stir till thickened.

Serve over drained noodles with a veg. and salad.

FETTUCCINE A LA BOLOGESE
(serves 6)

This recipe requires:

    3 c. 3 grain (spiced to 'Meatloaf' recipe page 231)

Prepare and sauté in a skillet or wok:

    1 c. onion (diced)   1 tbsp. oil
    ½ c. celery (¼" slice)
    ½ c. carrot (sliced on a large grate)

Tamari while frying.
Sauté vegetables till cooked, yet still crisp, add:

    3 c. 'meatloaf' grain (crumbled, not ground)
    1 tbsp. oregano
    1 tbsp. chopped garlic

Fry grain, stirring constantly. Scrape the bottom of the skillet each time so the grain will not stick.
Tamari once or twice. Done properly, this will give the grain the flavour of a 'singe', but it will not taste burnt.
When the grain is 'singed', add:

    28 oz. can whole tomatoes
    4 tbsp. miso (mixed with ¼ c. tom. liquid)
    cayenne to taste

Cook with a cover for 15 min. Stir occasionally.

In a saucepan boil:

    8 c. water   1 tsp. salt

Add: fettuccine noodles (to the quantity needed for the number of servings)

Remove cover from skillet and add:

    1 tbls. flour mixed with ¼ c. water

Simmer on a reduced heat, stirring till thickened. Keep hot till noodles are cooked.

When cooked, drain noodles, rinse and serve with sauce. Accompany with salad and a side vegetable.

WINTER TEMPEST

It had been a cold, snowy day and the guys had been working outside since morning. When they started eating this meal, they called it such,, saying it was just what they needed to match the day they had spent outside.

Pre-thaw:

  2~8 oz. pkg. of tempeh

Prepare a batch of:

  'No Cheese' cheese sauce (page 284)

Cut the tempeh into 1" pieces and steam cook for 15 minutes.

Peel and cut into 1" wedges:

  2 onions

Sauté onions in a little oil.

Wash and slice into ¼" thick diagonals:

  3 c. zucchini   2 c. carrot

Add to the onions when they're half cooked. Tamari and add a little water. Cover and steam cook for 5 minutes.

While the vegetables are frying, bring to a boil:

  6 c. water   1 tsp. salt

When boiling, add:

  1 8 oz. pkg. of spinach fettuccine ndls.

Drain noodles and arrange in a margarined dish. Layer with the fried vegetables,, then the tempeh. Cover with the blended cheese sauce. (You may not need the whole batch).

Bake at 350° till golden brown and hot. Serve with a side vegetable and salad.

SALISBURY STEAKS
(makes 8~10 steaks)

Commonly known as a hamburger steak. Traditionally it is served with gravy, mashed potatoes, a side dish of vegetables, plus salad and hot, garlic bread. What a satisfying meal.

For this recipe ,, you will need :

8 c. of precooked 3 grain (page 67)

Peel and dice finely :

2 onions   4 cloves garlic

Sauté onions and garlic in a little oil till cooked. Crumble grain into a large bowl.

Add : ¼ c. tamari   2 eggs (beaten)
      1 tsp. corriander   ½ tsp. celery sd.
      1 tsp. thyme   ¼ tsp. carraway pwd.
      ½ c. beet (grated fine)

Add fried onions and garlic. Mix well. Test texture, it should hold together well, if not, grind it.

Mix in a flat bottom bowl :

2 eggs, beaten   ¼ c. tamari
¼ c. water

Combine in a shallow pan :

1 c. durham fl.   1 c. cornmeal

Shape grain into 3" x 5" oval patties about ¾" thick.

Dip each patti into liquid mixture and then gently roll in the dry mixture.

Place on an oiled tray, cover and bake at 350° for 30 min. Remove cover and bake 20 min. more. Turn if needed.

Any left over steaks are very good the next day reheated in a skillet with a little oil and water.

MOCK CHICKEN CROQUETTES

Prepare the grain for this recipe early in the day so it has time to chill properly.

Combine in a saucepan:

4½ c. water	1 tsp. sage
1½ c. millet	½ tsp. savory
½ c. onion (diced)	½ tsp. paprika
1 tsp. salt	½ tsp. garlic pwd.

Bring to a boil and simmer for 30 min. Stir occasionally. Preheat oven to 350°.

When millet has cooked, turn it into an oiled bread loaf pan and bake for 30 min.
Remove from the oven and chill.

Later, cut the chilled millet into 1″ x ¾″ x 3″ pieces.

Prepare a mixture of:

3 eggs (beaten)	⅓ c. water
¼ c. tamari	

Combine in a shallow pan:

1 c. flour	1 c. bread crumbs

Dip each piece in the egg mixture, then roll in the dry ingredients. Place on an oiled oven tray.
Bake for 30~40 min.

Serve with tahini~miso (page 291) or your favorite barbecue sauce.

Lentil Balls

Very tasty served on spaghetti or on their own as a main course with a cooked vegetable and salad.

Combine in a bowl and mash till consistent:

2 c. cooked green lentils
⅓ c. whole wheat bread crumbs
¼ c. parsley (chopped fine)
¼ c. grated cheese (optional)
2 eggs (well beaten)

With wet hands, form into 1" balls.

Heat in a skillet:

3 tbls. oil

Fry the lentil balls till evenly browned. Drain on a paper towel.

If lentils are not your favorite or do not sit well in your stomach ,,, use cooked millet instead.

HABITANT TOURTIER
(serves 6)

To make these traditional french 'meat pies', you will need :

~ a batch of pie pastry (page 224~226)
~ 4 c. 2 or 3 grain (p. 67~68)

Crumble cooled grain into a large bowl and add:

1 tbsp. thyme	1 tsp. gr. bl. pepper
1 tbsp. carraway pwd.	1/8 tsp. clove pwd.
1/2 tsp. sage	1/8 tsp. cayenne
tamari or salt to taste	1 egg (beaten)

Mix grain well, then heat a skillet with :

4 tbsp. marg. (or butter)

Add spiced grain and singe fry for 3~5 minutes.
Add tamari while frying if needed for taste.

Prepare and singe fry :

2 onions (diced)   1/3 lb. mushrooms (1/4" slices)

Line pie plate with crust, add grain mixture and press lightly into place. Layer with fried onions and mushrooms. Moisten pie rim and add top crust. Seal the edges with a fork and perforate the center.

Mix a baste of :

1 egg (beaten)	1 tbsp. water
1 tbsp. tamari	1 tsp. honey

Use half now and the other half when partially baked.

Bake at 325° for 35~45 min., or till the crust is golden brown (baste again mid~way of baking)

Serve with gravy, mashed potatoes and turnips ,. a side vegetable and salad.

PHEYLONIAN MEATLOAF

The many recipes which incorporate this grain mixture will nicely revolutionize the main meals you cook for your family.

Prepare: a batch of 3 grain (page 67)

This should be cooked early in the day or the day before as it needs to be completely chilled.

When ready to prepare the grain, crumble it into a large bowl. If the edges or top are crusty, it is best to skim it off.

Mix together:

¼ c. miso	1 tbls. basil
¼ c. grated beet	1 tbls. garlic pwd.
(grated as you would	2 tsp. thyme
lemon rind to produce	1 tsp. carraway pwd.
a wet pultch.)	1 tsp. salt
⅓ c. tomato paste	

Work into the grain with your hands:

   ½ c. of 80% gluten flour

Add the spiced mixture and work it in.

At this point depending on the texture and what you want to make, you have to decide if the grain will hold together as is, or whether it needs to be passed through a meat grinder. If you are making lazagna, stuffed peppers or shepherds pie, etc.,, it should not be ground. For meatloaf, burgers, salisbury steaks, meatballs, etc., grinding will produce a more finely grained texture which will form patties or burgers better, however it is not necessary. The spiced 3 grain (ground or unground) can be cooked and kept refrigerated for 5~7 days, or it can be frozen ready to use. To use, thaw, shape and recook.

Some items like burgers and lazagna can be prepared, cooked and frozen. Having a few dozen grain burgers in the freezer can be very handy.

MEATLOAF STEW
(serves 6~8)

In the morning, cook an:

    8 c. batch of 3 grain (page 67)

Let cool.

In the early afternoon,, crumble cooled grain and spice as for 'meatloaf' recipe (page 231) Grind if necessary to get a good texture.

Place on an oiled tray and shape into a rectangular loaf 3"~4" high.

Bake at 350° for 35~45 min. Coat with a tamari baste (p. 377) every 10~15 min. When it has a crusted surface, remove from oven and let cool, refrigerate if possible.

Meanwhile, wash and prepare:

- 5~6 potatoes ~ cut into 1½" chunks
- 4~6 carrots ~ halved or quartered lengthwise, then cut in 2" pieces
- 3~4 onions ~ cut in ¼'s or ⅙'s
- 2 c. turnip ~ cut in ¾" squares
- 3~4 parsnips ~ cut same as carrots
- 1 lb. mushrooms ~ whole or halved

Place cooled meatloaf in an oiled roasting pan. Arrange vegetables around meatloaf (vegetables shouldn't be higher than the meatloaf.)

Sprinkle vegetables with:

½ c. tamari	1 tbsp. sweet basil
1 tbsp. thyme	sprinkle of cayenne
1 tsp. coriander	10~12 cloves garlic (sliced thin)

Add water to almost half the level of the vegetables. Cover and bake at 375° for 1 hour.

If you like gravy, remove the juice with a gravy siphon. Thicken with browned flour and return to stew. Serve.

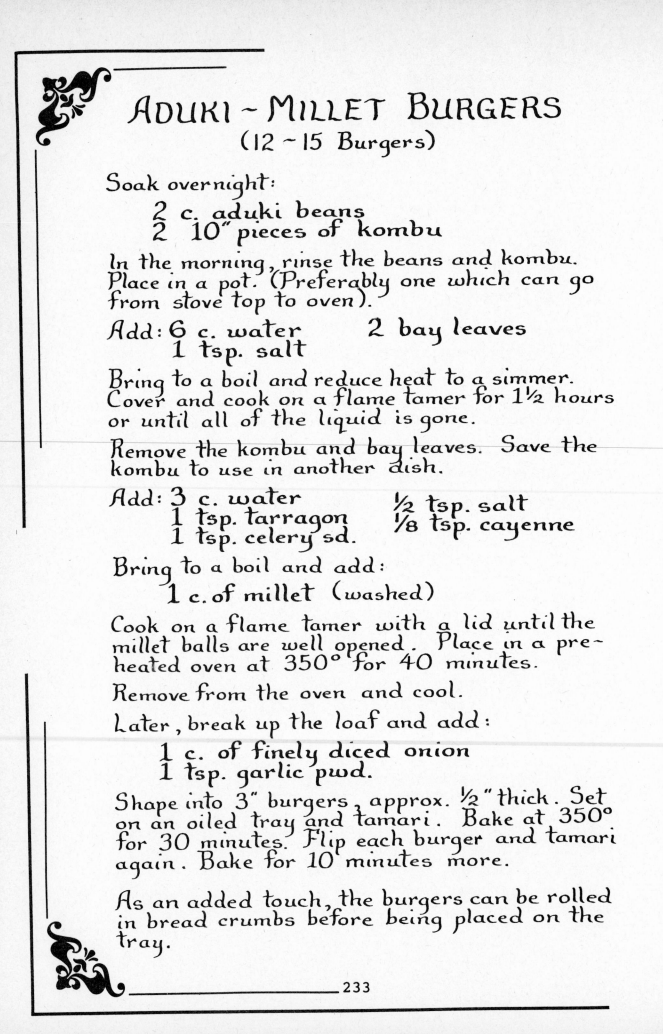

ADUKI ~ MILLET BURGERS
(12 ~ 15 Burgers)

Soak overnight:

    2 c. aduki beans
    2 10" pieces of kombu

In the morning, rinse the beans and kombu. Place in a pot. (Preferably one which can go from stove top to oven).

Add: 6 c. water   2 bay leaves
       1 tsp. salt

Bring to a boil and reduce heat to a simmer. Cover and cook on a flame tamer for 1½ hours or until all of the liquid is gone.

Remove the kombu and bay leaves. Save the kombu to use in another dish.

Add: 3 c. water   ½ tsp. salt
      1 tsp. tarragon   ⅛ tsp. cayenne
      1 tsp. celery sd.

Bring to a boil and add:

    1 c. of millet (washed)

Cook on a flame tamer with a lid until the millet balls are well opened. Place in a pre-heated oven at 350° for 40 minutes.

Remove from the oven and cool.

Later, break up the loaf and add:

    1 c. of finely diced onion
    1 tsp. garlic pwd.

Shape into 3" burgers, approx. ½" thick. Set on an oiled tray and tamari. Bake at 350° for 30 minutes. Flip each burger and tamari again. Bake for 10 minutes more.

As an added touch, the burgers can be rolled in bread crumbs before being placed on the tray.

KASHA AND BOW TIES

Put to boil in two separate saucepans:

    4 c. water   and   6 c. water
    1 tsp. salt   1 tsp. salt

In a bowl, beat:

    2 eggs

In a dry skillet, or wok, roast:

    2 c. buckwheat (groats or cracked).

Roast, stirring constantly till grain is slightly browned and good 'n hot.

Add the beaten eggs and continue stirring till all of the granuals are separate and lose again.

Remove from the heat and add to the saucepan with the 4 c. of boiling water.

Cover and slow cook till all the liquid is gone.

When the 6 c. pot of water is boiling, add:

    2 c. bow tie or rotini noodles

Simmer till cooked, then drain and rinse.

Meantime, slice and fry:

    3 onions

Preheat oven to 350°.
Mix all cooked ingredients together and add:

    1 c. grated cheese
or ½ c. good tasting nutritional yeast
    1 tsp. garlic pwd.
    tamari to taste

Mix well and turn into an oiled casserole dish.
Bake at 350° for 25 to 30 min.

BLINTZES

The preparation of this dish is more time consuming then most, however they are well worth it for special occasions and festivities.

BLINTZ STUFFING
(TOFU AND CHEESE)

When making these, you should make enough for two meals, because one serving is just a teaser and they are excellent cold in lunches.

You will need a double batch of batter to make enough wrappers for this quantity of stuffing.

Traditional blintz stuffing is made with cottage cheese, but considering the ingredients of commercial cottage cheese ,, we use tofu and cheddar cheese.
If you do not eat dairy ,, you can use strictly tofu (add 1 tbls. of nutritional yeast per tofu chunk).

Start by combining :

    6 c. tofu (crumbled fine)
    2 ~ 3 c. grated white cheddar cheese
        (depending on how 'cheesy' you want them)
    2 c. finely chopped fresh parsley
    2 tbsp. tarragon
    2 tbsp. maple syrup
    1 tsp. salt
    ¼ tsp. cayenne

Mix thoroughly.
Refrigerate mixture while making wrappers.

BLINTZ WRAPPERS

This is a single batch, double for the above quantity.

To make batter, beat well :

    3 eggs

cont.,

Add : 1⅓ c. soy milk
    ¼ tsp. salt
Stir in with a wisk :
    1 c. flour

The knack to making a proper blintz wrapper is the same as making a good crepe. Use a thin, steel frying pan with a 6" or 8" bottom surface. The pan must be moderately hot. Pass a stick of marg. around the pan in between each one cooked.

It is also important to get the proper amount of batter in the pan. You want to have a nice, thin flexible crepe (1/16" to ⅛" thick)
I've watched Tseanah make them and she pours about ¼ of a cup of batter into the center of an 8" pan, then she quickly,, but gently, tilts the pan so the batter runs evenly to the edges. Return to the heat and cook. As it cooks,, loosen the edges all around. When it can be loosened completely, flip it gently being careful not to tear. Cook till browned lightly.

Repeat until all of the batter is gone.
Stack wrappers on top of each other. This keeps them soft and flexible.

Putting blintzes together :

Place a small handful of filling along the width of one end. Roll moderately tight, being careful not to tear. Each blintz should be 1½" wide when finished. Continue filling each wrapper. Place blintzes on a margarined casserole dish, 1 layer only. They may touch but should not be crammed.

Combine in a saucepan and heat till thickened.

    1 c. water   ½ c. marg.
    ½ c. maple syrup   ¼ c. tamari
        or honey   1 tbsp. arrowroot fl.
Ladel over blintzes, cover and bake at 350° for 25 min.

Pheylonian Knishes

This recipe is made in keeping with a traditional knish, however, we have altered the ingredients to eliminate the eggs and added to the spicing to enhance the flavour.

Since the knish dough has baking powder in it, prepare the stuffing first.

Knish Stuffings

Either of these stuffings are delicious, well worth making a batch of each.

Each stuffing recipe is sufficient for one batch of dough and serves 4 people.

Potato and Cheese Stuffing

Scrub or peel :

> 4 large potatoes

Peel and dice :

> 1 onion

Boil potatoes and sauté onion till well cooked. Drain potatoes. (Retain ½ cup of the potato water).

Add :

½ c. grated cheese	½ tsp. savory
4 tbsp. dried parsley	¼ tsp cayenne
2 tbsp. margarine	salt to taste
1 tsp. tarragon	

In place of the cheese you can substitute :

> ¼ c. good tasting nutritional yeast.

Mix well with a potato masher and add enough of the potato water to make 'em smooth and creamy.

Set aside and prepare dough.

KNISHES:

MEATLOAF AND ONION STUFFING

For this recipe you need precooked 2 or 3 grain.

Dice and sauté :

   2 medium onions

Crumble : 3 c. precooked 2 or 3 grain (p. 67~68)

Add : ½ tsp garlic pwd   ⅛ tsp. cayenne
      ½ tsp. thyme   tamari to taste
      ½ tsp carraway pwd.

Sauté spiced grain with onions. Add a little oil if needed to keep grain from sticking.

Remove from heat and add a few tablespoons of tahini ~miso (p. 291) Prepare dough.

KNISH DOUGH

Sift : 2½ c. flour   ½ tsp. salt
       1 tsp. baking pwd.

Mix separately :

   1 egg (well beaten) ½ c. oil
   ½ c. water   1 tsp. honey

Combine both mixtures and knead just enough to form a soft dough.

Roll out to a thin ¼".
Cut into 3" squares.
Place a heaped tbsp. of filling into the center of each square. Fold up the four corners to form a pyramid. Pinch corner seams together and place on an oiled tray.

Bake at 350° till golden brown.

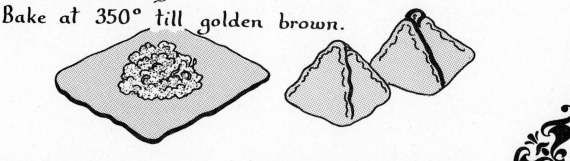

PATÉ

This is a rich and spicy dish which we make every Christmas and on other special occasions.
It is excellent incorporated into hors d'oeuvres or served on rye bread.

You will need:

8 c. precooked 2 grain (millet and bulghur) (page 68)

Crumble the grain and add:

4 eggs (beaten)	2 tbls. grd. bl. pepper
1/4 c. miso	1 tbls. tarragon
1/4 c. maple syrup	1 tsp. celery sd.
1/4 c. marg.	1 tsp. carraway pwd.
8 cl. garlic (diced)	1/4 tsp. clove pwd.
1 tsp. salt	

Mix well and pass through a meat grinder.

Use the shape of baking dish you want the paté to come out looking like. Loaf pans, round bottom steel bowls or specialty shaped baking molds are all suitable.

Margarine the choosen pan(s) and press the mixture into the pan. Level the top surface.

Make a mixture of:

2 tbls. marg. (melted) 2 tbls. tamari
2 tbls. maple syrup 1 egg (beaten)

Baste the top(s) and cover with a lid or tin foil.

Bake at 325° for 1½ hours.

Baste two or three more times while baking. Be sure to let some run down the sides of the loaf.

Cool briefly before removing from the pan.

When cooled completely store in a container, a plastic bag or foil. Refrigerated, this will keep for 7-10 days.

For daily use, half the marg. and syrup quantities.

PHEYLONIAN ONIFOO PIE
(serves 6~8)

Prepare a batch of :
> Yeast Raised Pie Crust (page 426)

Drain : 2   9 oz. cubes of tofu

Cut tofu into ¼" squares, bake on an oiled oven tray at 350°. Tamari and turn occasionally. Bake till browned.

Prepare : 2 onions (¼" slices)
> ¼ c. almonds (chopped)

Saute in a skillet with a little oil. Fry till cooked, tamari singe and remove from the pan.
Do likewise with:

> ½ lb. mushrooms (¼" slices)

For some color, wash and boil till tender :

> ½ lb. green beans (1" diagonals)
> or brussel sprouts (quartered)

Add all fried ingredients, boiled vegetables and tofu squares back to the skillet.

Combine in blender and liquify till smooth :

¾ c. parley (coarsly chopped)	juice of 1 lemon
½ c. water	1 tbls. corriander pwd.
2 tbls. tamari	2 tsp. arrowroot fl.
2 tbls. tahine	1 tsp. thyme
	¼ tsp. cayenne

Heat skillet and ingredients. Pour in the sauce and stir till thickened.

Line pie shell with crust, add the filling and top with another crust.

Fork edges to seal. Poke top crust and bake at 350° till crust is cooked.

SWEET N' SOUR MEATBALLS
(serves 6)

Early in the day, prepare a:

4 c. batch of 3 grain (page 67)

Later in the day, crumble cooled grain and spice it according to 'meatloaf recipe' (page 231).

Mix well and shape into 1" balls. Roll each one in an egg, tamari, water mix (page 377) then roll in bread crumbs.

Place on an oiled oven tray and bake at 350° for 30 min. Turn once or twice while baking. Cool briefly.

While meatballs are baking, make sweet n' sour sauce. Combine in a saucepan:

6 c. tomato juice (blend fresh tomatoes and strain them or use canned juice)

2 c. diced onion	6~8 cloves garlic
½ c. miso	(chopped fine)
½ c. apple cider vinegar	1 tsp. basil
¼ c. honey	1 tsp. thyme

Bring to a boil and simmer for 25~30 min.

Bring to boil in a saucepan:

2 qts. water	1 tsp. salt
1 tbsp. oil	

When boiling add:

350 oz. fettuccini noodles

Mix: ½ c. water   4 tbsp. arrowroot fl.

Add to the simmering sauce and stir until thickened.

When noodles are half cooked, add meatballs to the thickened sauce and simmer till noodles are done.

Drain noodles. Melt 2 tbsp. margarine into the noodle. Serve while hot with the meatballs and sauce.

This can also be served over rice.

GERMAN MEAT BALLS
(serves 6~8)

Prepare early in the day :

    8 c. batch of 3 grain (page 67)

Bake grain and set to cool.

Combine together :

¼ c. ch. parsley	1 tbsp. lemon juice
2 eggs (beaten)	1 tbsp. garlic pwd.
¼ c. grated beet	1 tsp. lemon rind
1 onion (diced)	1 tsp. paprika
2 tbs. miso	

Add mixture to grain and stir well.
Tamari or salt mixture to taste.

Pass grain thru grinder if texture doesn't hold a ball.

Shape into 1½" balls. Bake on an oiled oven tray for 30~40 min., turning once or twice.
Chill briefly.

Meanwhile, start a batch of gravy (page 285).

Boil : 2 qts. water   1 tsp. salt

Add an appropriate amount of :

or   Fettuccine noodles

    Broad egg noodles

Once gravy is thickened and noodles are cooking, add meatballs to the gravy and reduce to a simmer.

Occasionally stir the gravy, gently, being careful not to break the meatballs.

Drain and rinse the noodles. Serve immediately with the gravy and meatballs.

A side vegetable and salad would round this meal off nicely.

WILD RICE A LA IILAH
(serves 6)

The first time we ever had this was on my 25TH birthday when Iilah was cooking and in one of his creative moods. For this occasion he used some fresh scallops which were quite a treat, especially when combined with the other trimmings and special sauce. (You can use baked tofu squares as an alternative to the scallops if you don't include seafood in your diet).

These dishes are very attractive looking for when you have special guests to dinner and are a meal in themselves ,, requiring only salad and fresh garlic bread on the side.

First off, boil together :

4 c. water   1 c. wild rice
½ tsp. salt

Simmer with a lid till all of the liquid is gone ,, do not stir the rice as it will make it stick.

Peel and wash:

6 medium sized potatoes

Boil whole till cooked ,, but not falling apart. Remove from water and cool as soon as cooked.

Meantime , rinse :

1½ lb. scallops (depending on the size of the scallops, there should 8-12 per serving)

Heat a cast iron skillet with ample butter to cover the bottom. Sauté scallops, turning as they become brown, tamari once or twice. Do not overcook as they cook more on the plates.

Wash and squeeze dry :

1½ - 2 lb. mushrooms

cont.,

Leave mushrooms whole and sauté in margarine till cooked, tamari singe on a high heat then remove.

Combine in a blender :

3 c. water   3 cloves garlic
1 small onion (cut in 4)

Blend till smooth. Add and continue blending:

1½. c. millet (cooked)   1 tbsp. maple syrup
2 tbsp. marg.   ½ tsp. salt
1 tbsp. tarragon   ⅛ tsp. cayenne
½ tsp. black pepper.

Strain through a medium-fine strainer.

Last step. You need 6 6" (or 8") ovenware plates.

Margarine each plate and place a potato in the center of each one. (As an added touch, each potato can be pan fried in margarine, turning as each side becomes brown.)

Arrange rice around each potato to the edge of the plates. Set the fried scallops and mushrooms onto the rise around each potato.

Pour sauce evenly over each plate.

Optional - top with a sprinkle of grated cheese.

Bake at 350° for 20 - 30 min.

Bon apetite.

KUBAHSAH AND BEANS
(serves 6-8)

This is a traditional Slavik peasant dish which is quite hearty.

Start this recipe the day before.

Prepare: an 8 c. batch of 3 grain (page 67).

When baked and cooled,, crumble and spice the grain to the 'sausage' recipe. (page 211) For this recipe, it is best to grind the spiced grain.

Shape into 1½" wide rolls and place on an oiled oven tray. Cover with foil and bake at 325° for 40 min. Let cool and then refrigerate overnight.

Also,, the night before, soak:

2¼ c. pinto beans

Next day, in the early afternoon, rinse the beans and put them in a saucepan with:

7 c. water	1 tsp. savory
10" strip of kombu	in a tea ball:
10 cloves garlic	7 chillies
¼ c. maple syrup	3 bay leaves
1 tbls. basil	1 tsp. carraway sds.

Simmer for 3 hours or pressure cook for 1 hr.

Half an hour before meal time, slice sausages into ½" rounds. Fry in a little oil or heat on an oiled tray in the oven. Tamari lightly while cooking.

Serve on top of the hot beans.

This dish goes well with sauerkraut or a vegetable, fresh salad and a loaf of a good, dark rye bread.

MOCK CHICKEN A LA KING
(serves 5~7)

Start preparing this dish the day before.

Thaw: 6~9 oz. chunk of frozen tofu

Bring to a boil:

a batch of Tofu Chicken Marinade (p. 79)

Add the tofu cubes and simmer for 20 min. Let the tofu and the marinade cool together.

When cooled,, tear the tofu into 1" pieces. Return to the marinade and refrigerate overnight.

Next day, remove the tofu pieces from the broth and let them drain well.

Place on an oiled oven tray and bake at 350° for 30 min. Tamari lightly and turn twice.

Meanwhile, wash and squeeze dry:

1 lb. mushrooms (cut in ¼" slices)

Singe fry the mushrooms in a large skillet.

Blend: 2 c. marinade sauce
1 c. cooked millet
1 egg

Repeat 1 more batch of sauce.

Reheat the skillet with the mushrooms and add:

4 tbls. margarine
baked tofu pieces
blended sauce

Turn the heat to low and simmer for 15~20 min.

Serve over hot rice or noodles. Serve with a vegetable dish and salad.

GRAIN PUPPIES

Prepare : 4 c. of 3 grain (or 2 grain)
          to 'sausage recipe' spicing (page 211)

Shape into 1" sausages about 4" long.
Place on an oiled oven tray and bake at 350°
for 30 min.
Remove from oven and chill briefly.

Meanwhile, prepare and boil :

    6~8 potatoes   1 tsp. salt

When cooked, drain, saving 1 c. of the potato
water.
Mash the potatoes, adding:

    2 eggs   2 tbsp. marg.
    1/4 c. dry parsley   1/4 c. flour
    a little potato water (if needed)

Roll each sausage in the potato mixture to
coat 1/2" thick.

Roll in bread crumbs and place on an oiled oven
pan. Bake at 350° for 20~30 min.

These are just as good made ahead of time and
reheated when needed.

Serve as is or with gravy (page 285).

BLACK RUSSIAN SAUSAGES
(serves 4)

This is a different variation of the 'sausage' recipe. They are quicker to make because you don't need to grind the grain as the wrapper holds them together.

They have a very unique appearance and are very good to eat cold in lunches.

Prepare a : 4 c. batch of 3 grain (page 67).

Spice according to 'sausage' recipe (page 211).

This recipe should use approx :

10 sheets (1 pkg.) of nori seaweed

Lightly roast each sheet over a stove burner till it turns to a slight greenish color.

Cut them all in half widthwise.

Shape grain into 1" x 3" rolls.

Place grain on lengthwise edge of nori. Fold in the ends and roll up. Wet sealing edge so it will stick.

Place on an oiled oven tray (they should not touch) and bake at 325° for 30 min.

Tamari half way through baking.

Serve as is with a vegetable and salad ,, or top with cream sauce (page 283) or cheese sauce (page 283) and bake uncovered for 15 min. more.

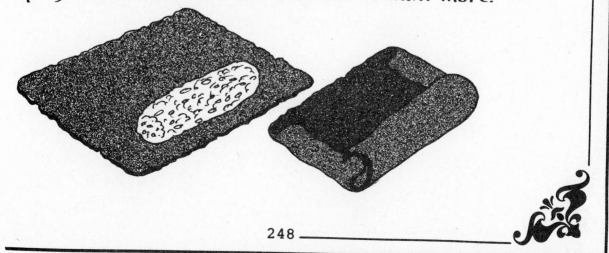

SHISH KEBABS
(serves 6)

To make these properly, you will need:

    6 ~ 16" stainless steel skewers

This recipe utilizes seitan as a substitute for the beef, so the day before you intend to eat this, prepare:

    a 4 c. batch of seitan (page 87)

Before boiling the seitan, cut the gluten into 1½" chunks. Boil in the regular broth till most of the water is gone. Cool and refrigerate overnight.

When ready to prepare the shish kebabs, first remove the seitan chunks from the broth. Drain.

Prepare a sufficient amount of these ingredients for each skewer:

    Tomatoes ~ cut lengthwise in ¼'s or ⅙'s
        (they should be ripe but not too soft).
    Green peppers ~ cut in 1½" squares
        (thick, crisp peppers are the best).
    Onion ~ cut lengthwise in ¼'s or ⅙'s

Arrange on each skewer in the order of:

    pepper, seitan, onion, tomato.

Repeat 4 or 5 times. (We always put the onion next to the seitan as it enhances the flavour).

When all skewers are full,, wrap them in plastic and refrigerate till ready to cook them.

The tastiest way to cook shish kebabs is over an open fire pit ,, turning as needed and basting with the following sauce.

Melt together:

3 tbls. marg.	1 tsp. dijon mustard
2 tbls. tamari	½ tsp. fresh ground
1 tbls. umebosi vinegar	black pepper

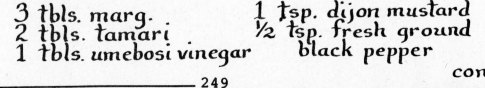

cont.

The shish kebabs should be basted before going on the grill and each time they are turned. (Turn often).

If you don't have an open pit in your kitchen or backyard,, they can be oven broiled on an oiled tray, turning and basting as needed.

As a finishing touch of gourmet flare, flame them while on the table.
Do this using a mixture of :

    1 ounce of cognac or Armagnac
    1 tsp. maple syrup

While arranging cooked shish kebabs side by side on a serving platter, heat above mixture. Do not let it boil.

Timing is crucial with this part, as the heated liquor must be sprinkled evenly over the skewered deli-cacies and then lite immediately.

Bring hot shish kebabs to the table, add the heated liquor and light while your guests delight in the show of flames, bring on the rest of the meal and dig in.

The flame will go out after 1 minute or so.

The use of liquor in this manner eliminates the alcohol and leaves just the flavour.

Me Wild Irish Rose
(serves 6)

In a saucepan, boil:

    6 c. water   1 tsp. salt
    1½ c. wild rice

Simmer with a lid till all liquid is gone, do not stir. Remove from heat, uncover and let cool.

Prepare:

    5~6 cloves garlic (minced)
    1 c. almonds (halved lengthwise)
    ½ c. raisins (washed)

Using a skillet or wok, sauté the above ingred. in:

    2 tbsp. marg.

Fry till browned, tamari, fry another minute and remove from the pan.

Prepare:

    3 onions (½" dice)
    3 stalks celery (¼" diagonal slices)
    2 green peppers (1" squares)

In same pan, singe fry the vegetables till cooked yet still crispy.

Prepare in ¼" slices:

    1 lb. mushrooms

Singe fry mushrooms.

Last but not least, margarine the skillet and fry the cooled rice on a medium-high heat. Work constantly with a spatula so it doesn't stick. When well heated, tamari and add all the fried ingred., plus:

    2 tsp. ginger pwd.

Continue cooking till all is hot. Arrange on a serving tray and keep hot till all else is ready to serve.

MOCK CHICKEN CACCIATORE
(serves 4)

This recipe requires:

    4 ~ 9 oz. sq. of Marinated Tofu Chicken

The day before, thaw tofu and marinate in Chicken Tofu Marinade overnight (page 79).

Mid-afternoon, set the tofu squares to drain.

When ready to start cooking, tear the tofu squares into 1" pieces, onto an oiled oven tray. Bake at 325° for 30 minutes. Turn every 10 minutes.

Prepare and sauté in a large oiled skillet:

    1 onion (¼" slices)
    1 green pepper (½" square pieces)
    4 cl. garlic (chopped fine)

Remove from pan. Prepare and sauté:

    ½ lb. mushrooms (washed, ¼" slices)

When mushrooms are cooked, tamari-singe them. Add tofu and vegetables back to the skillet. Also add:

    14 oz. can of whole tomatoes
    1 tbls. miso   1 tsp. basil
    1 tsp. oregano   ½ tsp. sage
    ¼ tsp. cayenne   ½ tsp. margoram

Cover and simmer for 25 min.

This dish should be served over fettuccini noodles, or cooked rice.
Prepare a sufficient quantity of your choice to suit the amount of people being served.

As a final step, mix:

    ½ c. water   2 tbls. arrowroot fl.

Add to simmering mixture and stir till thickened. Serve over drained noodles or hot rice.

BOEUF BOURGUIGNON

This is a gourmet stew,, fit to be served to royalty.

lilah wanted me to mention that one of the essential ingredients called for in this stew is a bottle of dry red wine. Even if you do not drink alcohol, it's all right as all of the alcohol will be cooked off, leaving only the flavor of the wine which enhances the whole dish.

This recipe utilizes seitan which has been cooked in small chunks (1"~1½" pieces) You may make a fresh batch or utilize what you have pre-prepared and frozen.

Prepare and combine in a casserole dish or roasting pot:

4 c. seitan pieces (1"~1½" pieces)
2 c. onion (¼ RD or ⅙ TH's, lengthwise)
1½ c. carrot (¼ RD lengthwise in 2" pieces)
2 c. potato (¾" chunks)
1 lb. mushrooms (washed, halved and singe fried in a little oil)
2 cl. garlic (peeled and sliced in ⅛" pcs.)
1 c. seitan juice
½ c. tamari
2 tsp. tarragon

Add, in a tea ball:

4 bay leaves   24 bl. pepper balls
4 cloves

Last, but not least, add:

3 c. of a dry, red wine (the better the wine, the better the sauce).
4 c. water

Cover with a lid and bake at 375° for 1¼ hours.
Serve with fresh rice, salad and garlic bread.

SQUASH - TEMPEH STEW

Thaw:

   2 8.5 oz. blocks of tempeh

Prepare:

   3 c. winter squash (peeled and cut
      into 1" chunks)
   2 c. onion (1" chunks)
   1 c. carrots (¾" diagonal slices)
   1 c. parsnips ("   "   "   ")

Combine the vegetables in a large pot and add:

   tempeh (cut into 1" squares)
   4 c. water
   ¼ c. tamari
   5 cloves garlic (slivered)
   1 tsp. thyme
   ½ tsp. celery sd.

Bring to a boil and reduce the heat to a simmer
Cover and cook for 30~40 minutes. (When
cooked,, the vegetables should be tender and
the squash will turn the broth creamy).

While the stew is cooking, prepare:

   1 c. of parsley (finely chopped)

Add the parsley to the stew once it has boiled
for 20 minutes.

Serve the stew as is with bread and salad
or over noodles or rice.

For a thicker stew,, add a little arrowroot
flour dissolved in some cold water. Stir in
and simmer till thickened.

Steak au Pouirve Flambé

This is another one of those exceptionally delicious gourmet dishes which Iilah has made on special occasions.

A day ahead of time, prepare:

a 4 c. batch of gluten (page 85).

After refrigerating the gluten, cut and shape it into 5 oz. steaks.

Prepare the broth using the 'spiced seitan' mixture. (Do not add any spicing to the gluten) Boil gluten till most of the water is gone and refrigerate.

One hour before it's time to start cooking, remove the seitan slices from the broth, let drain saving all liquid. Meanwhile, prepare all the other dishes for your meal. The steaks should be prepared last and served as soon as they are cooked.

Such a meal as this should be accompanied by a special potato dish, like 'sauted mini potatoes' or 'potatoes a la onions'. Also a vegetable dish such as 'Endives de Papa Leon',, plus garlic bread and a watercress ~ endive salad.

Traditionally: this would be made using:

1 pint of whipping cream

however, when we make this here at Philoxia,, we prefer to use the following, mix:

2 c. soy milk   1 tsp. arrowroot fl.

Next, crack or grind coarsely for each serving:

2 tbls. black pepper balls

Place pepper on a plate and press a steak into it, then do the other side. Place the steak on a dry board and press firmly to ensure the pepper is well adherred. Do this to each steak.

Make sure there is an equal amount of pepper on each piece. Don't worry about there being too much pepper, because it can be scraped off before being eaten. It is the flavor which the pepper imparts while being cooked that we're after.

For each steak, peel and chop:

½ tsp. garlic (finely chopped)

In a well buttered (soy marg.) skillet, fry the seitan steaks and chopped garlic. Fry till each steak has a well chard singe. Tamari a little while frying.

The next step is to flame them. For each serving use:

½ oz. Grand Marnier
or
½ oz. Armagnac

Preheat the liquor till almost steaming. Pour over the steaks and light with a match. While they are flaming, baste them with the sauce. Let the flame burn till it goes out on its own.

Put the steaks on a serving platter and keep warm in the oven while you prepare the sauce.

While your pan is still hot and sizzling, add per serving: **1 tsp. maple syrup**

Using either the whipping cream or the soy milk mixture, pour slowly into the simmering pan. It is important to stir this constantly, in one direction, especially if using the whipping cream, as it will curdle easily.

While stirring, the sauce should never boil, it should just simmer for about 3~5 minutes till thickened and turns a rich milk chocolate color.

When thickened, add a few tablespoons onto each steak. Any extra can be served on the side.

Serve while all is hot.

Buckwheat with Mushrooms and Sauerkraut

Prepare a 'small' batch of 'crumbly' buckwheat. (page 66) early in the day. Chill thoroughly.

While the grain is cooking, prepare and sauté together:

    1 lb. mushrooms
    2 onions

When onions and mushrooms are cooked, add:

    1~2 c. sauerkraut
    1 tsp. thyme

Fry till sizzling.
Add the buckwheat and continue frying till hot.

Serve with a vegetable dish and salad.

Mushroom Patties

Prepare, dice finely and sauté:

    ½ lb. mushrooms   3 cloves of garlic
    1 onion

Combine in a bowl:

    2 c. cooked millet   1 tbls. tamari
    2 eggs   ½ tsp. celery sd.
    2 tbls. flour   ⅛ tsp. cayenne

Add the fried ingredients and mix well. Shape into 2" patties and bake on an oiled tray at 350° for 15 min. Turn and bake 15 min. more.

As an alternative, these can be dipped in a tamari ~egg baste, then rolled in bread crumbs and pan fried in ⅛" of oil.

Salt

You hear a lot nowadays about low salt diets,, and the concerns are justly warranted. High iodized salt intake creates high blood pressure, heart problems, water retention, hypertension, etc. Whatever amount of salt you do use in your diet should be sea salt. It contains many natural trace minerals such as potassium, calcium, and manganese in a proper proportion with sodium.

Commercial salt contains excessive sodium with no potassium to balance it. The use of inorganic iodine used in iodized salt can act as an irritant, contributing to various digestive and assimilative problems. Consumption of a whole grain diet, including a variety of seaweed, green vegetables, and some fruits, will supply an ample amount of natural iodine. If you eat a little seaweed regularly you get plenty of iodine. Commercial salt is also bleached, and the granules are coated with emulsifier so that "when it rains, it pours".

We use sea salt primarily for cooking grains and beans, for making breads, cakes, etc.,, and in some sauces or dressings where tamari affects the colour.

Wherever possible,, use tamari or miso to salt and flavour foods. There is salt in each of these products,,, however once it has been through the aging process tamari and miso go through,, the salt is converted, and when digested, is more easily eliminated from the system. Regardless,,, it is still wize to keep any source of salt to a minimum.

MISO

A moderate consumption of miso each day in your soup, sauces, or on toast is very beneficial for the natural minerals and enzymes they contain. There are many kinds of miso on the market made of different grains: soybean (hacho), barley and soybean (mugi), soybean and rice Kome. Each have different flavours depending on which grains they are made with,, how long they are aged,, and to what degree they are processed.

Miso is a healthful salt substitute which is an excellent source of iron, Vitamin B12, and protein. It builds intestinal flora which aid digestion and absorption. It alkalizes the system and balances metabolism.

Commercial misos are pasteurized and tend to have a smoother texture. These are usually imported from the Orient. On the other hand,, there are numerous small miso producers operating throughout the States and Canada who are making very delicious unpasteurized misos. These usually have a coarser texture plus a deliciously sweet, aromatic flavour,, and altho they are more expensive, they are certainly worthwhile buying to use wherever you do not cook the miso, such as soup, sauces, toast, etc. These misos have live enzymes which are very beneficial to your digestion. For this reason you should never boil foods containing miso. (Miso should always be added to soup after it has completely cooked and been turned off.) For cooking purposes, the use of the pasteurized misos is sufficient and less expensive. We use miso in certain stews, casseroles, and grain dishes for the flavour it imparts,, and in some cases, to balance the acidity of meals which contain tomato sauce or paste.

OH~SOH~NOWA

CHAPTER 7

Oh~Soh~Nowa

Lilah's Famed
OSONAWA DISHES

These dishes are synonymous with the ancients of both the Great Eastern and Western civilizations.

Those oriented with this system of cooking in the East call it "OSŌNĂWĂ" altho,,,

when the Great Western Plains Indians prepared such deelites they called it,, "O~SÓH~NĂW~WĂH" and as we of the re-established first world of white Mayas call it,,, "Oh~ so now what we gonna make for dinner." "Hmmmm"

MILLET STEAKS

Millet is a mainstay of our diet, however, fresh cooked millet is rather porridge-like. We prefer millet served in this fashion as it has a firmer texture. It is definitely more appealing to the palate of people who are new to natural foods.

This recipe is designed to utilize millet which has been boiled and then baked as described in the grain section under millet (page 54).

These are two different methods by which you can reheat precooked millet:

1) ~ Oil an oven tray.

Slice cooked millet into 1" thick slabs.

Place millet on the tray and tamari each piece.

Bake in a 350° oven till browned. (How long you cook them depends on how crispy you like your millet steaks.)

2) Slice millet into 3/4"~ 1" thick slabs.

On a low flame, heat a skillet with about 1/16"" of an inch of oil.

Arrange millet steaks in the skillet so they all rest squarely on the bottom. Tamari each one and add a few tbsp. of water to the pan. Cover and simmer. Check frequently and loosen with a flipper if they seem to be sticking. Add a little water if needed.

Re-oil pan and flip each piece. Tamari again, add a little water and continue simmering. Serve when good and hot.

Either of these methods produces a very tasty, crisp and firm main meal item which is quite appealing.

261

on its own or simply served with tahini~miso.

Here are also a few different ideas we have used to add some other interesting flares to the millet steaks.

~Using method one, tamari millet steaks when on the tray and add the chosen sauce. Bake for 25~30 min.

~Using method two,, cook the millet steaks as described on one side. Flip the steaks and add the chosen sauce on top of steaks. If some of the sauce flows over,, let that supply the water needed for the second half of the cooking. Simmer till good and hot.

In each case use the quantities suited to your own taste.

1) leftover Cream Sauce mixed with chopped parsley.

2) leftover Cheese Sauce with chopped shallots.

3) leftover Sweet and Sour Sauce.

4) leftover spaghetti sauce or tomato sauce sprinkled with oregano, basil and garlic powder.

5) a spreadable mixture of miso, water, parsley and 'good tasting' nutritional yeast.

6) leftover gravy with fried mushrooms on top.

7) sprinkle with garlic pwd, tarragon and cayenne.

8) tahini~miso with tomato slices.

9) tofu mayonnaise mixed with chopped chives.

MILLET CUBES A LA VEGGIES

This is an ideal way to reheat and use millet which has been cooked a day or two before.

Using precooked millet, (page 54) cut into:

    1" squares (1 ~ 1½ c. / serving)

Place on a well oiled oven tray and bake till golden. Tamari and turn occasionally to brown evenly.

Meanwhile, prepare any or all of these vegetables for frying:

    onions (1" chunks)
    green peppers (1" squares)
    celery (½" diagonal slices)
    zucchini (¼" " " ")
    carrots (large grate or thin slice)
    mushrooms (halved)

(prepare 1 ~ 1½ c. of vegetables per serving.)

Steam-fry each vegetable as you would for Chinese cooking (so they are hot yet still crispy.)

Depending on the quantity you are making, will influence whether you can cook all of these ingred. at once or fry them in smaller groupings, ie,. onions, peppers and celery; the zucs and carrots; the mushrooms.

When all is cooked, mix the vegetables and the millet cubes together. Reheat all of the ingredients till hot and serve.

Serve as is or with tahini ~ miso sauce.

This may seem like a very simple meal, however the variations that can be created from this basic idea are numerous.

No matter how often you eat this meal ,,, it can be different each time by utilizing leftover vegetables or sauces. Add seasonings of your own likes.

This is very good served on top of noodles.

Here are a few creative examples :

1) millet squares
     steam fried peas
         and carrot slivers
     garlic pwd, corriander
     ginger pwd.

2) millet squares
     singe fried mushrooms,
         onions and zucchini
     garlic pwd. thyme

3) millet squares
     singe fried celery
         and onions
     leftover broccoli

4) millet squares
     steamed corn
     leftover homefries
     leftover gravy

5) millet squares
     -singe fried onion
         and green peppers
     -steamed green beans
     -add leftover tomato
     sauce or stewed tomatoes
     -spice accordingly with
     basil, oregano and garlic

6) millet squares
     -steam fried onions
         and carrots
     -leftover greens
     -serve with leftover
     cheese sauce
     -garnish with chopped
         fresh parsley

7) millet squares
     -steam fried onions
         and brussel sprouts
     -leftover sweet and
         sour sauce.

8) millet squares
     -steamed corn
     -fried sauerkraut

Tamari or salt each dish as is needed.

In most cases you can cook each dish in one skillet. Fry ingredients first , add millet squares and any other vegetables. Stir-fry till hot , then add the sauce and simmer on a low flame till bubbling.

In place of millet, you can use precooked 3 grain, or leftover buckwheat cut into squares.

STUFFED SQUASH

The type of squash used for making this should be either: acorn ~ butternut ~ pepper

Each of these types provide a large stuffing area when deseeded.

Pick the size of squash keeping in mind that each halved squash is one serving when stuffed.

General Preparations:

Wash each squash, cut in half lengthwise and remove seeds.

Place on an oiled tray and bake at 350° for 20 min.

Meanwhile, prepare stuffing mixture.
Stuff each half after they have baked 20 min.

Top with sauce (if you're using one), continue baking till squash is cooked.

These are a few of the mixtures we have used as stuffings (try some of these, then create your own).

The quantity and proportions of grain, vegetables and spicing is up to you depending on how many you are serving and your own preference.

As a finishing touch on any of these stuffings, top with one of these sauces:

Tahini~miso	Cream Sauce
Toma-hini sauce	Cheese Sauce

(a sauce keeps the filling from drying out).

1) cooked rice
   grated carrot (steamed)
   diced onion (fried)
   ginger pwd., cayenne
   tamari to taste.

2) cooked millet
   onions and celery,
   diced and sautéd
   coriander, thyme
   tamari to taste.

3) cooked buckwheat
   sautéd onions
   corn
   carraway pwd.
   garlic pwd.
   tamari

4) tofu (crumbled and fried)
   steamed peas
   grated cheese
   tarragon
   curry, cayenne
   tahini ~miso (as a binder)

5) cooked rice and
      crumbled tempeh
   fried mushrooms
   garlic pwd., curry
   nutritional yeast.
   tamari

6) cooked 3 grain
   fried onions
      and peppers
   tomato sauce
   carraway pwd., basil,
   garlic pwd, tamari.

7) cooked millet
   left over mashed potatoes
   chopped chives or
      shallots
   basil, salt to taste
   bit of melted marg.
   cayenne or black pepper

8) leftover Kasha
   and bow ties

9) leftover fried rice
   and cooked
      greens.

To prepare any of these in a more special fashion, par~bake the squash for 30 min.

Tamari singe each of the vegetable ingredients.

Score the inside of each squash with lengthwise slices. Baste the inside with margarine and tamari.

Fill with stuffing and bake till squash is cooked.

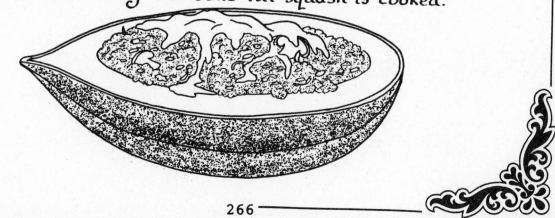

Sicilian Delights

This is a dish which Iilah tells me he first had the opportunity to experience in a small family restaurant in Naples, Italy.

To make this dish you need zucchini that has grown quite large (1½'~2' long). They don't generally sell these in the stores, however if you or a friend have a garden, it is quite often the case that they grow quite large in no time.

When they are this size, the removal of the seeds leaves a nice sized, stuffable hole in the center of each slice.

Wash zucchini and slice into 1" thick rounds. Scoop out the seeds from each slice (Two good sized rounds is usually enough per person).

Place on an oiled tray.

Spice an appropriate amount of cooked buckwheat (approx. 2/3 ~ 1 c. per serving) with:

> garlic pwd.   corriander
> cayenne   tamari to taste

Mix well and fill each ring spreading the mixture across the top of the round to the edge (about ¼" to ½" thick).

Put a layer of thinly sliced onion rounds on each one,, then a layer of tomato slices.

Sprinkle with : tamari
                powdered tarragon

Top with grated cheese.

If you don't eat cheese, use some cream sauce with nutritional yeast or mochi (page 328).

Bake at 350° till zucchini is soft and the cheese (or sauce) is browned.

cont.

There are many other combinations which can be enjoyed in this type of dish. Some of our most favorite have been from using and combining leftovers.

Here are a few ideas,, but do some experimenting and come up with your own.

1) 3 grain, ground and spiced to the Meatloaf recipe.

  ~ layer with sautéd : onions
                     mushrooms

  ~ top with leftover gravy.
  ~ serve any extra gravy on the side at the table.

2) cooked rice, spiced with :

     curry   garlic pwd.
     corriander   tamari to taste

  ~ add : sautéd onions

  ~ garnish with broccoli tops stuck in the rice.

  ~ top with leftover cream sauce or cheese sauce.

3) 3 grain mixed with leftover spaghetti, pizza or lasagna sauce. (don't add so much that the grain becomes sloppy).

  ~ layer with : thin onion rounds
                thin pepper slices

  Top with grated cheese or cheese sauce.

4) fill zucchini rounds with leftover "Tofu and Cheese" blintz stuffing.
  ~ top with tahini ~ miso.

RICE BALLS

There are numerous variations that can be used in making rice balls.

All rice balls are best made with a creamy, well cooked rice, as they will hold together better.

When forming rice balls,, have a bowl of water near to dip your hands in. It is much easier to form balls if the rice doesn't stick to your hands.

PLAIN RICE BALLS

These are quick to make and are a nice alternative to plain steamed rice.

Spice lightly with any of these combinations:

basil and thyme	curry and tarragon
garlic and carraway	oregano and savory
dried parsley	garlic and celery sds.

Mix well, tamari to taste, then shape into 1½" balls.

Place on an oiled tray and bake till browned. Do not overcook as the outside will get very 'chewy'.

SESAME~RICE BALLS

Make as in above recipe.

Moisten each ball with wet hands and roll in a plate of sesame seeds. Bake on an oiled tray.

BREADED RICE BALLS

Spice rice with	savory	cayenne or black pepper
	salt	some melted margarine

Shape into balls and roll in bread crumbs.
Bake on an oiled tray till good and hot.

UMEBOSI~NORI RICE BALLS

These are quite tasty hot or cold and because they are wrapped in nori (seaweed) they do not fall apart easily and are therefore great for lunches or for traveling with.

When eaten cold,, they are best with a tofu mayonnaise sauce to dip them in.

You will need 1 sheet of nori for every 2 rice balls (1½" to 2" size balls).

Roast each sheet over a stove burner till it turns a slight green color. (This par cooks the seaweed and makes it less chewy.)

With scissors or a sharp knife,, cut the sheets width~wise..........

These need no other spicing than the umebosi paste.

Place some rice in the palm of your hand.
Add a finger of umebosi paste to the centre.

Add more rice on top and shape into a ball. Do not make the ball bigger than 2".

Wrap one half sheet of nori around the rice ball. Moisten the edges so they will stick.

Repeat till all of the nori sheets are used.

Place on a plate and refrigerate if they are to be eaten cold, or place on an oiled tray and bake at 350° for 20~30 min. to enjoy them hot.

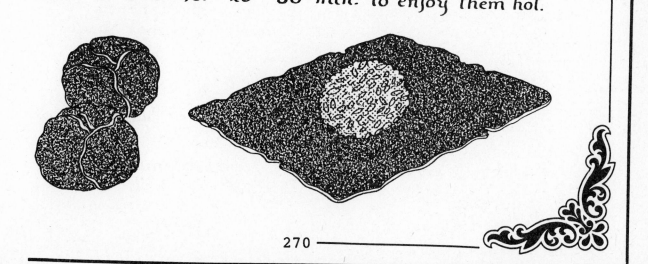

AH~SOH~NOODLE~NOW

These are certain types of dishes we have made and enjoyed in so many various combinations ,, that I'd still be writing this here book if I was to detail all of them to you.

These have consisted of everything from freshly prepared noodles, grain and vegetables to using up leftovers to make new and interesting dishes.

Now, with all this in mind and the various sauces, vegetable dishes and your favorite types of noodles at hand , be creative and surprise your family with a new and interesting meal.

Here are a few suggestions to get you started. Once again,, proportions and spicings are up to you in accordance with what you have to work with and the number of people being served.

Most of these can be simply combined or layered in a casserole dish and heated in the oven 'till hot.

1) vegetable shell ndls.
   steamed: carrots
                 peas
   cream sauce

2) spinach fettuccini ndls.
   cooked spinach or
                 swiss chard
   cheese sauce

3) rottini noodles
   cooked buckwheat
   fried : onions
                 mushrooms
   leftover gravy

4) leftover spaghetti ndls.
   baked tofu cubes
   steamed: broccoli or
                 green beans
   sweet and sour sauce

5) buckwheat (soba) ndls.
   fried : 3 grain
                 sauerkraut
   Zabro's horseradish
   tahini ~ miso

6) broad egg ndls.
   steam fried: zucchini
                 carrots
   toma~hini sauce
   chopped tomato

STEW A LA LEFTOVERS

This stew turned out just super and was very quick to make because we used:

- ~ last nights remaining gravy
- ~ the night before's meat balls
- ~ and the juice leftover from a Baked Broccoli Casserole.

Place in a pressure cooker:

- ~ Broccoli Casserole juice (2~3 cups)
- ~ 3 potatoes (1" chunks)
- ~ 2 carrots (1" chunks)
- ~ 2 onions (1" chunks)
- ~ 1 c. turnip or parsnips (½" chunks)

(the juice should be about ⅔ the depth of the vegetables).

Mix well and pat to be level.

Add the gravy on top of the vegetables but do not stir.

Place the meat balls on top of the gravy.

Add pressure cooker top and pressure for 20 min.

This is good served as is with bread, or over top of rice or noodles.

This is simply one example. There are endless combinations that can create very tasty, quick meals and also use up any leftovers.

As Iilah has always said ,,, the true art of cooking is making do with what you have to work with, making it interesting to the eyes and tempting to the palate.

CREAMY TOFU DELIGHT
(serves 4)

Rinse and towel dry:

     3 ~ 9 oz. cubes of tofu

Cut the tofu into squares, place on an oiled tray and tamari.

Bake at 350° for 30 min. Turn and tamari twice.

Prepare and singe fry:

     3 medium onions

Prepare a batch of:

     Cream Sauce (page 283)

Bring to a boil in a saucepan:

     2 qts. water   1 tsp. salt

Add: enough fettuccine noodles for 4 servings.

Boil: 2 c. peas

Blend sauce and return to the pot.

Add the tofu squares,, fried onions and cooked peas (drained).

Simmer till noodles are cooked, drain them and serve with the sauce.

Although this recipe is a meal unto itself, I put it in the Oh~soh~nowa chapter because there are so many variations which can be adapted to it. This is also a very tasty and quick meal to make if company shows up.

You can also serve this over freshly cooked rice or steamed rice.

Any variety or combination of vegetables will go well with this dish, carrot slivers, corn kernels, spinach, chard or broccoli.

Re-Incarnation

Men of science have long known that when a person passes on,,, there is a noticeable amount of weight loss,,, approximately the same amount of weight you lose when you're asleep.

Some 20 years ago,, an idea was thought of which might possibly shine more light onto the disappearance of this invisible mass which instantly leaves us in death, and slowly leaves while one's asleep.

Since Kerillian and infrared films have revealed many new revelations dealing with the science of energies,, these researchers decided to hook up a specially designed, highly sensitized camera system to a person who was next to death. As soon as the heart stopped beating, the shutter started to click frames of newly found dimensional truths. Upon development of this film,,, they, after the reversion of infrared colour to natural colour, saw a purplish haze leaving the body at the exact point of death,,, yet unaware at that time of what they were discovering. Scientifically, they had just proven that your spirit, life, atomized being, energy, or cosmik self (it's all the same) leaves your body at point of death. This light mass is also a molecular structure, and it goes back to the material elements from which it came,, as your material body goes back to its source. At this point,, the game of life and death is reset. The players, be they unconscious of life's meaning, are returned to play the cycle of kreashon again.

Now, a singular atom has not yet been seen,, but it is known that all material forms are composed of an atomic structure,,, and accepting this truth, we are brought to the awareness that in life or death we have another form which is energized atomically. It is that which leaves us in death and also represents the weight loss to the body. But then what happens to it? Well,,, there are millions of examples from which I could choose from,, but only one in simplicity is needed.

If you have not released consciousness of this atomized form in life,,, in death, it has no longer the physical bodily structure to confine its energy,,, so, off your seven billion atoms go,, scattering themselves into the wind, sea, and land,,, still unconscious and oblivious to any self realizations.

For those of you in life who have reached the limited level of believing in ghosts or demons,,, in death, for a time, you shall become that which you only knew of in life,,, a ghost or demon of one form or another. You must remember,,, because of the limitations in one's mystical beliefs,,, the atomized structure is still stuck to the Earth's gravitational pull. One cannot utilize one's seven-stage, atomized rocket ship which can, if properly programmed, travel at speeds seven times faster than light. Our last and final journey away from this kreative module will crash the light barrier which surrounds the Bardo Planes of our solar'd system,, thus allowing the spirited, atomized structure to leave off its stages one by one, as well,, until one is freed of all weight matter, and can emanate with only pure soul to the gates of Eternal Heaven.

This is still beyond most concepts,,, so first should be explained about what happens to your seven billion atoms after the illusive death of unconsciousness. Before I begin,,, I would like you to simply accept the fact that within one of your atoms lies the complete knowledge and wisdom of the Universe relative to yourself, both past and future. All which is conceivable to the infinite mind is housed within the nucleous of the material atom. (The nucleous is that which has no materialistic, egotistical form.)

Let us say that just one of your seven billion atoms gets caught up in the dance of the winds,, when it suddenly starts to rain. Low and behold,, you,, I mean your still unconscious atom is hit by a raindrop, then taken immediately Earthward, and soon finds itself snuggled next to a simple little celery seed planted not too long ago by Farmer John. The seed becomes energized, and Mother Nature begins her work of nourishing and protecting this seedling within her Earthly womb of warmth and tenderness. Soon,, up comes a full grown, living vegetable, still housing within it the spark of life which was a part of the unkonkshus one who passed on. (Is man not sometimes called a living vegetable - action-reaction.)

Now,,, a wandering brother comes a'boppin' down the roadway,, just digging life to no end, and lays sight upon this gorgeous celery stock being sold at his roadside stand. Soon afterwards,, down by the old mill stream,, several pieces are eaten with his lunch,,, of which one still houses the particular atom in question. Later, after digesting all this goodness,,, he finds himself in a freshly cut hay field and joyfully makes a bed of aromatic comfort. Entering a deep euphoric sleep and enjoying the astral travel within his galactic dream worlds,,, our young friend is startled into an awakening by the clanking of a milk pot,,, and upon focusing his eyes, he is confronted with visions of radiant beauty, as she, the ever so fresh, warm, and beautiful daughter of Farmer John (farmer's daughter joke, or is it?) says,, "Oh,,, I'm sorry,, I didn't mean to wake you. My name is Celene, what is yours?"

Well,, to make a timeless story shorter, she or he is soon subdued willfully,, and the spark of life, which by now has entered into his sperm cell,, is soon found to be within the tender vibrations of she,, who, here on Earth as it is in Heaven,, has the power to kreate life once again to your own image. Shortly after,,, the child is born, and within him still lies this same atom of complete, unconscious knowledge, which is once again humanized and is being given a chance to gain consciousness of its eternal developing character.

Upon gaining consciousness of this life cycle,,, all conceivable awarenesses relative to the infinite mind is then made available to you as a warehouse of knowledge which can be utilized as you wish. To reach the dwelling place of wisdom and nobility on Earth means one qualifies to go beyond life and death. Many are in training, as well as helping others to get their free passage haum, because all of worth is soon to be taken, whether they have awareness of it or not. To have done for the self is worth more than to have it done for you at a later date.

Many people have put a debatable word to such a circle of life and death, which is called "re-incarnation",,, but nah,, it couldn't be,,, it's all too simple to accept or believe. Well that it is,,, and the celery plant is symbolical, and is but one representation of the many ways from which this spark of life is passed on and on.

Once consciousness is released in life, one then knows in completeness that he or she will never have to go through the illusive, dualistic life and death cycle again, unless they choose to do so. From this point of simple acceptance begins one's true enlightening pathway of becoming the happy, healthy, eternally conscious character one would like to share with others forever after.

As the spirit of life leaves a human at point of death,,, so it does to the slaughtered animal people eat as a so-called whole food. In other words,,, what grows from dead meat does not equate what grows from a seed.

More scientific facts:

One atom utilized with chain reaction destroyed Hiroshima.

Two atoms utilized as such, can destroy four times Hiroshima.

Three atoms - 12 times,,, etc., etc., etc.

The seven billion atoms within each of us,,, if utilized,,, has the force not only to change the Earth and its solar system,,, but computerized, it is known where at will, we possess enough atomic energy to change the atomic structure of the Universe,,,, "Uni" meaning one, and "verse" meaning many as one. Interestingly enough,,, "Universe" spelled backwards is "esrevinu". If the Great One ain't changin' things, other than for the self,, no human should try, either,,, because such things as basic awareness have to manifest naturally from within for it to be of an eternal value to anyone.

ii,,,, the awareness of it, to whatever degree, has no real relevancy, either,,, until it is reflected through a common sensed, gritt-on-truth diet.

Garlic Breath

In learning about natural foods,, people acquire an appreciation and understanding for what they put into their systems. Likewise,, what you apply on the outside is just as important.

In the early 70's,, Iilah was invited to attend a world health symposium at Berkeley, California, hosted by Herman and Cornelia Aihara. One of the experiments they conducted was designed to prove what effect external substances have on the internal body.

A large quantity of garlic was peeled and crushed. It was spread onto two towels. Just before bed,, each cloth was wrapped around the feet of one person. This person went to sleep like this. In the morning, everyone was amazed at how strong the smell of garlic was on his breath. Imagine what effect some of these sprays, perfumes, and deodorants have upon your internal organs and brain cells.

SAUCES DIPS and DRESSINGS

CHAPTER 8

Sauces, Dips and Dressings

Salad Dressings:

HOT SAUCES

Each of these sauces are completely non-dairy and are very nutritious.

The method of these first two recipes are interchangable. The latter is quicker but not as 'creamy'.

CREAM SAUCE

Combine in a saucepan:

4 c. water	½ c. washed millet
1 onion (diced)	

(will make approx. 5 cups of sauce).

Add to sauce:

3 tbls. soy marg.	½ tsp. salt
1 tsp. tarragon	½ tsp. garlic pwd.
or ¼ tsp. bl. pepper	¼ tsp. curry pwd.
⅛ tsp. cayenne	1 tsp honey (opt)

Simmer with a cover for 25 ~ 30 mins.
Stir occasionally.

Blend half at a time, till smooth and creamy.
Keep warm till ready to serve.

CHEESE SAUCE

Blend: 2 c. water   1 c. cooked millet
       ½ onion (chopped)   (or rice)

Strain into double boiler and repeat one more batch.

Add to sauce:

2 tbls. soy marg.	1½ c. grated cheese
1 tsp. basil	½ tsp. salt

Double boil till piping hot.
The amount of cheese used can be altered to your own taste.

CHEESY "NO CHEESE" SAUCE

Combine in a saucepan:

4 c. water	1 c. onion
1 c. millet	2 cl. garlic
1 tsp. salt	1 tsp. tarragon

Simmer with a cover for 25 minutes.

Blend till smooth and creamy. Return to the pot and add:

½ c. grated mochi
½ c. good tasting nutritional yeast
(Farm yeast)
2 tbls. soy marg.

Stir well and simmer for 5~10 minutes on a flame tamer.

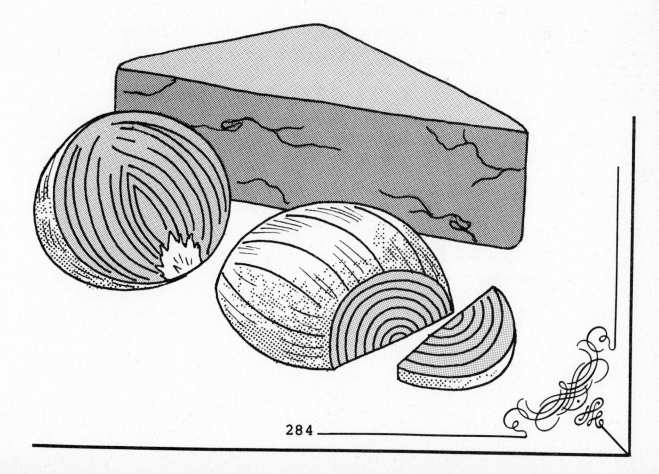

DELICIOUS BROWN GRAVY

As good as any gravy made from a meat stock providing you cook the onions properly.

Put to boil:

    10 c. water   1½ tsp. salt

Peel and slice for frying:

    4~5 med. onions in 2 tbls. oil

(the trick to this recipe is to achieve the flavor from the onion by frying them till well browned and 'syrupy'. This will impart a sweet, flavorful taste.)

While the onions are frying, wash and ¼" slice:

    ½ lb. mushrooms

Add onions to boiling water. Also add:

2 bay lvs.	½ tsp. celery sd.
½ tsp. thyme	4 cl. garlic
1 tsp. basil	¼ tsp. bl. pepper

Let simmer for 20 ~ 30 minutes.
Sauté mushrooms in a little oil. Tamari singe.

Meanwhile, dry roast: (preferably in a cast iron pan)

    1 c. durham fl. or wh. wheat fl.

(Be sure to stir constantly, scraping the flour as it browns. By browning, I mean simply to a golden beige. The darker the browning the stronger the taste will be.)

Sift browned flour into a bowl. Slowly add 1½ cups cold water while stirring. A wire wisp will help to avoid lumps.

Remove bay leaves from pot and add cooked mushrooms. While sauce is boiling add ¾'s of the brown flour batter. Stir till it thickens. Add more batter if a thicker gravy is desired. Tamari or salt to taste.

This gravy freezes well in single or family size servings.

Asparagus Sauce

This sauce is designed to be served over freshly steamed asparagus, however,, if you have your own asparagus patch, this is an excellent way to utilize overgrown or woody asparagus stems. Serve as a sauce on another vegetable, such as broccoli or cauliflower, even over meatloaf or noodles.

Combine in a saucepan and bring to a boil:

4 c. water   1 tbls. marg.
½ c. millet   ¼ tsp. salt
1 onion (diced)   ⅛ tsp. bl. pepper
2 c. asparagus (tops or stems, cut into
     1" pieces).

Simmer for 30 min. with a cover.

While sauce cooks, prepare the asparagus, or whatever you are serving the sauce on.

When cooked, remove sauce from the stove and let cool for 10 min.
Blend sauce and strain through a metal sieve to remove any fibrous asparagus pieces.

Reheat and serve when all else is ready.

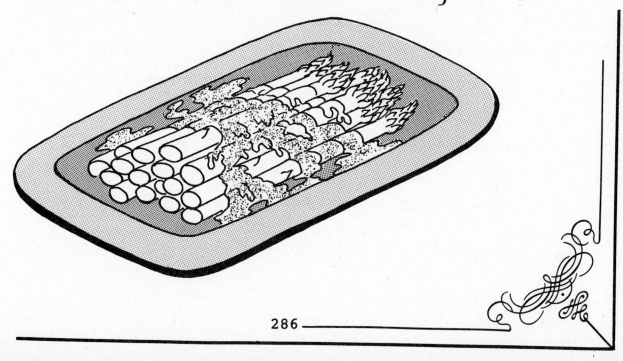

SWEET N' SOUR SAUCE

This sauce is designed for a few specialty dishes, such as: SWEET AND SOUR TEMPURA BALLS
  "   "   "   MEATBALLS
  "   "   "   BEETS
however, if you have guests drop by, it is a quick, easy sauce to make any vegetable and/or grain dish special.

Combine in a pot:

4 c. water	1½ c. apple cider vinegar
1½ c. honey	1½ tbls. garlic
2 tbls. tamari	1½ tbls. grated beet
1 tsp. lemon rd.	2 tsp. tarragon
1 tsp. thyme	¼ tsp. black pepper

Simmer for 15 to 20 minutes.

Mix: ½ c. cold water   7 tbls. arrowroot fl.

Add to the simmering mixture, stirring till it becomes thick and clear.

Pour over the meal or serve on the side.

PINEAPPLE
SWEET N' SOUR SAUCE

Combine in a saucepan and bring to a boil:

4 c. pineapple juice
1 c. vinegar (apple cider, brown rice,
              umebosi or combination of)
¼ c. finely grated white radish (loh bok)
      (grate as you would lemon rind to
          produce a watery pultch)
1 tbls. tarragon
1 tsp. salt

Simmer with a cover for 10 minutes.

Mix: 1 c. water   4 tbls. arrowroot flour

Add to the pot and stir till thickened. Serve.

UMEBOSI SAUCE

An excellent sauce on freshly steamed vegetables. It is a healthy sauce to serve with a meal which is a little oily.

This may be prepared ahead of time,, however, wait till 10 minutes prior to meal time to cook it as it does not take long.

Mix in a small pot:
    3/4 c. water
    1 tbls. umebosi vinegar
    1 tsp. tamari
    1 ume plum or 1/2 tsp. umebosi paste
    (break meat off the plum pit)

Bring to a simmer.

Mix together:
    1/4 c. water   1 tbls. arrowroot fl.

Add slowly to the pot, stirring constantly until thickened and clear. Simmer till ready to use.

Add steamed vegetables to the sauce. Toss lightly and serve.

UMEBOSI PLUMS

MAYONNAISE

Here are three alternative recipes, suitable for the rich creamy palate to that of a light, no oil mayo.

'THE REAL THING'

Combine in a blender or food processor:

1 egg (med. size)	½ tsp. prepared mustard
½ tsp. sea salt	¼ tsp. honey (opt.)

Measure into separate cups:

1¼ c. light vegetable oil (chilled)
¼ c. apple cider vinegar (chilled)

With blender lid on, but the small center hole open, blend on slow speed for 10 seconds, slowly add some oil, then vinegar, each alternately and proportionately so as to run out of both at the same time.

Pour into container and refrigerate.

This can be made into a thicker consistency by stirring in 1-2 tbls. of tahine.

TOFU MAYONNAISE

Combine in a blender or food processor:

1 c. tofu	¼ c. water (approx.)
1 tbls. vinegar	1 tsp. lemon juice
1 tbls. tahine	½ tsp. prepared mustard
½ tsp. salt	

Blend on high speed. If using a blender, it is necessary to assist this mixture to blend by stirring around the edge with a chopstick.

Besides replacing mayonnaise in any recipe,, this makes an excellent sauce on vegetables or grain.

Vary the quantity of water you use according to the consistency of the tofu to achieve the texture you desire.

TOFU MAYONNAISE, ½ and ½

This is our preference when it comes to mayonnaise.
It has the 'REAL' flavor yet is lighter and has less oil.

Combine and blend:

1~2 tbls. water   9 oz. tofu (crumbled)
2 tbls. oil   ½ tsp. salt
1 tbls. vinegar   ½ tsp. prepared mustard
½ tsp. honey (opt.)

Blend, assisting with a chopstick. Refrigerate.

SOUR CREAM A LA TOFU

Quite satisfying in any recipe or fashion in which
you would use sour cream, without the cream.

Combine and blend till smooth:

3 tbls. sauerkraut   2 tbls. vinegar
2 tbls. sauerkraut juice

Pass through a wire strainer.

Return liquid to the blender. Add:

1 c. tofu   ½ tsp. salt
¼ c. oil

Blend till creamy and smooth. Store in a
jar and refrigerate.

TAHINE SAUCES

TAHINE is made by grinding sesame seeds with their own oil content to produce a pourable liquid which has a delicious, nut-like flavor.

~It is very nutritious in that it supplies both protein and calcium, which many people feel can be missed in a vegetarian diet.

~As a spread on toast or sandwiches, it is much more nutritious and more easily digested than peanut butter.

~Tahine can also be used as a sauce on vegetables or grain, yet to make it more palatable and less oily, here are some sauces using tahine which will have your family asking for it as an everyday addition to your table.

~Kept refrigerated, these sauces are good for 5~7 days.

TAHINI~MISO

Blend or stir:

1 c. water   2 tbls. miso

Slowly add tahine till sauce is thick.

approx. 1 c. tahine

Refrigerate.

TAHINA

Combine in blender:

1 c. water   ½ c. chopped parsley
1 clove garlic   ½ tsp. salt
1~2 tbls. lemon juice   or 1 tbls. miso

Blend till smooth, then add tahine slowly:

approx. 1 c. tahine

Refrigerate.

These next two recipes are ideal for people who are on a low oil diet.

TAHINI-GRAIN SAUCE

Blend together :

    1 c. water   2 tbls. miso
    ½ c. cooked millet

When smooth,, add tahine till thickened :

    approx. ⅓ c. tahine

Refrigerate. This mixture is best used within 3~4 days.

NUTRI-GRAIN SAUCE

Blend together :

    1 c. water   1 tbls. gomasio
    ½ c. cooked millet

When smooth, add and continue blending :

    2 tbls. 'good tasting' nutritional yeast
    1 tbls. lecithin granuals
    ½ tsp. umebosi paste
    2 tbls. tahine

Add a little soymilk pwd. if a thicker texture is desired. Refrigerate. Use within 3~4 days.

TOMA-HINI SAUCE

Blend together:

    ¾ c. water   ½ c. cooked millet
    1 tbls. miso

Blend till smooth and add:

    ¼ c. natural ketchup   ½ c. tahine

Refrigerate.

DIPS

An assortment of these dips served with a variety of fresh vegetables, crackers, cheese, paté and bread makes a very nice spread when you are having a party, or for a light, cool meal during the summer.

PARSLEY~GARLIC DIP

Blend till smooth:

1 c. ch. parsley	2 tbls. oil
½ c. water	1 tbls. lemon juice
6 cl. garlic	1 tbls. vinegar
or 1 tsp. garlic pwd.	

Add and continue blending:

1 c. tofu	½ tsp. honey
1 tsp. salt	

Pour into a serving dish, cover and refrigerate.

SPICED~CHEESE DIP

Blend till smooth:

1½ c. grated cheese	¼ c. vinegar
½ c. water	¼ c. oil
1 green onion	

Add and continue blending:

½ ~ ¾ c. tofu
hot salsa sauce to taste

4 cl. minced garlic	1 tsp. salt
1 tsp. dill seed	½ tsp. curry pwd.

Refrigerate. (This dip usually disappears very fast, so make a double batch.)

ONION~CHEESE DIP

Blend till smooth:

    1 c. grated cheese   2 tbls. vinegar
    ½ c. water   2 tbls. oil
    ½ c. diced onion

Add and continue blending:

    1 c. tofu (crumbled) 1 tsp. salt
    1 tbls. dried parsley

Place in a bowl, cover and refrigerate.

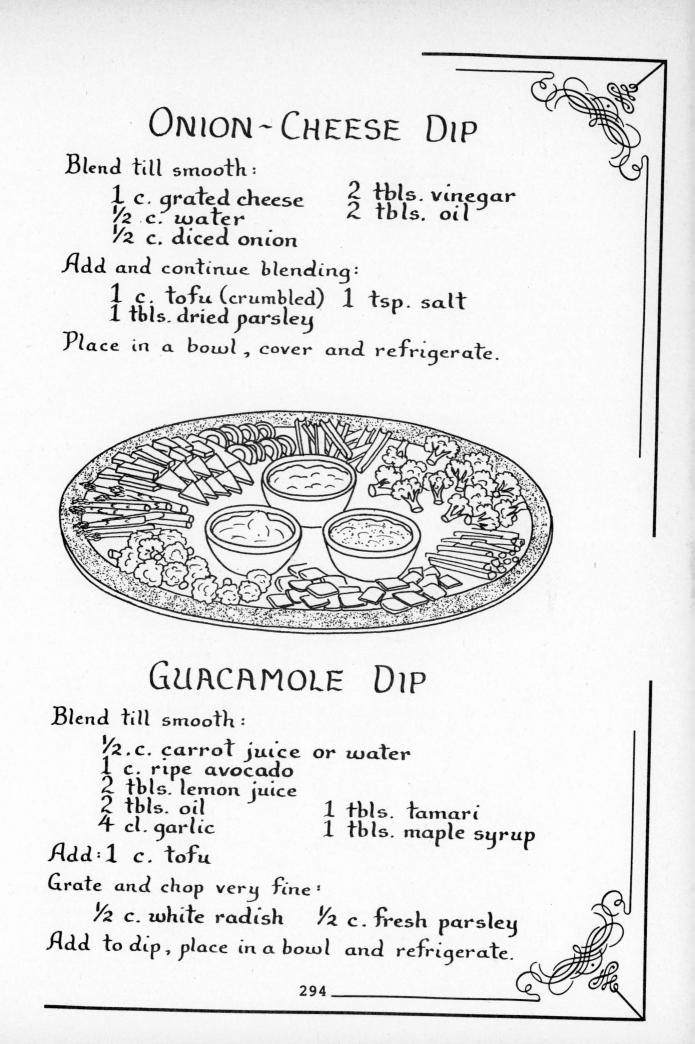

GUACAMOLE DIP

Blend till smooth:

    ½ c. carrot juice or water
    1 c. ripe avocado
    2 tbls. lemon juice
    2 tbls. oil   1 tbls. tamari
    4 cl. garlic   1 tbls. maple syrup

Add: 1 c. tofu

Grate and chop very fine:

    ½ c. white radish   ½ c. fresh parsley

Add to dip, place in a bowl and refrigerate.

SALMON AND CHIVES DIP

Blend till smooth:

½ c. carrot j. or water	2 tbls. oil
¼ c. chopped chives	1 tbls. vinegar
2 tbls. lemon juice	½ tsp. salt

Add and blend till creamy:

1 c. tofu (crumbled)
1 ~ 7.5 oz. can of red salmon

Place in a serving bowl, cover and refrigerate.

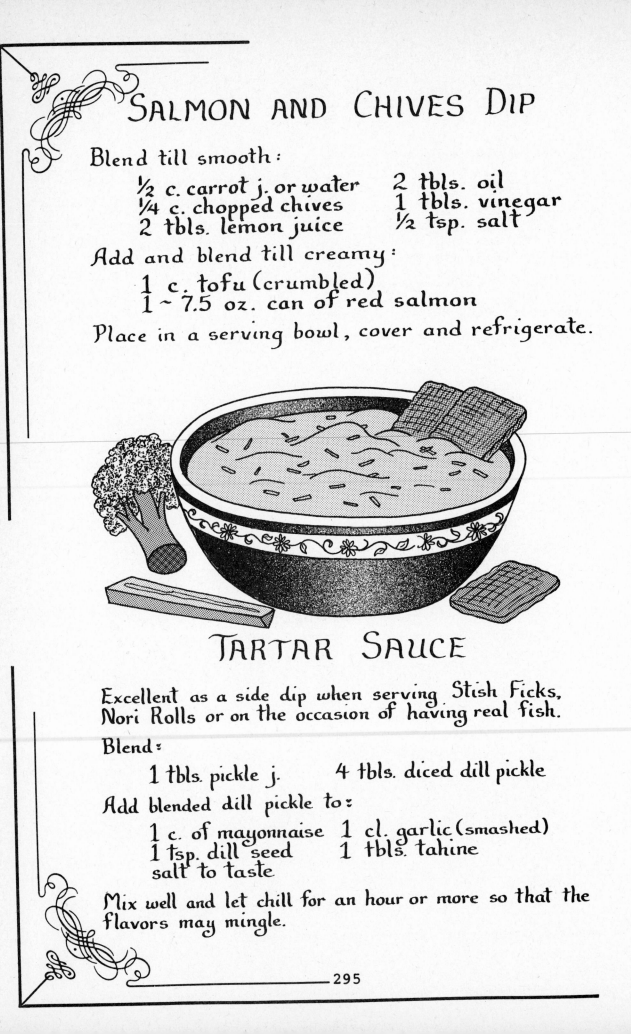

TARTAR SAUCE

Excellent as a side dip when serving Stish Ficks, Nori Rolls or on the occasion of having real fish.

Blend:

1 tbls. pickle j.	4 tbls. diced dill pickle

Add blended dill pickle to:

1 c. of mayonnaise	1 cl. garlic (smashed)
1 tsp. dill seed	1 tbls. tahine
salt to taste	

Mix well and let chill for an hour or more so that the flavors may mingle.

TOFU SAUCE

A light, low oil sauce using tofu as a base. Tasty on vegetables or grain.

Combine in a blender:

1 c. water
1 c. parsley
3 tbls. tahine

1 tbls. ume vinegar
½ tsp. garlic pwd.
½ tsp. salt

Blend till smooth.

Add crumbled tofu while blending till a pourable sauce is achieved:

approx. 1 cup

Bottle and refrigerate.

HUMUS

Humus is a traditional arabic side dish. It can also be used as a sandwich spread, or eaten in a pita bread with some chopped vegetables. With the addition of a little mayonnaise, it makes a very delicious vegetable or chip dip.

1 ~ 19 oz. can of chick peas
    or 2 c. of cooked chick peas
1 tsp. minced garlic
    or ½ tsp. garlic pwd.
2 ~ 3 tbls. chick pea juice
1 tbls. tahine
salt to taste

Blend till smooth and creamy. Bottle and refrigerate.

SALAD DRESSINGS

Any of these dressings will taste better if made ahead of time and allowed to marinate so that the flavors mellow and blend.

The oil and vinegar (or lemon) based dressings can be made in double or triple batches and kept on hand in the refrigerator. They improve with age.

Light oils such as sunflower sd. or safflower oil are preferrable as they won't impart a heavy flavor. Olive oil is traditionally favored for many salad dressings because of it's flavor,. however,, this oil is very hard to digest and should only be used occasionally.

Vinegars are available in numerous varieties. The commercial type of white vinegar should never be used. It is synthetically produced, bleached and of no nutritional value.   Use any good quality, apple cider, wine or grain (eg.~ brown rice) vinegar.

Garlic should always be put through a garlic press, or sliced widthwise and smashed. Either method will bring out the juice of the garlic and will reduce the pulp to small pieces. A chunk of raw garlic in a salad is not pleasant.

FRENCH DRESSING

Combine in a salad shaker or jar:

¾ c. oil	3 cl. garlic (smashed)
¼ c. vinegar	½ tsp. tarragon pwd.
¼ tsp. salt	¼ tsp. black pepper
¼ tsp. mustard	¼ tsp. maple syrup

Shake well and refrigerate.

Be sure to drain, shake or spin dry all salad ingredients, before adding the dressing. It will make the dressing coat the salad better and it will not dilute the dressing.

Pheylonian House Dressing

This is the house dressing which we serve in our restaurant. It is an excellent all-round dressing.

This is a good size batch which keeps well and gets better with age.

Combine in a bottle:

2 c. apple cider vinegar
⅓ c. umebosi or red wine vinegar
1 c. sunflower oil
⅓ c. maple syrup (or honey)
juice of 2 lemons
1 tbls. minced (or smashed) garlic
1 tbls. tarragon
1 tsp. prepared mustard
1~2 tsp. salt
½ tsp. finely ground black pepper

Shake well and refrigerate.

Iilah's Caesar Dressing

Mix in a bottle:

½ c. Pheylonian House Dressing
1 c. mayonnaise ('real' or '½ and ½')

Add: 1 tbls. pernod (anise liqueur)
1 tsp. garlic pwd.
¼ tsp. finely grd. black pepper

Mix well and keep refrigerated.

The next three recipes are each of a mayonnaise type base. They are creamy and make a nice change from the regular "oil and vinegar" type dressings.

CREAMY PARSLEY DRESSING

Blend together:

½ c. vinegar	½ c. chopped parsley
¼ c. oil	⅛ tsp. salt
2 cloves garlic	¼ c. water

When parsley is well blended, add and continue blending:

   ½ c. tofu (crumbled)

This will keep for 3~5 days in the refrigerator.

DRESSING OF MANY ISLES

Blend together:

½ c. vinegar	1 tbls. tomato paste
¼ c. oil	or 2 tbls. ketchup
¼ c. water	¼ tsp. thyme
1 tbls. parsley	¼ tsp. salt
¼ tsp. garlic pwd.	

While blender is mixing add:

   ½ c. of tofu (crumbled)

Bottle and refrigerate.

BLUE CHEESE DRESSING

This is very delicious, yet not too rich.
Blend together:

   ½ c. wine vinegar   2 oz. blue cheese

When smooth, add: ½ c. mayonnaise
Salt to taste, bottle and refrigerate.

ITALIAN DRESSING

Combine:

1/2 c. vinegar	4 cl. garlic (smashed)
1/4 c. lemon juice	1/4 tsp. basil
1/4 c. oil	1/4 tsp. celery sd.
1/4 tsp. thyme	1/4 tsp. salt

2 tbls. finely chopped fresh parsley
   or 1 tbls. dried parsley

Shake well and chill.

SIMPLE LEMON DRESSING

Combine:

1/4 c. lemon juice	1/8 tsp. salt
2 tbls. oil	1/8 tsp. garlic pwd.
1/4 tsp. honey (opt.)	pinch mustard pwd.

chopped chives or shallots

Shake well and marinate in fridge for 10 min.

NO OIL DRESSING

Combine in a blender:

1/4 c. lemon juice	1 clove garlic (smashed)
1/8 tsp. salt	2 tbls. parsley (chopped)
1 med. tomato (decored)	1 tbls. cooked millet

Pass thru strainer if you want to remove the tomato skin and seeds.

This dressing should be used within a few days.

As a substitute for the salt in any of these recipes, you can use tamari, miso, umebosi paste,, or gomasio. Each will impart their own flavor.

LYNDEN'S CAESAR DRESSING

Good and garlicky, creamy and rich. A delicious dressing which was shared with us by our friend It is a family recipe handed down from her mother.

Cook till soft boiled: (3 minutes)

　1 egg

Mince or smash:

　3 cloves of garlic

Combine in a blender:

　1 c. oil
　1 c. grated cheddar
　　cheese
　⅓ c. apple cider
　　or wine vinegar
　boiled egg
　1 tbls. lemon juice

　1 tsp. dry mustard
　1 tsp. salt
　1 tsp. honey
　1 tsp. oregano
　4 pinches cayenne
　1 tsp. finely ground
　　black pepper

Blend till smooth and creamy. Bottle and refrigerate.

COLESLAW DRESSING

Most people simply add mayonnaise, which is fine if you're in a hurry ,,, however ,, this variation will put a little more 'pizzaz' in the slaw.

Coleslaw is more palatable if premixed with the dressing and refrigerated for a couple of hours.

To each cup of mayonnaise ('real, tofu or ½ + ½') add :
- ¼ c. finely chopped dill pickle
- ½ tsp. celery sd.
- ½ tsp. black pepper

Mix well and refrigerate.

COLESLAW A LA ISABEL

This is an alternative recipe for coleslaw that is very good, quite different and much less oily.

It is very nice in the summertime when you feel like using a lighter dressing than mayonnaise.

Have quantity of cabbage and carrots precut to a coarse grate or fine slice.

Combine in a saucepan :
- 1 c. apple cider vinegar
- ¼ tsp. celery sd.
- 1 tsp. mustard pwd.
- 1 tsp. salt
- 1 tsp. honey

Simmer for 5 minutes.
Add :
- ½ c. oil

Simmer till it starts to thicken.

Pour as much as is appropriate over the cabbage and carrots. Toss well and chill immediately.

Remainder of the sauce will keep well refrigerated.

Antibiotic Story

For those of you who still eat meat,, a story of interest worth considering:

For the past decade or two, the Cattle Breeders' Association has allowed many medical and chemical alterations for the "betterment" of the industry. One of these was the use of antibiotics to inhibit the diseases which inflict cattle when they are raised under the stress of the unnatural conditions and dietary specifications of the Association.

The consequence of this overuse and sometimes excessive application of antibiotics was the creation of something termed an "anti-recessant gene". This gene is still present in butchered meats and is not destroyed by cooking.

Scientists have found a modern day malady arising out of this. People who have a high intake of beef in their diet were finding when they were in need of antibiotics for personal health reasons,, the antibiotics have no effect.

As it collects in cattle flesh,, so does this gene accumulate in human flesh. What effect this has on reproductive genes is unknown,, however, they do find that the mother's milk of some women is unfit for babies' consumption, due to additives and chemicals within the mother's diet.

A VITAL NOTE OF INTEREST

Years ago, I was told a story by a university professor about these fast cooking white rices, white sugars, and salt,,, one well worth passing on to you. No matter how much you steam or cook natural brown rice,, it will always stay brownish,,, so how do they make it so white and flaky, and able to cook in only a few minutes? Well,,, yawl have heard of a product called borax,, of course,, you buy it packaged at 10% of its natural strength to use as a bleach in your washings. At full strength, it would burn hell out of your clothes. Now when they bleach rice and sugar,, this same product is used at full strength,, mind you, they do rinse it off real good,, but think about it: What does it do to the innards of each grain, as well as to the nutritional value? In this commercial processing of rice, sugar, and salt,, after bleaching, the granules are dried on large tables,, then a synthetic coating of emulgeon (page 17) is sprayed on so's to keep them from sticking together. Sickening, isn't it?

Some of you can still remember 30 years back when white sugar used to stick together and get hard after a rainstorm, or if kitchen vapours got to it. Of course you do. Then,, like magic,, when these synpathetic emulsifires came onto the market, this never happened again. If yawl have come this far in the book, I'm sure you've got the picture,, so I won't go on with this, because it's just too depressing,, yet it has to be told.

Yeast Story

One of today's growing health problems is Candita. In simplicity, this is caused by an imbalance of the body which is affected further by the lack of proper bodily yeasts (bacteria), and an abundance of detrimental ones.

Yeasts are incorporated into so many foods which are eaten daily that the body cannot tolerate them. There are active yeasts in breads, doughnuts, cereals, prepared sauces, deserts, vitamins, etc. Coupled with the secondary yeast products which are fermented, such as pickles, sauerkraut, yogurts, cheeses, etc.,, the digestive system gets over-loaded.

When a person is prescribed antibiotics to kill a particular infection or bacteria,, what doctors don't tell their patients is that it also kills all the good bacteria as well as the bad bacteria. This in effect leaves the body defenceless and open territory for any yeasts to settle in.

The solution to this is more complex, but prevention is the wisest course. First, eliminate as much active yeast foods as you can or keep them to a minimum. Eat sour dough breads instead of yeasted breads. Eat foods which reinforce proper bacteria within the stomach and intestines to aid indigestion. Tempeh, natural sauerkraut, kosher pickles, etc. are all beneficial to proper digestion.

CONDIMENTS

CHAPTER 9

Condiments

Condiments

Condiments are food items which are used to complement other foods by adding flavour, texture, or nutrition to an otherwise simple meal.

They usually enhance your appetite and/or aid digestion.

We generally have most of the condiments in this section available near our dinner table. Which ones are used and how much, is up to the individual tastes of each person. Keep in mind that each should be used in moderation.

Most of these condiments can be bought in your health food store,, however, many are far nicer and more nutritious when made fresh,, and are much cheaper. Nutritional yeast and lecithin are beneficial for their taste, but most importantly for their nutritional value. Both of these should be bought, as they are not easily processed at home.

PRIMARILY GROWN NUTRITIONAL YEAST (Good Tasting)

Non-active yeast, such as brewer's yeast, has been used for centuries as a dietary supplement, for its B-vitamin, amino acid, and protein value. These yeasts were actually a by-product of the beer brewing industry, and quite frankly, didn't taste all that great.

Primary Nutritional Yeast has a very pleasant taste and has a higher nutritional value than brewer's yeast. This yeast contains all of the elements of the Vitamin B complex and is a rich source of complete protein. It also contains 16 of the 20 amino acids necessary for resistance to disease and proper tissue building. Nutritional yeast is claimed to have more nutritional power than any other food known to mankind. Even the ancient Egyptians are known to have used these special yeasts for their nutritional value.

The combination of nutrients which yeast offers helps build strong nerves and calmness,, plus it is beneficial in alleviating depression, fatigue, muscular weakness, and skin problems.

Nutritional yeast is very pleasant to add to soup, sauces, and main dishes. I have used this in many recipes to impart a "cheesy" flavour. It can also be added on top of porridge, or can be drank, stirred into a cup of juice. If drank on an empty stomach, its nutritional value is more thoroughly assimilated.

LECITHIN

Lecithin is available in two forms: liquid and miniature dry granules.

The liquid is used as an emulsifier in many products.

The dry lecithin is primarily used as a condiment on top of grains or in sauces.

Each are made from soya and are prized for the fact that they contain natural Vitamin E, and because they remove fatty acids from within your system.

GOMASIO

Delicious sprinkled on vegetables ,, grains or porridge. Being made of sesame seeds, it is a good source of calcium and protein. Prepared in this fashion ,, salt is more easily assimilated and eliminated from the system.

Rinse in a strainer and then soak in a bowl overnight:

   1 c. sesame seeds

Early in the day ,, drain the seeds. (It is not necessary to soak the seeds, yet they should be washed and drained for 30 min. or more). The nutritional value of sesame seeds are much better when soaked).

Heat a cast iron frying pan and roast till darkened:

   1 tbls. sea salt (or less)

Place the salt in the suribachi and grind till very fine.

In the same skillet ,, roast the sesame seeds on a medium flame, stirring constantly till evenly browned. They are cooked when they crush easily and taste good. Be careful not to burn them.

Add roasted seeds to the suribachi and grind till 2/3 RD of the seeds are crushed.

Cool and place in a glass jar.

TEKKA

A dark, bold flavored condiment with a savoury difference created by slow cooking a combination of vegetable, roots and miso.

Prepare each of these ingredients ,, chopped or grated as fine as possible:

   1 c. burdock rt.
   2 tbls. fresh or soaked lotus root
   ¼ c. grated carrot
   1 tsp. grated ginger

In a heavy bottom skillet, preferably cast iron, heat:

   ½ c. oil

Add the burdock and sauté for 5~7 min.

Then add the lotus root ,, carrot and ginger. Sauté another 10 minutes.

Add: ½ c. hacho or mugi miso

Mix it thoroughly with the vegetables. Cook on a low flame for 3~4 hours, till it is dry and crumbly. Stir frequently and scrape the bottom well. Cook on a flame tamer.

Cool and store in a jar. Use sprinkled on top of grain, cereal or vegetables.

NORI CONDIMENT
(NITSUKE)

Very tasty served on the side with grain.

You need:

    1 pkg. of nori

Tear the sheets of nori into 1" squares and soak for 20 minutes in:

    2 c. water

After soaking, bring to a boil and simmer without a lid for 20 minutes.

Add: 2~3 tbls. tamari soy sauce

Cover and simmer for 20 mins. more.

If the nori is still watery, remove the cover and simmer till the excess water evaporates.

This can be served hot or cold.

TOASTED NORI

A tasty garnish to sprinkle on grains.

Toast: 2 sheets of nori seaweed

Toast on a medium flame,, moving quickly till the nori changes from black to a slight green color.

Cut the nori into 1" squares or ¼" thick strips 2" long.

Sprinkle the nori with tamari. Serve or cool and store in a jar.

TEMPURA SAUCE

This is a delicious sauce to serve with any fried food, tempura or other oily meals. It can be used to dip in or pour onto.

Very beneficial in aiding digestion with these types of meals.

Grate on a very fine grater:
   4 tbls. diakon radish
Grate and strain:
   1 tbls. ginger juice

Add: 1 tbls. tamari

Marinade for 1 hour before using.

Variation: replace ½ tbls. of tamari with ½ tbls. umebosi plum vinegar

FLAX SEED CONDIMENT

Flax is high in fibre and is very beneficial for the intestines. It also contains linoleic acid which is very beneficial for removing fatty acids from the arteries.

Use sprinkled on grains and vegetables.

Roast in a dry skillet till lightly browned:
   1 c. flax seed
Cook with a cover as they will pop out of the pan otherwise. Stir frequently.
Grind in a suribachi till 2/3RD of the seeds are crushed.

MISO PICKLES

To make these pickles ,, you need a quantity of miso, about 10 lbs. Buy it in bulk from a distributor ,, or through your local health food store.

Empty the miso from its bucket ,, into a large bowl or pot.

The vegetables which pickle the best are diakon radish, cucumber, carrot, turnip and burdock.

Prepare 2~3 cups of vegetables, preferably one choice. Cut into 1/4" thick diagonal slices.

Replace 1" of miso back into the bucket.

Add 1 single layer of vegetables. Top with a 1" layer of miso. Repeat till the bucket is half full. Fill the rest of the bucket with just miso.

Store in a cool place and use the miso as you would normally. By the time you get to the vegetables ,, they should be pickled.

DRIED WAKAME

Place dried wakame on an oven tray and bake it at 250° till it crumbles easily.

Remove from the oven and cool.

Crush with a rolling pin or bottle till finely crumbled.

Bottle and use in soup or sprinkle on grain dishes or salad.

MISO PICKLED TOFU

A unique way of serving tofu as a marinated side dish.

Preparing tofu this way alters the texture slightly so it has a more cheese like consistency, plus it imparts a delicate flavor.

Cut the tofu into 2" x 1" x 1" squares.

Ice each square with a ¼" layer of miso. Do this with 4 or more pieces and arrange them on a plate ,, side by side so they touch.

Cover with a bowl and marinate in the refrigerator overnight.

Just before using, scrape as much miso as possible from each slice of tofu. Store this miso in the fridge and use within a week or so.

Slice the tofu into desired sizes. This can be used in numerous ways.

　★ ¼" cubes in salad

　　★ slices for sandwiches

　　　★ 1" squares a ¼" thick
　　　　for hors d'oeuvres

　　　★ ½" cubes for soup

Or just as they are for a snack.

CROUTONS

Croutons are the ideal use for stale or moldy bread. Remove the crusts and any moldy areas. Cut the bread into ½" thick slices.

Preheat oven to 325°.

Mix in a bowl:

    ½ c. soy marg.   1 tbls. garlic pwd.

Butter each slice and cut into ½" squares. (How thick you spread the margarine will depend on how 'buttery' you want them to taste.)

Place on an oven tray, one layer deep only.

Bake till golden brown. While baking, turn them occasionally and move them around, as the ones on the edge always brown faster.

Cool, then place in a bag or jar.

TOFU PEPPERONI'S

We make these to use on pizza in place of real pepperoni. Just a dozen or two slices on a pizza gives a very unique flavor.

Cut tofu weiners into ⅛" thick diagonal slices. Heat a large skillet and add enough oil to coat the bottom thinly.

When hot, add tofu slices. Sprinkle with a good bit of garlic pwd. and some cayenne. Fry, turning as needed. Halfway through the cooking, sprinkle with tamari. Cook till nicely browned.

Use on pizza as you would pepperoni. Any extra will keep well frozen.

Chopped up into small bits, we use them as you would bacon bits in a Caesar Salad.

CHILI SAUCE

This is a large batch ,, well worth putting up for the winter . Best made when tomatoes are in season and fresh ripened.

Wash, decore and blend :

  1 bushel of tomatoes

Pour through a wire mesh strainer or a tomato press. Strain into a large pot. Bring to a boil. Let simmer while you prepare the other ingredients.

Prepare and dice finely :

  3 lbs. onions
  2 heads of celery
  6 lrg. green peppers
  6 hot peppers

Add the vegetables to the tomato puree , plus :

  1 c. whole mixed spices (in a cloth)

Boil till the sauce is reduced to a thick and flavorful consistency, then add :

  ½ c. miso or salt (adjust amount to taste)
  4 c. apple cider vinegar
  2 c. honey

Simmer for ½ an hour longer.

Bottle in sterile jars while sauce is hot and seal tightly. Store in a cool place.

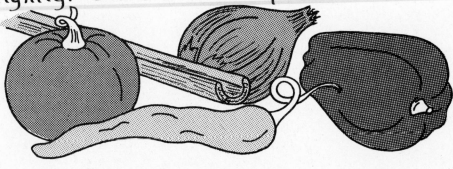

MUSHROOM ANTIPASTO

Makes a good spread for sandwiches or on crackers for hors d'eourves.

Prepare and mix:

> 1 c. natural ketchup
> 1 c. sweet mixed pickle (diced fine)
> ½ c. sliced black olives

Prepare and cook in a saucepan:

> 1 lb. mushrooms (chopped fine)
> 1 c. carrots (¼" dice)
> ½ c. celery (¼" dice)
> ½ c. water
> ½ tsp. salt

Simmer till the carrots are soft. Combine the two mixtures and add:

> 1 c. millet paté (page 239)
>   or 1 ~ 14 oz. can of tuna
> 2 tbls. oil
> 2 cl. garlic (smashed)
> salt and pepper to taste

Combine all the ingredients and toss lightly. Store in a jar. Refrigerate.

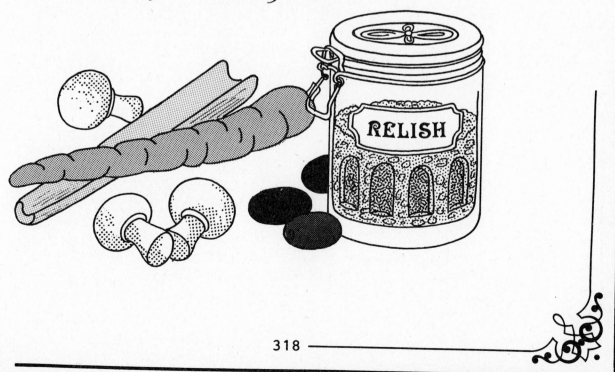

KOSHER DILL PICKLES

Shanola and Zabro have shown us how to make these pickles. They have no vinegar and are the best pickles I have ever tasted.

The most important step in preparing pickles this way is to make sure each pickle is well scrubbed and any blemishes or marks are removed, including the nub end where it attaches to the plant.

This is especially important since there is no vinegar, as any bad spots or blemishes will turn the whole jar bad. It is always best to use freshly picked pickles.

Wash and clean the pickles.

Soap wash and rinse the jars thoroughly.

Peel the appropriate amount of garlic needed and slice each clove into 3~4 pieces.

Wash whole stalks of dill and remove any browned parts.

Fill the bottles with cleaned pickles. You may want to grade them by size into different jars.

Here are the proportions of spicing according to the different size jars. The quantity of chillies used for each jar gives a slight 'hot' to each pickle. Increase or decrease to your own likes.

	1 qt.	2 qts.	1 gal.
salt	1½ tsp.	1 tbls.	2 tbls.
chillies	2	4	8
bl. pepper balls	8~10	16~20	40 or so
dill	1 sprig	2 sprigs	4 sprigs
garlic	3~4 cloves	4~6	12 or more

SNACKS

CHAPTER 10

Snacks

TEMPEH SANDWICH SPREAD
(MOCK TUNA SALAD SPREAD)

The first time I made this for the guy's lunch, they came home and said „ "Where'd you get the tuna for the sandwiches." When I told them it was tempeh „ they said „ "Boy, you had us fooled."

Thaw and steam cook:

    1 8.5 oz. pkg. of tempeh
      (preferably 3 grain tempeh)

Cool and then mash with a fork.

Prepare and dice finely:

    1 stalk of celery

Combine the tempeh and celery.

Add: ¼ c. cooked millet (or rice)
     ½ tsp. prepared mustard
     3~4 tbls. natural relish
    mayonnaise ~enough to hold it all together

Spread on toast, or bread as a sandwich with sprouts „ or use on crackers as hor d'oeuvres.

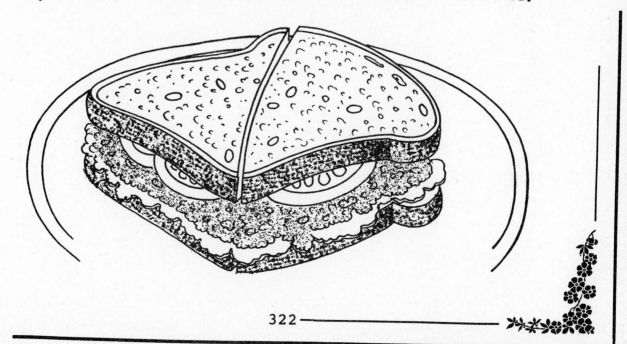

EGG SALAD SANDWICH SPREAD

Ideal for people who want to minimize the amount of egg they eat.

Hard boil:
    3 eggs (8~10 min.)
Cool the eggs in cold water, then remove the shells.

Mash the eggs in a bowl with a fork.

Add: 1 c. of cooked rice (or millet)
        or 1 c. scrambled tofu (page 77)
    ½ c. celery (diced)

Stir in enough mayonnaise to hold it together.

SALMON SALAD SANDWICH SPREAD

If you eat fish on occasion ,,, this is a tasty alternative to your standard version.

Open a:
    7.5 oz. can of salmon
        or use 1 c. of cooked salmon
Add: ¾ c. cooked rice or millet
    ½ c. finely diced cucumber
    ¼ c. chopped green onions

Stir in enough mayonnaise to hold the mixture together.

OVEN FLATS

These are some of our favorite snack meals,, and are reproduced often, especially in the summer for a quick, light lunch.

They're also a great way to use day-old 'flats'(pg. 384).

(Any of these ideas can be duplicated using a slice of bread, however, flats are much better.)

PIZZA FLATS

Spread a thin layer of tomato sauce, leftover spaghetti sauce or natural ketchup onto each flat.

Sprinkle with: oregano   basil
     garlic pwd.   cayenne

 -add amount of spicing in accordance with how much spicing is in the sauce you are using.

Sprinkle lightly with cooked millet, rice or 3 grain.

Layer with any combination of thinly sliced:

  onion   mushrooms   broccoli
  peppers   tomatoes   zucchini

Sprinkle with tamari.

Top with grated cheese or mochi (see 328).

Place on an unoiled tray and bake till sizzling and nicely browned.

MEATLOAF FLAT

Butter each flat with margarine.

Layer with 1/4" slices of meatloaf. Spread a thin layer of mustard over the meatloaf.

Top with tomato slices and grated cheese.

Bake on a tray till golden brown.

ITALIANO ~ TOFU FLAT

This is for when you have left over spagetti noodles.

Chop noodles into approx. 1" pieces and place in a bowl.

Add: chopped chives or green onions
     cooked greens (spinach, chard, collards, etc.)
     chopped tomatoes

Blend a sauce of :

1 chunk of tofu
1 tbsp. miso
1 tbsp. tomato paste
  or 4 tbsp. tomato sauce or ketchup
1 tbsp. tarragon
enough water to make it blend

Add sauce to noodle~vegetable mixture. Mix well. (Make another batch of sauce if needed).

Spread on flats, ½" to ¾" thick.

Place on oven tray and bake as is, or topped with cheese. Cook till good and hot.

GRAIN 'N GRAVY FLAT

Mix leftover gravy with rice, millet or meatloaf grain.
Spread mixture on flats.

Top with fried mushrooms. Bake till good and hot.

UKRAINIAN FLAT

Place ¼" slices of meatloaf on flats.

Spread a layer of Zabro's Horseradish followed by a layer of sauerkraut.

Top with left over gravy or tahine~miso. Bake till hot.

SHEPHERD'S PIE FLAT

This is an interesting way to us leftover shepherds pie. It is a good way to spruce it up and make it more appealing to the kids for lunch.

Mash the leftover shepherds pie together.

Baste the flats with margarine or tahine~miso.

Spread the mixture 3/4" thick on each flat.

Tamari and place on an oven tray.

These can be topped with leftover gravy, grated cheese or cream sauce.

Bake till good and hot.

VEGETATED~GRAIN AND TAHINE FLAT

Baste each flat with a layer of tahine~miso.

Layer with cooked millet, rice or 3 grain (add some spicing to your own likes).

Top with any type of cooked vegetable or greens which are at hand.

Evenly coat the grain with more tahini~miso.

Place on oven trays and bake till sizzling.

NORI ROLLS
(makes approx. 6 rolls)

Ideal for lunches or to take along on trips.

Combine:

- 3 c. cooked rice
- 2/3 c. grated carrot
- 2 tbls. chopped pickled ginger
- 1/2 c. tahini~miso
  - or 1/2 c. of tofu mayonnaisse

Toast: 6 sheets of nori
(roast each sheet over a flame till it turns a slightly green.)

Spread 1/6 TH of the rice mixture on one nori sheet. Leave 1" of the thinner end empty. Roll up into a sausage shape. Moisten the 1" edge and seal the roll. Repeat with the remainder of the mixture and the nori.

Refrigerate till ready to eat. Cut into 3" rolls for individual portions or slice into bit size rounds to serve as hor d'oeurves. (If making these rolls into hors d'oeurves, use 1/3 RD of the amount of tahini~miso or mayonnaise.

NUTRITIONAL POPCORN

Popcorn is a relatively healthy, occasional snack food if popped using a minimum of oil and not too much salt.

To add flavor and nutrition ,, we add a few tbls. of good tasting nutritional yeast while it is still hot. You can use kelp instead of salt or pop it with a few tbls. of gomasio in the pot from the beginning.

MOCHI

Mochi is made from sweet rice. It is prepared by pounding cooked sweet rice for a long time till the grains open and stick together.

Mochi is also available in dried form from most health food stores, in a variety of makes and combinations including nuts and other grains.

Mochi can be added to soups to thicken their consistancy, plus it adds flavor and nutrition.

Baked, grilled or fried, it puffs up and softens. 'Tis a tasty treat on its own or with a meal.

Mochi is a high energy food,, ideal for active people, especially children.

Nori Wrapped Mochi:

Bake mochi in a 320° oven till softened and slightly puffed. (Cut into 2" x 3" squares).

Roast 1 sheet of nori for each 4 pieces of mochi. Roast till slightly green.

Cut the nori into 2" strips.

When the mochi is cooked,, wrap a nori strip around each piece of mochi. Eat as is or dip in a diakon~tamari~ginger sauce (page 313).

ROASTED SEEDS AND NUTS

Roasted nuts and seeds are good snacks and make tasty garnishes for your meals.

Ideally,, seeds and nuts are much healthier and easier to digest if soaked first,, allowing the life force within to germinate. (12 hr. or more).

Almonds, pumpkin seeds, sunflower seeds and pecans are the best suited for roasting. Pecans and almonds should be chopped slightly.

Wash and soak the seeds overnight.

Drain in the morning.

Roast in a dry skillet till evenly browned, stir constantly.

Sprinkle with tamari and saute 1 min. more.

Remove from the heat. Cool and store in a jar.

TOASTED RICE

A good treat for munching on inbetween meals or while traveling.

Wash and soak overnight :

    1 c. short grain brown rice

In the morning, rinse and drain the rice in a strainer.

Heat a cast iron skillet and add the rice. Toast, stirring frequently till dried. Continue cooking till evenly browned and golden. Sprinkle with tamari, saute another minute then remove from the heat. When cooled, place in a jar.

RICE CAKE SNACKS

Rice cakes make an ideal base to hold a variety of tasty treats.

Spread 'em with:

Almond butter
rice syrup

tahini~miso
maple syrup

peanut butter
apple butter

tahini~miso
alfalfa sprouts

mayonnaise
cucumber slices

Zabro's horseradish
grated mochi
~bake under a grill
till browned.

carob icing
banana slices

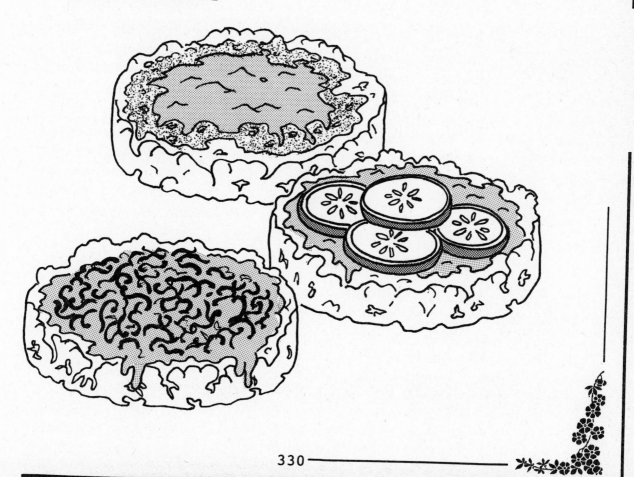

Georgia, Georgia

Another short story worth relating about beez in Georgia,, is when the Philoxians were invited to partake in a huge fair over in the next town of Ackworth. They had set up their 55-foot tent, displaying their art works and invalued artifacts which had been acquired throughout their world travels. People would enter through their gypsy wagon,,, and as they came out of their mystical adventure, they were met with the aromatic smells coming from the portable kitchens, housed between Mohtar and the big top. The menu of the day consisted of "The Nile Saucer", a flat bread with honey-spiced beans and coleslaw, garnished with succulent onion rings. This was 49 cents,,, then, for a quarter, one could get a huge, fresh made donut, dipped in a honey-cinnamon sauce.

Here they were, centre of attraction and ready to cook,, when all of a sudden, the beez started comin'. ii,,, first the scouting parties from various hives,,, then came the first swarm within an hour, as did the people. By 11 o'clock, there must have been a few thousand people mullin' about, and all kept an eye on the Philoxians, because there must have been 10 times as many beez. They were beginning to swarm over the honey jars, donut bins, on the plates as they were being served to the people,,,, Gad Zooks,,,, they was just everywhere. The good people of Ackworth weren't the only ones out havin' a picnic that day.

Now,,, while all of this excitement be goin' on,,, from early set-up, Iilah had noticed this here sweet li'l old lady sittin' on this li'l ol' hill about 50 feet away, just a'watchin' all the goin's on. She looked like she was the type who had seen an awful lot,, yet she sat there knowin' she dun never seen the likes of this act at no fair, nor on the TV.

Well,,, the day went on, and more and more people were comin' by. Some dared to step up and order food because each tantalizin' bite was worth the gamble of a bee sting,, while most just sat back and watched. By mid noon,, they was really going full tilt,, and no one had got bit yet,,, so more and more people were bravin' it. Why some were even daring and betting others to go get some of this good lookin', good smellin' grub from these Lovable Strangers. So out from where I bee watchin' all these goin's on,,, you should have seen those in the open kitchen, keepin' up with their part of the bargain. ii,,, here again,, they were cookin', and the people were lovin' it, as were the beez. By now, they were swarming all over everything,,, and in order to pick up the pinchers needed to pick up a donut,,, a clear spot had to be brushed off the tool before being able to hold it,,, never mind the donuts.

As I glanced over now and then at that li'l ol' lady still sittin' on the li'l ol' hill,, I had to smile,, because she was just amazed, takin' it all in. I thought to myself,, if anyone had panicked on the inside or out,,, pandemonium would have broke loose. The only humorous dilemma was that finally someone did get bit,,, yet the whole while,, nee'r a word be said other than "Ooooh, that smarts!!". By now,,, there were hundreds of beez on the ground, slurpin' up the drops,, and here was Ishma, the only lady workin' along with the fellows in the kitchen,,, and wouldn't you know it,, she bee wearin' a ground-length skirt. Well, it wasn't too long until the inevitable had to happen,,, ii,, and folks,, till today I bee holdin' a deep respect for this here fine lady, because of how she be handling herself in such a situation.

The humour in it all could be appreciated more today,,, because she did get bit right where you thought she might've,,, making the pain no more easier to take. She carried on throughout the day with a smile on her face, along with the inner fear of it happening again.

Finally,,, the cool of the evening set in, and the people were going home, as were the beez,, and before dark, all the beez were cleared out and clean-up had started. Meanwhile,,, Iilah ducks under the table to go get some water, when this li'l ol' lady, who had bin sittin' on that li'l ol' hill, watchin' 'em all day,, comes up to Iilah and asks,,,,

"Where do yawl keep the beez?"

BEVERAGES

CHAPTER 11

Beverages

Cold Beverages:

Cocktail Drinks:

Beverages

As you vary the grains and vegetables you eat each day, so should you vary your liquid foods. With the varieties available between teas, seed and nut milks, vegetable and fruit drinks,, you need not have more than two or three from any one category within a given week.

As with any treat,, there is always the temptation to indulge yourself often. Remember though,, even if something is natural,, too much is not good. This is particularly true with juices because unlike milks or teas which are quite diluted,, juices are actually very concentrated.

Within this chapter we would like to acquaint you with the multitude of delicious, healthful drinks you and your family can enjoy.

These range from creamy, wholesome, non-dairy milks,, to beneficial herbal teas, hot and cold,, invigorating, fresh fruit and vegetable drinks,, onto some wonderful family traditionals to let's get down and boogie, cocktail drinks.

First, we would like to correct a widely believed misconception about the intake of liquids. Most people in general drink numerous glasses of liquid a day, be it tea, coffee, pop, milk, juice, or water. The volume of liquid people drink is in line with conventional dietary guidelines,, the norm being 6 to 8 cups of liquid a day. What people don't realize is that their bodies actually crave and require this amount of liquid because of the type of foods they consume. Heavily salted, fried, sugared, processed foods create a condition within your body which requires a flow of liquid to offset the extremeness of the foods,,, when, in effect, you are only adding insult to misery.

When eating a diet of whole grains, vegetables, and fruit in balance with the season,, one finds that one requires very little liquid intake. This is because all your grains are mostly water,, plus vegetables and fruits are also.

Keeping the amount of salt and concentrated sweets to a minimum also reinforces the need for less water, as the body does not have to flush these extreme elements from your hurting organs.

Excessive water due to wrong food intake puts extreme hardship on all your internal organs.

During a normal day at Philoxia,, I would say that none of us drink more than 1 or 2 cups of a tea or other type of drink per person,, and in honesty, sometimes I have had no craving to drink anything at all for several days.

Now,, if we're outside in the hot sun, planting the garden or mixing cement,, we certainly do drink more than our usual,,, but no where near 8 cups a day!

WATER, THE LIQUID OF LIFE

Water is a commodity that is taken for granted in most "civilized" countries. Throughout these cities and towns, water is abundant, and by government standards, safe for consumption. However, in reality, most city waters are far from pure. The chlorine added to purify simply masks the pollutants and waste matter in it.

If your water source is from a pure well or fairly unadulterated source,, you are certainly very fortunate. There are other alternatives you can use if your water source is offering you more than you really want, such as toxic waste, dioxins, flouride, excessive P.C.B., excessive mineral substance (sulpher, iron), radioactive isotopes, etc.

You can buy spring water, purchase a filtering system,, an ionizer, or a distiller,, as everything you prepare for yourself will be affected by the quality of your water.

In respect to eating foods with less chemicals and additives,, likewise, downtown chlorinated tap water sure doesn't make for a finely brewed herbal tea base,,, however, if one is going to continue drinking caffinated, white sugared, chemically milked drinks,, it really doesn't matter all that much.

Seventy-five percent of the human body is comprised of water. Pure water flushes out internal waste and purifies the cells, tissues, and organs.

Not until you've had the opportunity of drinking and cooking with good water do you appreciate it for real.

MILK, THE CREAM OF LIFE

Milk is an important beverage everyone worries about replacing when embarking into the way of eating as expressed in this book.

It has been scientifically proven that the consumption of cow's milk is not designed for human digestion,,, it's made for baby cows.

Have you ever wondered why it is that a baby cow leaves its mother's udder in one year,, and a human child does likewise before the age of two,, and yet adults and children alike stay suckled to a cow's udder all their lives.

It's quite simple. In looking for a nutritious alternative to boost the increasingly deficient dietary standards,,, government agencies and the economists of the civilized worlds have promoted milk and its by-products to great importance.

It has only been in the present century and primarily the last few decades that the consumption of milk has become commonplace in the every day diet of the majority of the population. Prior to this century,, milk was consumed in moderation as a drink. It was used more so in the production of cheese,, which acted as a way of preserving it in cooking. Unless a family owned a cow,, the amount of milk and milk products (cheese, cream, butter) used was usually a reflection of their financial status.

The prominence of milk in this century has been aided by the availability of refrigeration. The consumption of dairy products, particularly milk, has been promoted for reasons of economics. In light of common sense,, drinking milk is not a natural thing to do, and by far, it is not healthy, especially when taking into account the modern day processes and additives which are used to get milk to our tables. Plus, what people don't realize is that the process of pasteurization eliminates necessary enzymes, vitamins, and minerals. Milk drinkers are usually full of mucous, and experience coughs, colds, headaches, and flus more often. This is due to the fact that milk causes the intestines to create excessive amounts of mucous,, a lubricating substance produced to keep foods moving in the intestines. This material tends to harden and form a coating on the inner lining of the intestines which greatly restricts the nutrients from passing into the bloodstream,, thus you are not deriving the calcium and other nutrients which you are drinking the milk for. Plus,, the excessive buildup of mucous travels to and collects in the lungs, bronchial tubes, and head.

Some of the ailments attributed to the consumption of milk and milk products are high cholesterol, heart disease, diabetes, colds, asthma, skin diseases, adverse drug reaction and drug resistance, salmonella, anemia,, and even cancer. The ethics, general treatment, and quality of life which these animals exist in are also negative factors in the continued need for the production of milk,,, but that's another story.

There are so many tasty, nutritious, non-toxic, non-damaging alternatives which are so easy to prepare in our modern kitchens, such as soy milk, nut and seed milks,, and even grain milks (useful for some needs), that no one has to consume cow's milk nowadays. Due to the demand for an alternative,, organically made soy milk is readily available from many outlets nowadays.

In closing,, we know personally dozens of children brought up from birth who have never drank cow's milk. They were nursed on mother's milk for a year or so, then weaned. These children have grown to be strong, healthy, and vibrant on nut and seed milks, soy milk, and natural juices.

This beverage is what we use as a daily sub-stitute for milk.

NUT MILK

These milks are smooth and rich as well as being sweet and creamy. They are non-mucus forming and nutritious.

Nut milk can be used on porridge or cereal in the morning or as a nutritious drink through-out the day.

Ideally, nut milk is best made fresh each day, so make only what you need. Any extra keeps well in the refrigerator for 2~3 days.

Nut milk is not a homogenized liquid and the solids tend to separate when standing for any length of time, so when you drink it through-out the day it will need to be stirred.

Although we call this 'Nut Milk' there are a variety of seeds which we use also.

BASIC NUT MILK

Combine in a blender:

2 c. water
1/2 c. sunflower sds.
1/4 c. sesame sds.
1/4 c. almonds (chopped)
} wash and rinse the seeds and soak if possible.

Blend on 'liquify' for a minute or two.

Add: 2 c. water

Blend for 1 minute more and then strain.

This is the point at which you must decide on how refined (filtered) you like your milk. I've met some people who enjoy it rather coarse,, then there are others, like myself, who prefer it strained so it has no noticeable grit.

Nut Milk, cont.,

When being used for porridge or cereal,, or on top of rice pudding ,, straining the blended milk through a wire strainer is good enough.

For a smoother drink ,, we use a screening cloth which we keep just for straining milk with. It should be coarser than a jelly bag, yet finer than a cheese cloth.

The blended pulp in the strainer or cloth may be put back in the blender with 1½ cups of water. Blend well and strain again.

For a richer milk , combine in a blender :

    4 c. nut milk (strained)
    ¼ c. oil (sunflower, corn, etc.)
    1 tbls. honey or maple syrup
    1 tsp. vanilla
    pinch of salt

Blend till creamy and smooth.

Here are some combinations of nut milks we make, written in parts, rather then measurements. After you have made the 'Basic recipe' try some of these other blends or try your own.

★ 2 parts sunflower sds.
  1   "   almonds
  ½ "   coconut
  ½ "   currants
★ 1 part cashews
  1   "   sesame sds.

~this is the creamiest of all nut milks, however, cashews are not easily digested and should be only used occasionally.

★ 2 parts sesame sds.
  1   "   almonds
        (chopped coarse)

★ all sesame sds.

~blend the washed sesame seeds with boiled water. Strain and drink while hot. It is very relaxing just before bed.

Nut Milks, cont.,

* 1 part dried coconut
  1 " sesame sds.

When blending this mix
you may find a thick, white
cream sticking to the bottom
of the blender. This is coconut
butter. It is very tasty used
in cooking, sauces or on
toast. Use in moderation
as coconut oil is not
easily digested.

* 2 parts sunflower
  1 " pinenuts
  1 " raisins

A rich and creamy,
lightly sweet milk.

NUT AND SOY MILK SHAKES

Once you have your basic nut milk or soy milk
of your choosing, you can get creative and
prepare any type of milk shake your lil' ol'
taste buds crave.

To half a blender full of nut or soy milk
(approx. 2~3 cups) add:

    1 c. crushed ice
    1 c. fresh fruit   (strawberries, banana, etc.)
        or flavoring (carob pwd, vanilla, etc.)
    honey, maple syrup or rice malt to taste

* soy milk
  blueberries
  ice and honey

* coconut-sesame milk
  pineapple
  crushed ice

* sesame-almond milk
  banana
  carob pwd.
  crushed ice
  sweetener to taste

* sunflower-almond
  milk
  peaches
  crushed ice

NUTS AND SEEDS (Why They Should be Germinated)

Seeds and nuts contain almost every essential food elements necessary to proper health. They are high in calcium, Vitamin A, B complex, Vitamin E and F, phospherous, niacin, iron, lecithin, unsaturated fatty acids, natural oils, protein, and zinc,, and hard to get mineral necessary for the proper functioning of the prostrate gland.

Seeds and nuts should be always soaked overnight or longer. This increases their life force tremendously,, plus it eliminates the enzyme inhibitors that are natural within ungerminated nuts and seeds. These enzyme inhibitors are present to prevent seeds from germinating prematurely. When eating raw seeds or nuts,, these inhibitors neutralize certain valuable enzymes your body produces,, thus decreasing the digestibility of the nutrition they hold. They cause indigestion, constipation, and some skin problems. Soaking seeds increases their enzyme content, protein quality, and taste,, plus making them much easier to digest and assimilate.

THE CALCIUM QUESTION

Calcium is very necessary for maintaining strong, durable bone structure, nails, and teeth. It steadies the nerves, strengthens and firms the arteries and pulse, imparts endurance, will power, and good memory. It helps to heal wounds and strengthens the heart. It is especially important to pregnant women.

Lack of calcium causes poor teeth, anemia, ricketts, weak bones, and diseased bodies. Calcium needs Vitamin D for proper assimilation.

Taking into account that modern medicine requires a certain percentage of dairy products in our daily diet,, specifically milk and cheese,, to sustain "proper" calcium levels,, why do people of third world countries who consume little or no dairy products not suffer from these diseases which doctors claim are caused by lack of calcium?

These peasant folk live on primarily whole, unadulterated grains, relatively organic vegetables, seeds, nuts, fresh fruits, and seafoods where available,, such as fresh fish and seaweeds. They assimilate a sufficient quantity of calcium, as well as all the other nutrients needed for proper growth. These people do not consume dairy products on a regular basis, and yet in comparison to people of the civilized world,, these people show no or little sign of improper bone growth, poor teeth, or the ever increasing problem of Osteoperosis.

Articles I have read indicate that due to the general diet of the civilized countries,, the food sources which contain calcium, other than dairy products,, are either not eaten, or they are so processed that there is little left. Also,, even when foods are eaten with sufficient calcium intake,, the digestive system of the consumer is not properly assimilating the needed nutrients because of the imbalance and improper digestive system created by eating so many detrimental foods.

So,, judge for yourself and eat according to which alternate foods will supply calcium.

The foods rich in calcium are Canadian wheat, kale, swiss chard, green vegetables and their juices, oats, cabbage, cauliflower, sesame and sunflower seeds, egg yolks, garlic, dates, oranges, lemons, berries, apricots, buttermilk, and goat's milk.

If you were to visit any number of third world countries such as Jamaica, Guatemala, China, etc. and go into the villages (not the cities) where the people are poor, yet not living under undue political or economic stress,,, you would find happy, healthy, radiant people, with an exuberant spirit and reverence for life.

Goat's milk, drank in moderation along with a well balanced diet of whole grains and vegetables, will supply a good source of calcium and other nutrients. It is mucous forming,, however it has a composition closer to that of human milk than cow's milk has.

Soy Milk

This is an excellent milk for many purposes. It keeps in the refrigerator for 5 ~ 7 days, doesn't separate,, won't curdle when heated, is very nutritious and is quite inexpensive when made at home.

Soy milk offers 3/4's the amount of protein as cow's milk and has less fat.

The beans are best if soaked for 18 ~ 24 hours. Change the water once or twice.

1 lb. of dried soybeans will make about 1½ gallons of soy milk. This recipe uses this proportion. You can increase or decrease it to suit your own needs.

Measure beans and check for stones or bad beans.

1 lb. soybeans (2½ c. beans)

Wash and soak in ample water overnight. Drain and rinse the beans in the morning.

Blend in batches:

1 c. of beans   4 c. water

Strain through a cheese cloth or cloth sack into a 2 gallon pot or double boiler.

If in a pot, bring to a boil, stirring frequently. Simmer for 10 mins. Remove from heat and cool.

If in a double boiler, heat to the point to where the milk is too hot to keep a finger in it. Continue to heat for 15 ~ 20 min. Remove from the heat and cool.

When cooled, refrigerate in glass jars.

We like this milk as is, however some people like it a little richer and sweeter.

Before chilling, add to each quart and blend:

1 ~ 3 tbls. oil   1 ~ 2 tsp. lecithin
1 tbls. honey   pinch of salt

Farm Fresh Egg Nog

A truely rich drink worthy of sharing with family and friends during the Christmas Season.

Now,, to do justice to this age old, seasonal treat ,, you will need fresh milk, cream and eggs.

This recipe makes approx. 2 qts. Any extra keeps well in the refrigerator for a few days, that is ,, if it lasts that long.

Crack and separate:

6 country fresh eggs

Place the yolks in a 3 qt. bowl (or pot).

Combine in a jug:

4 c. whole milk } well chilled
2 c. 50% cream }
1 c. of your favorite rum or brandy (opt.)

Beat the yolks well. While beating, slowly add:

½ c. liquid honey or maple syrup

Continue beating while pouring in the milk and cream mixture. Whip till fluffy.

In a separate bowl, beat the egg whites till stiff. Add a pinch of salt and beat in.

Now, turn beaten egg whites onto the top of the milk mixture. Using a spatula, gently fold the whites in. (Do not stir).

Pour into a serving dish and sprinkle with fresh grated nutmeg. Chill till ready to serve.

If any of your family or friends do not partake of liquor, make this drink omitting the rum or brandy. It can be added to the individual glasses as wanted.

Non - Dairy Egg Nog

Lilah created this version of egg nog originally for his mom, as she can't drink milk or cream. And yet ,, most of us prefer this version because we can enjoy more of it with less ill-effect.

Being a special occasion drink ,, we use a cashew-pine nut mixture as it makes the smoothest milk.

Make 1 qt. of cashew-pine nut milk and strain it through a fine screen or cloth. Chill well.

Blend: 1/2 c. cashews   3 3/4 c. water
       1/2 c. pinenuts

This makes a very creamy mixture ,, or you may use: 4 c. soy milk

Now, separate into 2 bowls:

   3 farm fresh eggs

In a large bowl, beat:

   3 egg yolks

While beating, add:

   1/3 c. honey or maple syrup
   1/4 c. sunflower oil
   1/3 c. rum or brandy (opt.)
   1/8 tsp. salt

Continue beating and slowly pour in the milk.

In a separate bowl, beat the egg whites till fluffy and stiff. Gently fold the egg whites into the milk mixture. Sprinkle with freshly grated nutmeg and chill till served.

If you prefer not to use eggs, a similar texture can be achieved by omitting the eggs and blending in 3/4 of a cup of tofu. Blend till it is smooth.

TOFU SHAKES

Creamy and thick, quick to make. These are a high protein, nutritious drink.

An easy drink to whip up when you have no nut milk made or soy milk on hand. Regular tofu is fine for these drinks, however soft tofu will give a creamier texture.

Combine in a blender and liquify till smooth:

★ 2 c. water
1 c. tofu
1½ c. blueberries
1 c. crushed ice
4 tbls. honey

★ 1 c. pineapple juice
1 c. water
1 c. tofu
1½ c. banana
1 c. crushed ice

★ 3 c. apple juice
1 c. tofu
1 c. frozen
    strawberries
2 tbls. honey

★ 3 c. white grape
    juice
1 c. tofu
1 c. crushed ice
1 tsp. vanilla ext.

★ 3 c. orange juice
1 c. tofu
1 c. crushed ice

★ 3 c. water
1 c. tofu
¼ c. carob pwd.
¼ c. honey
1 c. crushed ice

★ 2 c. apple juice
1 c. tofu
1 c. papaya
1 c. crushed ice

★ and many more.

These are but a few of the possible blends. We hope you enjoy them as much as we have. Experiment and create your own combinations.

FRUIT AND VEGETABLE DRINKS

Liquid treats in a class unto their own. The variety and combinations are boundless.

Vegetable and fruit juices offer an excellent source of Vitamins A, B-1, B-2, C, E, and K, plus an abundance of organic mineral salts, trace minerals, alkaline elements, and enzymes. Any green vegetables are high in chlorophyll.

The nutritive values in juices are very quickly assimilated into the blood stream,, however,, juices are very concentrated, lacking the bulk and fibre they would be accompanied with if eaten whole. Juices should be consumed in moderation,, i.e., no more than 4 to 6 ounces per day,, preferably on an empty stomach,, or half an hour before a meal. More than 4 to 6 ounces of juice per day overworks the liver.

Specific juices have particular health benefits when used in moderation on a short term basis. There is not room here to expand on this,,, however, there are very good books which delve into the technicalities of this. Within this section, I am simply outlining the variety of juices one can moderate throughout one's daily diet.

Suggested combinations are given in proportions rather than exact measurements, so you can make your own mixtures to the volume you need.

Nut Milks

This beverage is what we use as a daily substitute for milk.

These milks are both smooth and rich,, as well as being sweet and creamy. They are non-mucous forming and nutritious,, containing a variety of elements from iron to calcium, phospherous, silicone, sodium, magnesium, zinc, and

Vitamin B's. Nut milk can be used on porridge or cereal in the morning, or as a nutritious drink throughout the day. Ideally,, nut milk is best made fresh each day, so make only what you need. It will keep two to three days in the refrigerator, though.

Nut milk is not a homogenized liquid,, and the solids tend to separate when standing for any length of time,, so if you drink some throughout the day, you need to stir it.

VEGETABLE DRINKS

As in anything, there are goods and bads. Such is true with vegetable juices also. They are categorized below. The 'Not Goods' should only be drank on the odd occasion as they are acidic or hard on the digestive system. The 'Moderates' should be used in small quantities as they are very strong. The 'Goods' can be used as the bulk or base.

Good	Moderate		Not Good
carrot	cabbage	parsley *	tomato
celery	beet	asparagus	potato
cucumber	turnip	parsnips	
broccoli	diakon	zucchini	
	alfalfa *	spinach *	
	squash	chard, kale *	
		or beet greens *	

* Vegetables with this symbol are best blended into a juice base and then strained. These vegetables don't work well in an extractor.

Try these blends:

* 6 parts carrot
  1 " beet

* 6 parts carrot
  2 " celery
  1 " beet
  2 " parsley *

* 2 parts carrot
  2 " apple
  2 " celery
(fruit and vegetable juices may be combined as they have no fibre.

* 4 parts carrot
  2 " cucumber
  1 " cabbage

* 4 parts carrot
  1 " beet
  1 " diakon or turnip
  1 " spinach *

* 3 parts carrot
  1 " broccoli
  1 " celery
  ½ " alfalfa *

Fruit Juices

Likewise with vegetable juices,, some fruit juices are better to drink than others. This is partially dependent upon the season and on what grows locally within your climate.

For example: bottled orange juice made from concentrate, using city water is extremely acidic. However, if you live in Florida and can purchase fresh, tree ripened oranges, a freshly squeezed drink on occasion won't hurt.

Good	Moderate	Not Good
apple grape pear cherry watermelon	lemonade cranberry prune orange grapefruit } fresh pineapple	orange grapefruit pineapple (if from concentrate)

Freshly squeezed juice surely is the nicest and has the most nutrition. However, there are numerous pure and healthful fruit juices on the market to enjoy,, both bottled and frozen.

The types of fruits suitable for making drinks are far more numerous than with vegetables. Not all are juicable but many can be blended with other juices, water or nut or soy milks to make delicious smoothies.

Fruits which are best blended with other liquids are:

canteloupe	cherries	pears
nectarines	pineapple	plums
raspberries	peaches	mangos
strawberries	honeydew	banana
blueberries	papaya	kiwi
watermelon		

SMOOTHIES

Listed here are some of our favorite blends.
Mix to your own proportions and quantities.
You may use frozen fruit for colder, thicker drinks.

★ Apple juice
strawberries

★ Pear juice
water
canteloupe

★ Grape juice (white)
cherries (pitted)

★ Fresh orange juice
mangos

★ Papaya
Water
Banana

★ Apple juice
blueberries

★ Watermelon juice
honeydew

★ Pineapple juice
water
banana

★ Lemonade (unsweetened)
nectarines

★ Prune juice
apple juice
slippery elm tea

★ Grapefruit juice
orange juice
squeeze of lime

★ Grapefruit juice
peaches

★ Cherry juice
papaya

★ and many more

Crushed ice may be added to any of these
mixtures to make them thicker and cooler.

Don't add too much ice, drinks should be cool
but not ice cold. Very cold drinks constrict
the digestive system inhibiting its proper
functions.

HERBAL TEAS

There are many herbal teas (plus grain and root coffees) which are beneficial to generally tone and strengthen your nervous system, heart, digestion, and specific organs or ailments. Teas alone cannot cure,, but they can help balance in conjunction with a proper diet.

The list of herbs used for specific health problems is a book in itself,, and there are many good ones on the market,, "Back to Eden" by Jethro Kloss being one of the best and easiest to understand. However,, in general, there are numerous tasty herbal teas which can be enjoyed in your daily diet simply for their flavour and general soothing effects. Teas should be used moderately and varied daily and season- ably.

When brewing herbal teas,, never boil any roots or barks on a hard, fast boil,, as this can give a harsh, bitter taste. They should be simmered on a slow, rolling boil. When adding herbs for steeping,, turn off the heat, stir in the leaves or flowers,, and cover. Steep for 10 to 15 minutes,, then strain the tea or remove the herbs (if in a tea bag), so the flavours will not become too strong or bitter.

HOT HERBAL TEAS

These are a few of our most favorite teas. They are delicious drank hot,, however, many are quite good served chilled as they are, or with a little sweetener and lemon added.

These measurements are for dried herbs. Use twice the amount if fresh.

★ Boil: 4 c. water
Steep: 2 tsp. lemon grass
2 tsp. St. Johns Wort

★ Boil: 6 c. water
2 tbls. kukicha
Very refreshing tea which can be drank hot daily. Has an alkalining effect, thus it is strengthening and refreshing.

★ Boil: 6 c. water
1 tbls. ginger (grated)
Steep: 2 tsp. mint
Hot or cold, this is good with a squeeze of lemon.

★ Boil: 5 c. water
1 tsp. licorice rt.
Steep: 1 tbls. mint

★ Boil: 5 c. water
1 tsp. sassafras
Steep: 2 tsp. melissa
1 tsp. borage

★ Boil: 4 c. water
Steep: 2 tsp. mint
1 tsp. comfrey
1 tsp. catnip

★ Boil: 6 c. water
1 tsp. sassafras
4 cloves
Steep: 1 tbls. St. John's Wort
Tastes similar to root beer when chilled.

★ Boil: 4 c. water
1 tsp. cherry bk.
1 tsp. calamus
Steep: 1 tsp. wood betony
(helps indigestion and gas)

★ There are numerous herbal tea blends available in tea bags. Try different ones.

TEA AND COFFEE - THE CONS (NO PROS)

Commercial teas and coffees are artificial stimulants that react directly on the heart, kidneys, bladder, liver, and intestines, causing acid forming substances to flow into the blood.

Tea contains tannic acid which interferes with the gastric juices in the stomach.

Coffee contains pyramidene, which is a smoke poison produced in the roasting process coffee goes through.

Caffeine weakens the nervous system by temporarily exciting it through false stimulation which is then followed by a physical and mental fatigue and depression. This is further complicated by the usual addition of refined sugars or artificial sweeteners (more stimulation), plus chemically produced coffee "whiteners".

These beverages not only waste vital energy,, they lower immunity and resistance to disease.

HERBAL TEAS, SOY AND NUT MILKS

Beverages are like foods,,, sometimes you have to acquire a taste for them. Often the difference between learning to like something or not is realizing that one really is a lot healthier for you than the other, and giving it an honest chance.

Also,, don't settle for the first example of say, a herbal tea, or soy milk, etc. There are many varieties of teas, and each company that makes soy milk is a little different,,, so check out a few at least.

HOT BEVERAGES

Here are a variety of healthful, hot beverages which we enjoy. They range from those made of a tea base ,, to fruit juices ,,. soy milk or amasake.

KUKICHA TEA
(JAPANESE TWIG TEA)

Kukicha is the roasted twigs (and some leaves) of a particular Japanese Bush. This is an every-day drinking tea in Japan. It has practically no caffeine so it is suitable for people of all ages, even children. Kukicha has an alkalining effect on the blood so it strengthens and re-freshes. Generally, it has many beneficial effects when consumed daily.

To make kukicha tea:

Bring to a boil:

> 4 c. water
> ¼ ~ ½ c. kukicha (the quantity depends on how strong you like it.)

Simmer on a low boil for 10 min. Strain and drink. The flavor is uniquely different from most tea, yet you will find it quite satisfying once you have acquired a taste for it.

Here are some very pleasant hot beverages we make using kukicha.

Bring to a boil in a pot and simmer for 10~15 min:

> 4 c. water
> ¼ c. kukicha twigs
> 1 tbls. ginger root (grated)
> 1 tsp. licorice root

Very soothing on the throat and beneficial when you have a cold.

Hot Beverages, cont.,

1 cup serving : Should be drank to alleviate mild stomach problems or tiredness. Will help to relieve some headaches.

Place in a cup:

 1 umebosi plum (remove meat from the pit)
   or ½ tsp. umebosi paste
 ½ tsp. tamari

Top the cup up with boiling hot kukicha tea,, mix well,, let cool slightly and drink.

HOT CAROB TODDY

We were served this at a friend's house one cold winter night. It was warming and made us feel very relaxed.

Reheat to a boil:

 4 c. kukicha tea

Combine and mix well:

 ½ c. soy milk
 4 tbls. brown rice syrup or amasake
 2~4 tbls. carob pwd.
 2 tbls. tahine

Add to the hot kukicha, reheat slightly and serve. (Do not boil as the soy milk will curdle).

As an added touch you can put a spoonful of tofu~whip cream on top.

APPLE~KUZU DRINK

Bring to a boil:

    3 c. apple juice

Mix in a glass till dissolved:

    1½ c. water   2 tbls. kuzu

Add to the simmering apple juice and continue stirring till thickened and clear.

Place on a flame tamer and simmer on a low heat for 10 ~ 15 min.

Drink while hot.

KUZU

Kuzu is a starch from a plant which originated in the mountains of Japan. It is easily digested and quickly absorbed by the intestines. It strengthens and regulates digestion, increases vitality, relieves tiredness and is beneficial to people with intestinal problems and colds.

TONIC FOR ALL SEASONS

This is a drink Lilah designed which is amply named. Drank hot or cold,, it is very uplifting.

Combine in a pot and bring to a boil:

6 c. apple juice	1 tsp. vanilla
2 c. water	⅛ tsp. nutmeg (grated)
¼ c. dried lotus rt.	¼ tsp. lemon rind (· ··)
2 tbls. grated ginger	4 cloves

Simmer for 15 min. Mix together till dissolved:

    1 c. water   4 tbls. kuzu

Add to the apple juice and simmer for 15 mins. Strain and serve.

Andy's Amasake Drinks
Hazelnut Toddy

To look at these ingredients ,, one might say, "That sounds like it tastes weird" but au contrer, these are deliciously refreshing and lightly sweet. Excellent hot yet very good cold also.

Available here in Ontario is a very good brand of organic amasake in different flavors. If such a product is not available to you, simply mix 2 cups of amasake with ⅓ cup of finely ground hazelnuts.

Combine in a pot:

    500 ml. of hazelnut amasake (2 cups)
    5 c. water
    1 tbls. umebosi vinegar
    1 tbls. gomasio (well ground)
    1 tbls. instant herbal coffee

Heat till good and hot. (Do not boil) Serve while hot or chilled.

Strawberry Delight

Combine in a pot:

    500 ml. of strawberry amasake (2 cups)
    4 c. water
    2 tbls. umebosi vinegar
    1 tbls. tamari
    2 tbls. almond butter
    1 tbls. mild miso (preferably smooth)

Heat till good and hot (Do not boil.) Serve while hot or chilled.

If you want to serve this cold, simply blend all of the ingredients.

CORN MILK

This recipe was redesigned in memory of a hot drink we would buy in the market of Solola, Guatemala. They make it using fresh milk, de-cobbed corn and white sugar, however,. this is just as tasty and healthier.

Husk and decob:

  2 c. corn

Combine in a saucepan and bring to a boil:

  2 c. water   few grates of nutmeg
  corn   pinch of salt

Simmer for 10 minutes with a lid.

Press through a metal sieve or blend and strain back into the pot.

Add: 2 c. soy milk
  1~3 tbls. sweetener (use rice or barley malt, honey, amasake or maple syrup).

Reheat till hot and serve. Do not boil as it may curdle.

We used to buy this from a beautiful, mayan woman. She would ladle it out of a big crock kept hot by thick cloths wrapped around it.

DRINKING AND EATING

Another widely abused habit people subject their bodies to is having a drink whenever they eat a meal.

Drinking of any liquid while eating dilutes the stomach acids which offsets the proper digestive processes. It further complicates matters when sweet or fruity beverages (such as apple or orange juice, etc.) are drank with a meal consisting of grains (or meats) and vegetables,, as different stomach acids are required to digest them properly,,, thus setting up a bit of a brewery right in your stomach. This is the cause of many stomach problems, indigestion, ulcers, etc.

It's humorous in a sad sense, how eating of the wrong foods creates a situation which wants to worsen itself. It is the consumption of oversalted, starchy, oily, acidic foods which creates an imbalance in your stomach that unconsciously says to your mind, "I need some liquid",,, thus the craving to drink with the meal, which only worsens the problem by diluting the situation, making the stomach and other organs work all the harder to digest everything.

A properly prepared meal of grains and vegetables, in balance, should leave you completely satisfied and wanting nothing more.

Any beverages drank should be had a half hour before or after your meal,,, or longer in the case of fruit drinks, before or after a grain and vegetable meal.

COLD BEVERAGES

We enjoy numerous different drinks throughout the year. Here are a variety of warm weather drinks which are satisfying and very refreshing.

We serve 100's of gallons of these next two drinks in our restaurant during the summer. It is lightly sweetened,. very refreshing and quite healthy also. They are an ideal drink to have on hand for children as an alternative to them drinking fruit juice all the time. (The one with the catnip is actually quite calming.)

ICED GARDEN TEA

To make this tea you need to have some fresh comfrey and catnip. It is very easy to grow in your backyard.

Boil: 8 c. water

Pick and wash:

> 4 comfrey leaves
> 2~10" catnip stalks

Fold washed leaves into a bunch and place on a wooden board.   Using a heavy knife handle or rolling pin "bruise" the leaves. (This means to pound them to release the juices within the leaves)

Remove the water from the heat and add:

> bruised leaves
> 3 tbls. St. Johns Wort herb

Replace the lid and steep for 20 min. Strain the tea through a clean cloth and bottle.

Add: 1 tbls. lemon juice
> 1~4 tbls. honey or maple syrup.

Mix well and refrigerate. Best used within 3~4 days.

Iced Root Tea

Bring to a boil:

    8 c. water

Add to the pot, cover and simmer for 20 min.

    2 tbls. sassafras
    1 tbls. grated ginger

Remove from the heat and add:

    ¼ c. lemon grass herb (melissa)
    3 tbls. St. Johns Wort

Cover and steep for 20 min.

Strain and bottle.

Add: 1 tbls. lemon juice
       1~4 tbls. honey or maple syrup.

Mix well and chill.

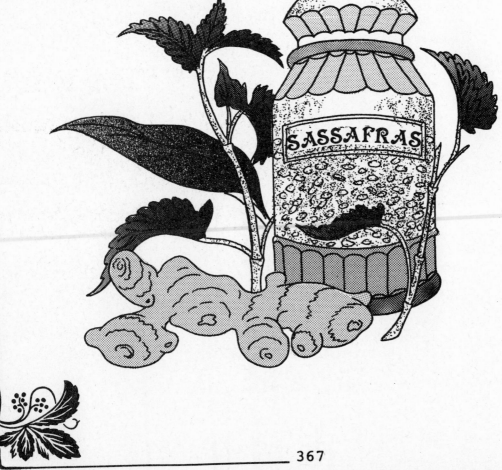

COCKTAIL DRINKS

BLANCANNAISE A NICHOLAS

This is a deliciously creamy cocktail which Iilah created for a gentle gypsy man who owned and ran a quaint gourmet restaurant in Beirut, Lebanon. Iilah gifted him with this recipe in return for the hospitality he had been shown by this man's establishment while Iilah was residing and lecturing there.

Combine in a blender:

    2/3 c. vanilla soy milk.
    1/3 c. natural vanilla ice cream
        or non-dairy ice cream
    1/3 c. crushed ice
    1 tsp. cointreau
    1/4 tsp. pure orange flavor

Whip till fluffy and serve immediately.

STRAWBERRY DACQUIRI

A pleasant alternative to the traditional style dacquiri.

Combine in a blender:

    1/3 c. sparkling white grape juice
        (we use a product called 'Vitale').
    1/3 c. crushed ice
    4 fresh strawberries
    2 tbls. egg whites
    1 tbls. maple syrup
    2 tsp. lemon juice
    1 tsp. rum or 1/4 tsp. rum flavoring

Blend till fluffy and serve.

Maylasian Jungle Juice

A refreshing and light fruit cocktail. Ideally suited to quench a dancing thirst.

Blend together:

    1 c. Berry-Berry juice (an apple juice, strawberry, raspberry blend).
    squeeze of lime
    3/4 c. pear nectar
    1/2 c. pineapple juice
    1/2 c. crushed ice

Serve in a tall glass with a slice of lime.

Afrodisiah

An exotic cocktail Iilah created which tastes like ambrosia.

Combine in a blender:

    1 c. vanilla soy milk
    1/4 c. frozen vanilla soy milk
    1 tsp. maple syrup
    1/2 tsp. Kahlua
    1 tsp. Grand Marnier
    1/2 tsp. instant herbal coffee
    1/4 tsp. pure orange extract
    pinch of nutmeg

Whip till creamy and serve.

Pina Colada

Blend together:

    1 c. pineapple juice   2 tbls. coconut
    1 c. vanilla soy milk   1 tsp. rum flavoring
    1/2 c. crushed ice   2 tbls. coconut butter
                                              (opt.)
    Serve and enjoy.

BREADS

CHAPTER 12

Breads

Pheylonian Baked Goods

Please read the general sponge method and Durham Bread recipe beforehand if you are not familiar with making bread. It will explain in better detail some points that are not mentioned in the succeeding recipes.

These recipes are an accumulation of our favorite breads, buns, and pastries. A couple of these recipes are traditional breads which Iilah grew up with, such as the Ukrainian Bolkah Bread and Kemel (Rye) Bread. The rest are unique recipes Iilah has devised which are delightfully pleasing.

All our recipes call for durham flour as a base,, however, you can use hard whole wheat flour or unbleached whole wheat flour.

When bread is rising it is important not to jar or bump it or allow any cold drafts to pass over it, as it may flop.

Each of the yeasted bread and bun recipes are started with a "sponge method".

GENERAL SPONGE METHOD

This is the easiest and most effective way of ensuring the yeast gets properly started.

- Heat the appropriate amount of water to a lukewarm temperature. It should feel hot when you stick your fingernail in it.

- Pour water into a large bowl and dissolve the honey into the water. When the water settles, sprinkle the yeast evenly over the surface.

-   Let set till the yeast "bubbles" to the surface (usually takes 4 to 8 min.).

-   At this point, add the initial amount of flour called for and stir it in with a wire wisk. The texture should be like a thick cake mix. This is a sponge.

-   Cover the bowl and place in a warm spot for a half-hour or so.

       All of the recipes in this chapter each differ from this point on. According to which recipe you are following, you will add a variety of flours, sweeteners, oils, salt, fruits (dried or fresh), nuts, seeds, etc.

   Once the sponge has sat for a half-hour or so, you add all of the ingredients called for, except the flour (i.e. salt, oil, eggs, honey, molasses, or malt, seeds, nuts, washed fruit [dried or fresh, chopped or whole], flavouring, etc.).

       This should be stirred till well mixed. Then proceed to add your flour. Each recipe has an approximate amount of flour. This may vary according to your ingredients. Stir in one-half of the flour recommended with a large spoon. The remainder is best worked in by hand. Add the remainder of the flour as needed. Knead the dough in the bowl (pull the far side toward you, then push it away,, turn the bowl slightly and repeat several times). When the dough has formed a ball, you may roll it onto the counter to knead it, or leave it in the bowl if it is large enough.

       Continue to knead, adding a little flour as necessary for 5 to 10 min. Scrape the mixing bowl clean and return the dough to it. Moisten the top surface with water,, cover, and set in a warm place to rise for 45 min. or more. It should rise till doubled.

HOW TO FORM A LOAF (FROM DOUGH TO OVEN)

Flour your counter and turn the risen dough onto it. Knead the dough by pulling the far side towards you on top of the close half. Push away from you using the palms of your hand. Turn the dough 1/4 to the left (counter-clockwise). Repeat this several times till the dough has lost the air in it. Divide the dough into loaves. Each loaf should fill the pan slightly more than half. Knead each loaf separately until it becomes sticky and appears to be forming a well rounded ball. Do not have too much flour on your counter or the dough will not become sticky. Finally, shape into an oblong ball and place in the pan. Any cracks or seams should be turned towards the bottom. This action of kneading is designed to stretch the outside layer of dough to form a smooth, tight skin.

Durham Bread

Into a large bowl, combine:

    2 c. warm water

    1 tbls. honey

Sprinkle evenly over the water:

    1 tbls. yeast

Let set for 10 minutes. When activated, stir in:

    2 c. durham flour
        or unbleached whole wheat flour

Set the sponge in a warm place for 30~60 min.

Stir down and add:

    1 tbls. oil   1 tbls. salt

Mix well and add:

    2~3 c. durham flour

Stir till thick, then knead with your hands. Work the dough till it has a smooth consistency.

Knead the dough in the bowl or on the counter for 5~10 minutes. Replace the dough into the bowl, moisten the top with water and cover. Set in a warm place till risen about double.

Turn the dough onto a floured counter and knead the air out of it. Cut into 2 even pieces. Knead each loaf till you have a smooth, oval shape.

Oil 2 bread pans and place one loaf in each. Moisten the top surface with water. (This allows the bread to expand easier as the top stays soft).

Place the pans in a warm spot and let rise till they crest the pans edge. (Basically doubled).

Preheat the oven to 350° 30 minutes before the bread is ready to bake.

Durham Bread, cont.,

When rising bread, never let a cold draft or breeze blow on it as it may cause it to fall. Also, do not bang or jar it when placing into the oven.

When the bread is risen, place gently in the oven and bake for 30 minutes without opening the door.

Tamari ~ Baste:

Prepare the tamari~baste by combining:

    1 egg (beaten)
    1 tbls. tamari
    1 tbls. water

When the bread is firm to the touch and crusted (approx. 30~40 min.) baste the top of each loaf with the tamari ~ baste and return to the oven for 5~15 minutes more till cooked.

How to test Bread:

Remove bread from the pan by turning it onto a cloth in one hand. Tap the bottom with your knuckles and see how it sounds. If it sounds hollow and light ,, it should be cooked. If it sounds heavy and dull, it needs more baking.

As a secondary check, till you are familar with the first, cut a 1" slice off one end. If the bread looks overly moist or gummy, bake it a little longer. It will always be slightly moist as fresh cut, hot bread is like that.

Always remove bread from the pan fairly soon after it comes out of the oven or it will sweat and make the crusts soggy. Cool completely before bagging.

Natural bread is best kept refrigerated.

WHOLE WHEAT BREAD

Warm and dissolve together:
    2½ c. water
    1½ tbls. honey
Add: 1½ tbls. dry active yeast
Let set for 10 minutes.
When activated, stir in:
    2 c. durham flour
        or unbleached whole wheat flour
Let set in a warm place for 30~60 minutes.
Stir down and add:
    2 tbls. oil
    1 tbls. molasses
    1 tsp. salt
Mix well. Add and knead in:
    4~5 c. whole wheat flour
Knead for 5~10 minutes. Moisten the top of the dough, cover and let rise till double.

Turn the dough onto the counter and knead into a ball. Cut into 2 loaves. Knead and shape each loaf and place in an oiled bread pan. Place in a warm spot and rise till doubled.

Bake at 350° in a preheated oven for 35~45 minutes.

TAMARI BASTE

Crack into a bowl:
    2 eggs
Whip till fluffy. Add and mix well.
    2 tbls. tamari   ¼ c. water
Use to baste bread just before it's fully cooked.

Raisin Bread

A delicious bread which always seems to disappear very fast.
Ideal for toast at breakfast.

Warm and dissolve together:
  2½ c. water
  1½ tbls. honey
Add: 1½ tbls. dry active yeast
Let set for 10 minutes.
When activated, stir in:
  2 c. durham flour
    or unbleached whole wheat flour
Let set in a warm place for 30~60 minutes.
Stir down and add:
  ¾~1 c. raisins
  ½ c. honey
  3 tbls. oil or melted margarine
  1 egg
  1 tsp. vanilla
  1 tsp. salt
Mix well. Add and knead in:
  4~5 c. durham flour
    or unbleached whole wheat flour

Knead for 5~10 minutes. Moisten the top of the dough, cover and let rise till double.

Turn the dough onto the counter and knead into a ball. Cut into 2 loaves. Knead and shape each loaf and place in an oiled bread pan. Place in a warm spot and rise till doubled.

Bake at 350° in a preheated oven for 35~45 minutes.

PHEYLONIAN MONKS HEAD BREAD

At Philoxia, we bake this bread in specially designed, round pans (6½" diameter by 3" high) When Lilah designed this bread, he named it thus because when it is finished it resembles the shaven head of a monk, as it is nicely rounded and dotted with poppy seeds.

It is a hearty, whole wheat~durham flour loaf with the chewiness of sunflower seeds through-out.

Warm and dissolve together:

    2½ c. water
    1½ tbls. honey

Add: 1½ tbls. dry active yeast

Let set for 10 minutes.
When activated, stir in:

    2 c. durham flour
      or unbleached whole wheat flour

Let set in a warm place for 30~60 minutes.

Stir down and add:

    ⅔ c. sunflower sds.   2 tbls. oil
    2 tbls. molasses   1 tsp. salt

Mix well. Add and knead in:

    4~5 c. whole wheat flour

Knead for 5~10 minutes. Moisten the top of the dough, cover and let rise till double.

Turn the dough onto the counter and knead into a ball. Cut into 2 loaves. Knead and shape each loaf and place in an oiled bread pan. Wet the top surface and sprinkle with poppy seeds. Let rise in a warm spot till doubled. Bake at 350° for 35~45 minutes.

Ukrainian Bolkah Bread

This is a delightfully fluffy ,, slightly sweetened, braided bread. It is traditionally made and eaten on religious holidays, however it is an ideal bread for guests or on special occasions.

Warm and dissolve together:
- 2½ c. water
- 1½ tbls. honey

Add: 1½ tbls. dry active yeast

Let set for 10 minutes.
When activated, stir in:
- 2 c. durham flour
  or unbleached whole wheat flour

Let set in a warm place for 30~60 minutes.
Stir down and add:

½ c. raisins	2 eggs
¼ c. oil	1 egg yolk (beaten)
3~4 tbls. honey	1 tsp. salt

Mix well. Add and knead in:
- 4~5 c. durham flour

Knead for 5~10 minutes. Moisten the top of the dough, cover and let rise till double.

Turn the dough onto the counter and knead into a ball. Cut in two. The dough can simply be shaped as you would a regular loaf and bake as usual or you may braid it in a variety of different ways.

If you have a round, straight sided pan about 7"~8" wide, with no handles, shape the bread as follows.

Shape the 1 loaf into:
- a 1½" wide roll

Cut off: 1 2" ball

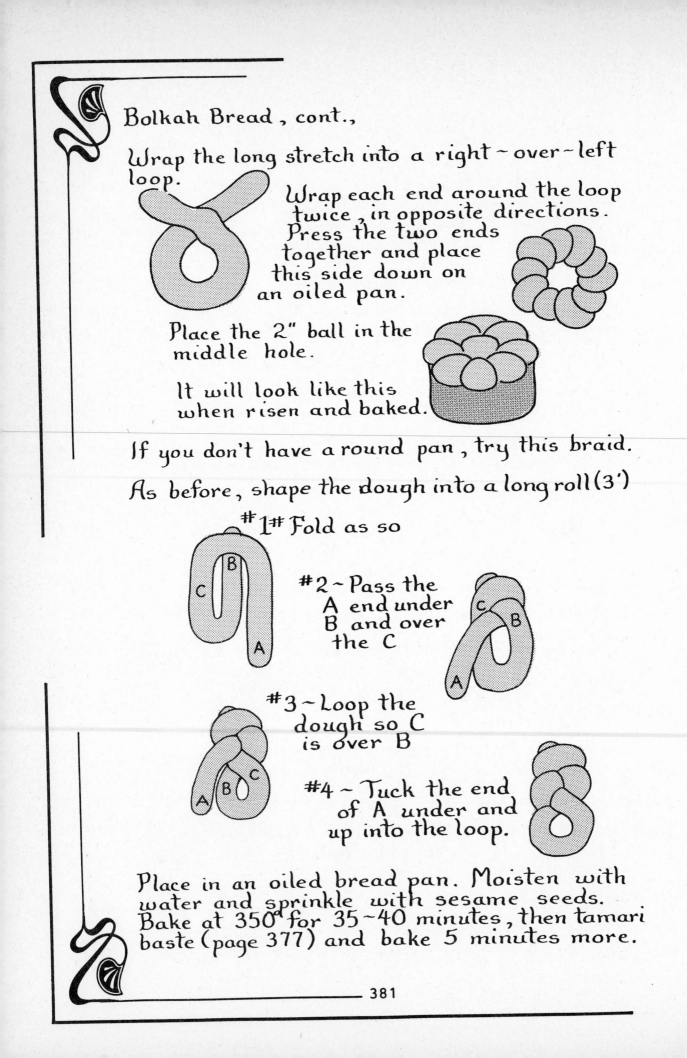

Bolkah Bread, cont.,

Wrap the long stretch into a right ~ over ~ left loop.

Wrap each end around the loop twice, in opposite directions. Press the two ends together and place this side down on an oiled pan.

Place the 2" ball in the middle hole.

It will look like this when risen and baked.

If you don't have a round pan, try this braid.

As before, shape the dough into a long roll (3')

#1# Fold as so

#2 ~ Pass the A end under B and over the C

#3 ~ Loop the dough so C is over B

#4 ~ Tuck the end of A under and up into the loop.

Place in an oiled bread pan. Moisten with water and sprinkle with sesame seeds. Bake at 350° for 35 ~ 40 minutes, then tamari baste (page 377) and bake 5 minutes more.

HAMBURGER BUNS
(approx. 6 buns)

Warm and dissolve together:

    2½ c. water
    1½ tbls. honey

Add: 1½ tbls. dry active yeast

Let set for 10 minutes.
When activated, stir in:

    2 c. durham flour
      or unbleached whole wheat flour

Let set in a warm place for 30~60 minutes.

Stir down and add:

    1 tbls. oil
    1 egg (beaten)
    1 tsp. salt

Mix well. Add and knead in:

    4~5 c. whole wheat flour

Knead for 5-10 minutes. Moisten the top of the dough, cover and let rise till double.

Turn the dough onto the counter and knead into a ball. Cut into eight even pieces. (Each piece should weigh approx. 3 oz.).

On a lightly floured surface, knead each piece into a ball. Then roll to a 3½" wide by ½" thick bun. Place each bun on an oiled tray, an inch or more apart. Moisten each bun with water and sprinkle with sesame seeds. Let them rise till doubled, then bake at 325° for 15 mins. Coat with a tamari baste and cook for 2~3 minutes more. Do not overcook as they will become very hard.

Store in plastic bags when cooled.

Don't be afraid to make a double or triple batch and freeze some. They thaw and reheat well.

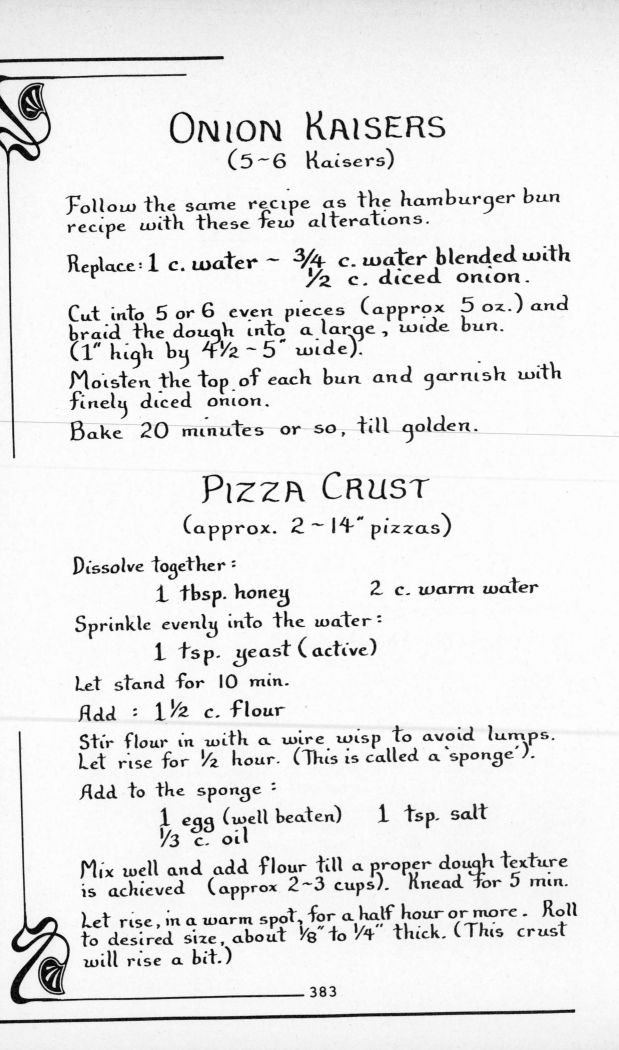

ONION KAISERS
(5~6 Kaisers)

Follow the same recipe as the hamburger bun recipe with these few alterations.

Replace: 1 c. water ~ 3/4 c. water blended with 1/2 c. diced onion.

Cut into 5 or 6 even pieces (approx 5 oz.) and braid the dough into a large, wide bun. (1" high by 4½ ~ 5" wide).

Moisten the top of each bun and garnish with finely diced onion.

Bake 20 minutes or so, till golden.

PIZZA CRUST
(approx. 2 ~ 14" pizzas)

Dissolve together:

    1 tbsp. honey   2 c. warm water

Sprinkle evenly into the water:

    1 tsp. yeast (active)

Let stand for 10 min.

Add : 1½ c. flour

Stir flour in with a wire wisp to avoid lumps. Let rise for ½ hour. (This is called a 'sponge').

Add to the sponge:

    1 egg (well beaten)   1 tsp. salt
    1/3 c. oil

Mix well and add flour till a proper dough texture is achieved (approx 2~3 cups). Knead for 5 min.

Let rise, in a warm spot, for a half hour or more. Roll to desired size, about 1/8" to 1/4" thick. (This crust will rise a bit.)

FLATS

Flats are our Pheylonian style of unyeasted, unleavened bread. They are so called because they are very "flat." Iilah designed these as a treat and as an alternative to eating yeasted bread. They became so favored that for quite a few years we seldom ate bread,, but we sure put away a lot of flats.

Unlike a chappati, flats are designed to be crispy (less flexible) which makes them ideal for putting foods on. In our Oh-soh-nowa section we explain some of the many meals we have made using flats.

They are very tasty on their own also.

Combine in a bowl:

    3 c. flour (one kind or a combination of)
    ½ c. sesame seeds
    ½ tsp. salt

Work in with your fingers:

    ¼ c. oil

Add: 2½ c. water

Work with your hands to form a soft dough.
Add,, if needed, up to:

    ¾ c. of water more

Knead slightly to form a well rounded ball.

Cut a 2" strip off the dough. Shape it into a 1½" wide roll and cut it into 1" pieces. Using a little flour,, roll each piece to a thin circle. The thinner they're rolled, the crispier they turn out.

Cook on an open grill in a dry skillet or on a cookie sheet in the oven. Cook till lightly browned.

Extra dough may be refrigerated and used daily, or make all of the dough into flats and refrigerate them in a plastic bag. Reheat in the toaster or oven before eating.

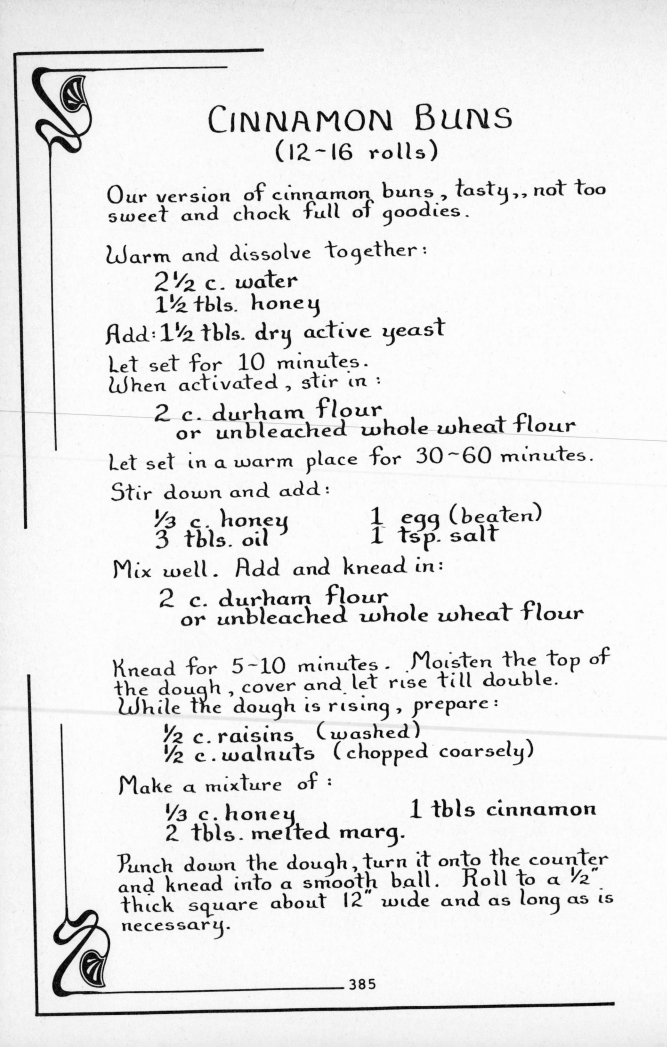

Cinnamon Buns
(12~16 rolls)

Our version of cinnamon buns, tasty,, not too sweet and chock full of goodies.

Warm and dissolve together:

    2½ c. water
    1½ tbls. honey

Add: 1½ tbls. dry active yeast

Let set for 10 minutes.
When activated, stir in:

    2 c. durham flour
      or unbleached whole wheat flour

Let set in a warm place for 30~60 minutes.

Stir down and add:

    ⅓ c. honey   1 egg (beaten)
    3 tbls. oil   1 tsp. salt

Mix well. Add and knead in:

    2 c. durham flour
      or unbleached whole wheat flour

Knead for 5~10 minutes. Moisten the top of the dough, cover and let rise till double.
While the dough is rising, prepare:

    ½ c. raisins (washed)
    ½ c. walnuts (chopped coarsely)

Make a mixture of:

    ⅓ c. honey   1 tbls cinnamon
    2 tbls. melted marg.

Punch down the dough, turn it onto the counter and knead into a smooth ball. Roll to a ½" thick square about 12" wide and as long as is necessary.

Cinnamon Buns, cont.,

If the dough seems very elastic and springs back each time you try to roll it out, take the rolling pin and pound the dough several times, across one way, then across the other way. This should help.

Pour the honey sauce onto the dough and spread evenly. Leave a 1" strip on the far side with no sauce.

Sprinkle evenly with the raisins and walnuts, then sprinkle with a liberal amount of poppy seeds (approx. ¼ c.)

Moisten the 1" bare strip with water. Starting at the closest side, roll up the dough evenly and pinch to seal the moistened edge to the dough.

Reshape the roll a little if needed to have a consistent thickness. The roll should be about 2½" in diameter.

Now, with a sharp, wide bladed knife, cut the roll into 1½" thick rounds. Lay each slice on an oiled pan, spaced with about 1" in-between.

Moisten each roll slightly and set in a warm place to rise.

Preheat the oven to 350°. When well risen, bake for 25~30 minutes. Coat with sweet baste (page 388) and bake 5 min. more till done.

A double or triple batch of these is just as easy to make. Ideal for party treats, plus they freeze well and reheat just as though they were fresh baked.

PHEYLONIAN FEAST BUNS
(approx. 12 buns)

A delicious, lightly sweet bun which Lilah created many years ago when we first opened our bakery here at Philoxia. He named these delicacies feast buns because they really are a feast in themself.

A sure hit for snacks, lunches or breakfast.

Warm and dissolve together:
- 2½ c. water
- 1½ tbls. honey

Add: 1½ tbls. dry active yeast

Let set for 10 minutes.
When activated, stir in:
- 2 c. durham flour
  or unbleached whole wheat flour

Let set in a warm place for 30~60 minutes.

Stir down and add:

1 c. dates (chopped)	2 eggs (beaten)
½ c. honey	2 tbls. oil
⅓ c. sunflower sds.	1 tbls. cinnamon
¼ c. poppy seeds	1 tsp. salt
¼ c. molasses	

Mix well. Add and knead in:
- 4~5 c. durham flour
  or unbleached whole wheat flour

Knead for 5~10 minutes. Moisten the top of the dough, cover and let rise till double.

Turn the dough onto the counter and knead into a ball. Cut into 12 pieces. These buns may be shaped as a rounded bun or in any variety of braided buns.

Feast Buns, cont.,

Using one of the 12 pieces, roll it to a 12" long roll. Loop the right hand end (A) over the left (B).

Pass the left end (A) under the loop and out to the side.

Tuck the right end (B) over the loop and into the middle. Tuck A under and up through the middle.

Once you've done a few dozen of these, it gets quite easy. Place them on an oiled tray 1" apart. Moisten with water and sprinkle with sesame seeds.

Let rise in a warm place till doubled. Bake in a preheated oven (350°) till golden brown. (Approx. 30 min.) Coat with sweet baste and bake for 5~10 minutes more.

SWEET BASTE

Use as a finishing touch on sweet buns, pie, raisin bread, etc.

Crack into a bowl and beat till fluffy:

    1 egg

Add and mix well:

    ½ c. honey   2 tbls. water

Baste buns, bread, etc., 5 minutes before they are fully cooked. Return to the oven and bake till golden brown.

HOT CROSS BUNS

Tasty and light, subtly sweet with a hint of lemon. Very good with breakfast,, for snacks, or with a meal instead of bread.

Preheat oven to 375°.

Sift together:

2 ½ c. flour	½ tsp. salt
4 tsp. bak. pwd.	¼ tsp. nutmeg

Add: 2 tbls. grated lemon peel
     ½ c. currants (scalded and drained)

Combine:

1 egg (beaten)	2 tbls. honey
½ - ⅔ c. soy milk	2 tbls. soy marg. (melted)

Mix liquid into dry ingredients to form a soft dough. (Add up to 3 tbls. of soymilk more to dough if needed.)

Knead lightly on a floured board. Divide into 1½" buns. Arrange on an oiled tray about ½" apart.

Cut a deep cross in the top and let stand for 10 mins.

Brush with a mixture of honey and margarine. Bake for 25 ~ 30 min.

Sour Dough Breads

For the last few years we have primarily been eating sour dough breads, as opposed to yeasted breads. We find sour dough just as enjoyable, if not more, and it digests better. (The guys claim they can eat more when it's sour dough.)

Once you know how to make yeasted bread,, sour dough is basically the same except for making the sponge and caring for the culture.

Here are a few general points about sour dough bread:

- The culture should be used or "fed" every 10 to 14 days.

- The culture should be kept refrigerated, preferably in a plastic container with a pop-on (not screw-on) lid. This is because a very active culture can pop a glass jar or sealed container if it builds up too much air.

- Keep your culture as pure as possible, preferably with only the culture itself and the water and flour which gets added each time. Try to keep only one kind of flour in your culture.

- A good culture should rise as well as any yeasted bread,, but takes a little longer. How fast sour dough bread rises is greatly affected by its surrounding temperature.

HOW TO MAKE A CULTURE

There are several methods for making a sour dough culture. This is how I made my culture a few years ago: I used some rice that had been kept in the refrigerator, but

that had gone distinctively sour -- not mouldy,, just good
and sour.

> Blend: 2 c. water
>   1 c. of the soured rice
>   1 tbls. honey

Pour this mixture into a dry bowl and add:

> **2 c. of durham flour**

Mix it well and cover with a lid,, and place in a warm
corner where it is out of the way. This should be stirred
two, three, or four times per day, each time with a clean
spoon.

Each day note the aroma of the culture. By about
four to six days, it should be getting a little stronger, and
you may notice some bubbles,,, plus the consistency of the
culture should be thinner.

At this point,, dissolve together:

> **1/2 c. warm water**
> **1 tsp. honey**

> Add: **1/2 tsp. dried yeast**

When activated, stir into the culture and add:

> **1/2 c. flour**

Continue to age, stirring daily.

When you notice a significant activity within the
culture, in one to three days more,, your culture should be
ready.

Proceed with it in any of these recipes, or store it in a container refrigerated. If you know of someone who has a good sour dough culture, ask if you may have some. Most bakers are glad to share a little culture.

MAKING A SOUR DOUGH SPONGE FROM THE CULTURE

As with many of the recipes in this book,, adapting from what I used to make using "so much of this" and "so much of that" to "1 c. of this and 2 tbls. of that" has been trying at best.

Likewise with the sour dough. When I make bread every seven days, I simply take the whole culture, add three times the amount of warm water, and enough flour to make a sponge texture,, and away I go, making anywhere from two to four kinds of bread, cookies, or muffins, etc.

The best method I figured to teach you from was to show you how to make different quantities of sour dough sponge and to start each recipe from that point.

Keeping a sour dough culture alive calls for versatility. The whole mixture should be added to and fed every 10 to 14 days. The proportions given below are general and should suit a small family's use on a weekly basis.

- Retain in the fridge:

2 c. of starter

- The evening before the day you want to make bread, remove the culture from the fridge and stir it up thoroughly. Pour into a large bowl or wok.

- Add:

6 c. of warm water

- Stir well and add:

6 to 8 c. durham fl.
(or unbleached whole wheat flour)

Mix well using a wisk, and cover.

- Set in a warm place overnight. (Make sure there is plenty of head room for the sponge to expand, as it can more than double.)

- By morning, the sponge should have risen and fallen. Stir it down a little and remove 3 cups of sponge to retain as your culture.

- Replace in a container and refrigerate immediately. (This amount of sponge will settle down and become approximately 2 cups of culture for your next batch.)

- You will be left with approximately 12 cups of sponge. Work from this point with each recipe.

Make a half quantity if this is too much, or use this quantity to make two or three different kinds of bread and cookies.

When making the sponge into bread,, if it calls for 4 c. of sponge and you have 5,, don't worry about it,,, just add a little extra flour and you will have enough dough for a few buns on the side.

SOUR DOUGH MONKS HEAD BREAD

Place in a large bowl:

    6 c. of sour dough sponge

Add to the sponge:

    1 c. sunflower sds.   2 tbls. oil
    1/3 c. molasses   1 tsp. salt

Stir well and add:

    1½ c. durham flour
    2½ ~ 3½ c. whole wheat flour

Knead till it forms a soft dough. Knead the dough for 5~7 minutes either in the bowl or on the counter. Scrape the bowl clean and return the dough. Moisten the top and cover.

Set in a warm place to rise for 1~3 hours until doubled.

Punch down and turn onto a floured counter. Knead dough lightly, then cut into loaves. (Each loaf should fill 3/5's of the pan,, as sour dough bread does not rise as much as do yeasted breads.

Moisten the tops and sprinkle with poppy seeds or sesame seeds. Let rise in a warm place. When risen, bake in an oven preheated to 350° for 40~60 minutes.

Coat with a tamari~egg baste and bake for 5 minutes more.

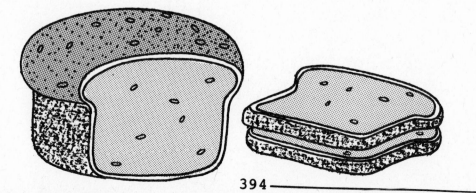

Follow the method of the preceding recipe using the specified ingredients.

SOUR DOUGH KEMEL
(RYE BREAD)

Place in a bowl:

6 c. sour dough sponge

Add and mix well:

⅓ c. molasses   1-2 tbls. carraway sds.
2 tbls. oil   1 tsp. salt

Mix in and knead till smooth:

¾ c. cornmeal
3½ - 4½ c. rye flour

(this dough is stickier because it has less flour. Rye flour is heavier [has less gluten] and needs a softer dough to rise easily).

Garnish with carraway seeds.

SOUR DOUGH CORN BREAD

Place in a bowl:

6 c. sour dough sponge

Add: ¾ c. barley malt   ¾ c. oil
     2 eggs   1 tsp. salt

Stir well and add:

3-3½ c. cornmeal   1 c. grated carrot
3 c. flour   ½ -1 c. currants
                     (washed and soaked)

Mix well. This is a very soft dough (like a thick batter). Spoon into oiled pans till ⅔'s full. Let rise till level with the top edge of the pan. Bake in a 350° oven for 40-45 min.

SOUR DOUGH COOKIES

These are an ideal inbetween meal snacks. They are lightly sweetened and very delicious.

These are just 2 versions which we have made. Once you have tried these, devise your own mixtures and have fun. If you stick to these basic proportions they are practically fool proof.

ALMOND CHEWS

Place in a large bowl:

2 c. sour dough sponge.

Add: 1½ c. rolled oats   2 eggs (beaten)
     ½ c. almond butter   ¼ c. oil
     ½ c. barley malt   ½ tsp. salt
     ½ c. almonds

Mix well and add:

1½ c. durham flour
     or unbleached whole wheat flour

Place batter to rise in a warm spot for 1~2 hrs.

When risen, stir the batter down and drop by spoonfuls onto an oiled tray. Flatten to ¼" thick and let rise for 30 minutes.

Preheat oven to 325°. Bake cookies for 10~12 minutes. Remove when cooked and cool.

SESAME DELIGHTS

Proceed as above substituting these ingredients:

Add: 1½ c. sesame sds.   ½ c. oil
     1¼ c. raisins   2 eggs (beaten)
     ½ c. barley malt   ½ tsp. salt

Mix well and add:

2 c. durham flour   1 c. cornmeal

Bred of de Camel

Now this is something yawl don't want to try unless you're riding a camel on route to some Bedowin village near the Valley of the Kings in Luxor, Egypt. Yet,, it's a cute story worth sharing with our spotless, irradiated, microwave'd society.

Some time ago,, as a quest of the people of Egypt,,, I had the opportunity to spend the necessary time needed to re-evaluate and affirm the ancient truths and untold secrets of this enchanting valley. Relative to the true analogies being confirmed within this mysterious valley,,, many of these startling facts are being revealed and elaborated on for the first time in the book, "Alpha, Mu, and Omega",, soon to be released through this same Pheylonian Publishing Kohr.

Each day on my way through this little Bedowin village,, I would stop on the edge of town and briefly visit with the aging aunt of Abdul Mohamed. He was my friend who was put in charge of the local free mileage, low cost rent-a-camel, or donkey business. Always being aware of my basic nutritional needs,, I had asked him where I could find a fresh grain'd bread, so's as to sustain my energies while on my extended journeys into the valley and desert beyond.

During the first few days, he came as my guide and friend,,, and always we would stop at his aunt's quaint little adobe villa, surrounded by palms and floral bushes,,, and we'd purchase some of the finest corn bread yawl ever did taste. The grain was stone-ground,, fresh each day,, and had a sun rising rather than a yeasted one. Then, she would bake these mounded little half-pound loaves in a nice little round clay oven, situated out back of her house.

When chomping into my first loaf,,, I couldn't help but comment to Abdul of just how tasty and fulfilling it was.

Silently, I detected a particular flavour which I couldn't quite identify,, and simply assumed it was her secret spice to make it so nice. I tell you,,, for people who are used to wholesome goodness,,, these mini loaves took the cake.

It wasn't until my fourth or fifth visit,, and getting the bread steeping hot out of the oven,, did I realize the essence of this aromatic, subtle flavour. Without a doubt,,, it was fresh clover. Well, as the months rolled by, and my visit to this breathtaking part of the country was coming to an end,,, an enlightening experience befell me one morning.

In wanting to absorb as much as I could before my departure,,, I had left an hour or so earlier than usual on my way to the Great Valley. Here I was, rounding the bend, coming into sight of Abdul's aunt's house,,, when I could see her on the sandy path in front of her home. I could see her crouched low, and very gently scooping a loose camel dung paddy onto a tin sheet. She was ever so careful so's as not to break its spiral pattern. I bid her good morning, and followed her into the back yard, where she scurried up these narrow clay mud stairs situated against the back of her house. Soon after, she returned with her tin filled with rock-hard, perfectly shaped camel paddies. As she walked by me, glowing her ever radiant smile,,, she removed the charred, blackened wood door to her oven, and gently placed these paddies in such an efficient manner over the existing coals, so's as to generate the exact heat needed to bake her next batch of corn bread.

ii,,, I was stupified there for a spell, and turned to look upward atop her little one-storey home,, and there, before me eyes, was a veritable gold mine of camel dung dried and drying. All these revelations of reality began flowing through my mind. I could just see myself standing there open-mouthed and dumbfounded for ever so long,,, because folks,,, there just is no burning wood in that neck of the desert,, and all they ever feed them there camels is fresh

clover, grown along the Nile,,, and here I was, after so
long,, ready to enjoy my last mouth-watering feast on this
clover-spiced corn bread. So help me,,, I hesitated but for
a moment,,, and for the last time before leaving this marvelous place,, I stocked up, so's as to have enough for the
next few days,,, and friends,,, I can't remember when I'd
ever bin happier and healthier.

Incidently,,, to put yawl at a comfort,,, whenever
Tawlia bakes our sour dow'd, currant corn bread in our brick
ovens here at Philoxia,,, rest assured,,, we use hard wood,
even though there's a real live Egyptian camel a'wanderin'
throughout our courtyards.

DESSERTS

CHAPTER 13

Desserts

PIE CRUSTS

PUDDINGS

CAKES

CAKES (Cont'd)

SQUARES AND ROLLS

COOKIES

COOKIES (Cont'd)

ICINGS

DESSERT TOPPINGS

PIES and TARTS

Treats like these are as traditional as the phrase "Mom's Apple Pie."

Within this chapter we have pies made of fresh fruit which have little or no sweetening, depending on the fruit used ,, some made from fruit juice and their rinds and a whole assortment of delicious cream pies which have no dairy products whatsoever.

Most of these recipes will make 2 9" pies. It's just as easy to make two pies as it is one, and besides, from our experience, pie is something that never goes to waste.

In each of these recipes, I specify how many pie crusts or tart shells are needed and whether it is just the bottom or a top crust also. The type of crust you use is up to you. You can prepare and use fresh pie dough, or,, utilize dough which you have refrigerated or frozen. I always keep some pie dough in the fridge or freezer as it comes in handy to make a quick treat when someone drops by unexpectedly.

FRUIT FILLED PIES

In choosing fruit, look for well ripened, yet unbruised produce. Avoid fruit which looks very glossy or coated, (esp. apples) as they have often been sprayed with a parrafin base substance to keep them fresh and shiny looking.

Wash fruit well before peeling to eliminate any surface dirt or chemicals which can get on the inner fruit while peeling.

If you can purchase or harvest organically grown produce, all the better.

Apple Pie

There are many ways to make apple pie. This is how Iilah's mom makes her's. Perhaps we're prejudiced, but we think her apple pie is the best we've ever eaten.

Prepare enough dough for 2 pies, tops and bottoms. (Dough should be about ⅛" thick).

Wash, peel, quarter and core:

   3½ lb. cooking apples

Rinse apples again and cut into ¼" slices. (You should have about 7 cups.)

Simmer sliced apples in a pot with:

   ¼ c. water or apple juice

(Depending on the type of apples you use,, this cooking time may take anywhere from 2 minutes to 10 min. As soon as the apples are 'softened' remove them from the heat.)

Add to the apples:

   ½ c. raisins   4 tbls. flour
   1~4 tbls. honey   1 tbls. vanilla ext.
      or maple syrup

Mix together. Preheat the oven to 350°.

Roll the bottom crusts and line the pie shells. (Do not cut the edges.) Roll the two top crusts.

Pour the apples evenly into the two pies, moisten the edge of the pie crusts and add the tops. Seal the edges. Perforate the tops with a nice design to allow air to escape. Bake for 30 min.

Mix together and baste the top of the pies with:

   1 egg (well beaten)   1 tbls. water
   2 tbls. honey

Return to the oven and bake till golden brown.

PEAR PIE

If apple pie has always been one of your favorites, then I'm sure you'll love pear pie.

Use nicely ripened pears and follow the procedure and spicing as in the 'Apple Pie' recipe.

Ripe pears are usually very sweet and should need little or no sweetener.

ALTERNATIVES AND TURNOVERS

Keep in mind you can combine fruits, like apples and pears, or peaches, to make a very nice taste combination for pie or turnovers. Speaking of which, turnovers are ideal for lunches, treats on outings and for picnics. They are very portable as individual servings.

Roll dough into 6" circles. Place some filling on one half, moisten the edges and fold in half. Seal edges well ,, pierce the top of each turnover and bake on an oiled cookie sheet till browned.

CHERRY PIE

Make and bake: 2 pie shells

Combine in a saucepan:

6 c. pitted cherries   1 tbls. cherry or
1/2 c. honey   vanilla ext.
3/4 c. water (or cherry juice)

Bring to a boil and simmer for 10 min.

Mix: 1/4 c. water   4 tbls. arrowroot fl.

Add to the cherries, stirring till thickened.

Pour into the cooked crusts. Cool and serve.

BLUEBERRY PIE

For this recipe you can use either fresh or frozen blueberries.

Prepare dough for 1 9" pie, top and bottom.
Combine in a saucepan :

½ c. water *   1 tbls. agar agar

Bring to a boil and simmer with a lid for 10 min.
Preheat oven to 350°. Remove agar mixture from stove.
Mix together and add to the agar mixture :

4 c. blueberries   ¼ c. water
⅓ ~ ½ c. honey   3 tbls. arrowroot fl.

Roll the bottom crust, line the pie shell and add the filling. Moisten edges and add the top crust. Seal the edges and cut a design in the top.
Bake for 30 ~ 40 min. till sizzling and golde. brown. Brush with pie baste (see below) 5 min. before pie is done.

* If using frozen blueberries ,,, drain off any liquid from the thawed blueberries and use it as part of the water content.

PIE BASTE

In a bowl, whip till light and fluffy
    1 egg
Add: 2 tbls. honey   1 tbls. water
Mix well.
Use to baste the top crust of pies. Apply when almost fully cooked. Bake 5 minutes more.

PEACH PIE

Prepare dough for 1 full pie.

Blanch:

> 6~8 peaches (approx. 4 c. when sliced).
> (drop into boiling water and simmer till the skins slip off easily.)

When skins are removed, cut peaches from the pits in 1/4" slices.

Roll bottom crust and line pie shell. Preheat oven.

Arrange peach slices in the crust.

Sprinkle evenly on top of the peaches:

> 10~12 grates of nutmeg
> or 1/4 tsp. ground nutmeg
> 2~4 tbls. honey or maple syrup
> 2 tbls. flour

Roll the top crust. Moisten pie edge and add the top. Seal edges and perforate the top with a nice design.

Bake at 350° for 30 min. Baste with "Pie Baste" (page 408) and bake 5~10 min. more.

Pie Top Designs

PUMPKIN PIE

Prepare a batch of Graham Cracker Crumb Crust (page 427) Press into 2~oiled 9" pie pans and set aside.

This recipe requires:

5 c. cooked pumpkin

Cook pumpkin by either baking or steaming.

Baked: cut in half, remove seeds and bake on an oiled tray. Cut a 'V' in the sides to allow the juice to run out of the pumpkin. Bake till soft. Let cool and remove from skin.

Steamed: cut into strips, peel and cut into 1" chunks. Steam till tender. (This method tends to be more watery).

Any extra pumpkin can be frozen or bottled in 5 c. batches.

Preheat oven to 400°. Separate 4 eggs.

Combine in a blender and whip till smooth:

4 egg yolks	1½ tsp. vanilla
1¼ c. tofu	1½ tsp. cinnamon
½ c. soy milk	½ tsp. ginger pwd.
½ c. honey	½ tsp. salt
or maple syrup	⅛ tsp. clove pwd.
3 tbls. arrowroot fl.	

Mash the pumpkin and add the blended mixture. Continue mashing till well mixed.

Beat egg whites till fluffy and stiff. Fold into pumpkin mixture. Pour into pie and bake for 20 min. Reduce heat to 350° and bake till done (approx. 40 min. Knife test,, a dry knife means it is cooked). Remove from the oven and let cool, then refrigerate. Serve as is or with Tofu Whip-Cream.

RHUBARB ~ STRAWBERRY PIE

Prepare and cook:

    2   9" pie shells

Wash the rhubarb stalks and cut into 1" pieces till you have:

    9 c. rhubarb

Place the chopped rhubarb in a pot and add:

    1 c. water   4 tbls. agar agar
    1 c. honey   ½ tsp. salt

Simmer for 20 minutes then add:

    9 c. washed strawberries
    (you may use fresh or frozen berries.
    If you use frozen berries, use the juice
    which thaws off the strawberries to
    replace some of the water called for).

Simmer for 5 minutes.

Combine in a cup:

    ½ c. water   6 tbls. arrowroot flour

Stir slowly into the pot while the fruit is still simmering. Cook till thickened and clear. Let it cool for 15 minutes, then pour into cooked pie shells.

Cool and refrigerate.

When cooled, serve as is or topped with tofu whip cream.

Shanola's Lemon Meringue Pie

This recipe is the most scrumptious lemon meringue pie you ever tasted.

Prebake: 1 pie shell

Combine in a double boiler and heat till boiling:

2½ c. water
grated rind of 1 lemon

Mix together:

½ c. water   3 tbls. durham fl.
6 tbls. arrowroot fl.

Add the flour mixture and cook till thickened; stir occasionally.

Meanwhile, separate:

2 eggs

Mix : 2 yolks
½ c. honey

When sauce has thickened, add the egg and honey. Continue simmering for 5-10 min.

Remove from heat and add:

⅓ c. lemon juice   ½ tsp. salt
1 tbls. marg.

Mix well and pour into precooked pie shell. Let cool for 1 hour.

When pie has cooled, whip the 2 egg whites till fluffy and stiff. Add while still beating:

1 tbls. maple syrup (or liquid honey)
1 tbls. corn starch (this prevents the meringue from being runny)

Top the pie with the meringue and bake at 325° for 10-12 min., or till golden brown. Chill.

MILLET CREAM PIES

Each of our cream pies are made from a millet base. They are deliciously creamy and contain no dairy products.

The sweetness of each of these recipes is suited to a moderate sweet tooth. If your tastes are sweeter, add a few more tbls. of honey. It won't affect the texture.

LEMON MERINGUE PIE

Precook: 2 pie shells

Combine in a saucepan:

6 c. water	grated rind of
3/4 c. millet	2 lemons
4 tbls. agar	1/4 tsp. salt

Bring to a boil. Cover and simmer for 20 min.

Meanwhile, separate:

4 eggs

Mix in a separate bowl:

4 yolks	juice of 2 lemons
1/2 c. honey	3 tbls. marg.

Add the yolk mixture and simmer for 10 min. Let the filling cool for 10~15 min. Blend half at a time. Re~mix and pour into the cooked pie shells. Cool.

When the pies are cooled, whip up the egg whites till fluffy and stiff. Continue beating and add:

1 tbls. liquid honey or maple syrup

Spread meringue on top of the filling, forming nice peaks. Bake in a preheated oven at 325° until the meringue is golden brown (approx. 10 min.). Cool, then refrigerate.

413

BLUEBERRY CREAM PIE

This recipe was always one of my favorites, seeing as blueberries are the fruit I like the most. Since blueberries are expensive even in season, this is a very satisfying answer to the blueberry lover,, which is less expensive, yet very tasty.

Prepare pie dough and bake 2 pie shells.
Combine in a saucepan:

6 c. water	4 tbls. agar agar
1 c. millet	1 tbls. blueberry ext.
½ c. honey	(or vanilla)
2 c. blueberries	½ tsp. salt

Bring to a boil and simmer for 30 min. Cool for 15 min. Blend 3 cups at a time and pour into cooked pie shells.

While pie is cooling, prepare topping.
Simmer in a saucepan for 5 min.

3½ c. blueberries	2~4 tbls. honey
½ c. water	

Mix: ¼ c. cold water   2 tbls. arrowroot fl.

Add to blueberries while simmering. Stir and cook till thickened. Pour on top of cream filling.

PINEAPPLE CREAM PIE

Bake: 2 pie shells
Combine in a saucepan:

6 c. pineapple juice	
2 c. water	
1 c. millet	4 tbls. agar agar
¼ c. honey	½ tsp. salt

Bring to a boil and simmer for 30 min.
Cool for 15 min., then blend 3 cups at a time.
Re-mix and pour into pie shells. Let cool.
Top with a layer of Tofu Whip Cream #2.

CAROB CREAM PIE

Prepare pie dough and bake: 2 pie shells.

Combine in a saucepan:

8 c. water	1 c. millet
½ c. carob pwd.	4 tbls. agar agar
½ c. honey	½ tsp. salt

Bring to a boil and simmer for 30 min.

Add: 1 tbls. lemon juice   1 tsp. vanilla
     1 tbls. margarine

Blend 3 cups at a time ,, re-mix and pour into the cooked pie shells.

Chill and top with Tofu Whip Cream #2.

CAROB-MINT CREAM PIE

Eliminate the lemon juice from the above recipe. Put 2 tbls. of dried mint into a tea ball and boil from the beginning with all the other ingredients.

STRAWBERRY CREAM PIE

Bake: 2 pie shells

Combine and bring to a boil:

5 c. water	4 c. strawberries
1 c. millet	4 tbls. agar agar
½ c. honey	½ tsp. salt

Simmer for 30 min.

Blend 3 cups at a time, re-mix and fill pie shells.

When filling has cooled ,, top with a layer of Tofu Whip Cream #2 and decorate with fresh strawberry slices.

BANANA CREAM PIE

Bake: 2 pie shells

Combine in a saucepan and bring to a boil:

6 c. water	¾ c. millet
¼ c. honey	4 tbls. agar agar
½ tsp. salt	1 tsp. vanilla

Simmer for 30 min.

Add to the saucepan:

3 c. banana (cut in chunks)

Let mixture cool for 15 min.

Blend a third at a time, re-mix and pour into precooked pie shells.

Decorate the top with ¼" thick banana slices
Let cool, then chill.

COCONUT CREAM PIE

Bake: 2 pie shells

Combine in a saucepan and bring to a boil:

8 c. water	1 c. millet
1 c. grt. coconut	4 tbls. agar agar
½ c. honey	1 tsp. vanilla

Simmer for 30 min.
Dry roast:

½ c. coconut

Add to simmering millet mixture:

2 tbls. marg. or coconut butter

Blend pudding, ⅓rd at a time, pour into shells.
Top immediately with roasted coconut.
Chill.
Serve as is or topped with Tofu Whip Cream.

Mocha Cream Pie

This is a scrumptious pudding which I devised after being treated with a chocolate mousse at a get-together. This isn't as rich but it sure is tasty.

Prepare pie dough and roll two bottom crusts. Bake till golden brown.

Combine in a pot:

8 c. water	4 tbls. agar agar
1 c. millet	1 tsp. vanilla
1/2 c. maple syrup	1/2 tsp. salt
1/4 c. carob	

Bring to a boil and simmer for 20 minutes with a lid.

Let cool for 10 minutes.

Add to the pudding:

1/4 c. of instant herbal coffee
2 tbls. soy margarine

Blend in 2 batches. Whip till creamy.

Recombine and pour into the cooked pie shells. Let cool to room temperature, then refrigerate.

Blend in two batches. (Whip till creamy and fluffy.)

BOSTON CREAM PIE

This is one of those gourmet desserts that always leave you speechless.

First off,, make the cake.

Preheat oven to 350°.

Sift: 2 c. flour   ½ tsp. salt
      3 tsp. bak. pwd.

Combine in a separate bowl:

3 eggs (well beaten)   1 tbls. vanilla
¼ c. oil   ¾ c. soy milk
¾ c. honey

Add liquid to the dry ingredients and mix well.

Pour into an oiled and floured, 9" cake pan
Bake for 35~40 min. at 350°. Cool.

While the cake is cooking, prepare the cream.

Combine in a saucepan:

3½ c. water   3 tbls. agar agar
½ c. millet   1 tbls. vanilla
½ c. honey   ¼ tsp. salt
1 tbls. marg.

Bring to a boil and simmer for 30 min.
Let cool for 15 min., then blend till smooth.

When cake has cooled, slice in half through the middle. Place bottom half back in cake pan.
Add cream filling.
Let set till firm enough to add the other layer (It's best to 'stir up' the top of the pudding so the cake has a moist surface to adhere to.

Chill for 3~4 hrs.

The final step is the icing.
Prepare a batch of Carob Icing.
Remove cake from the pan and ice the top and sides.   Serve chilled.

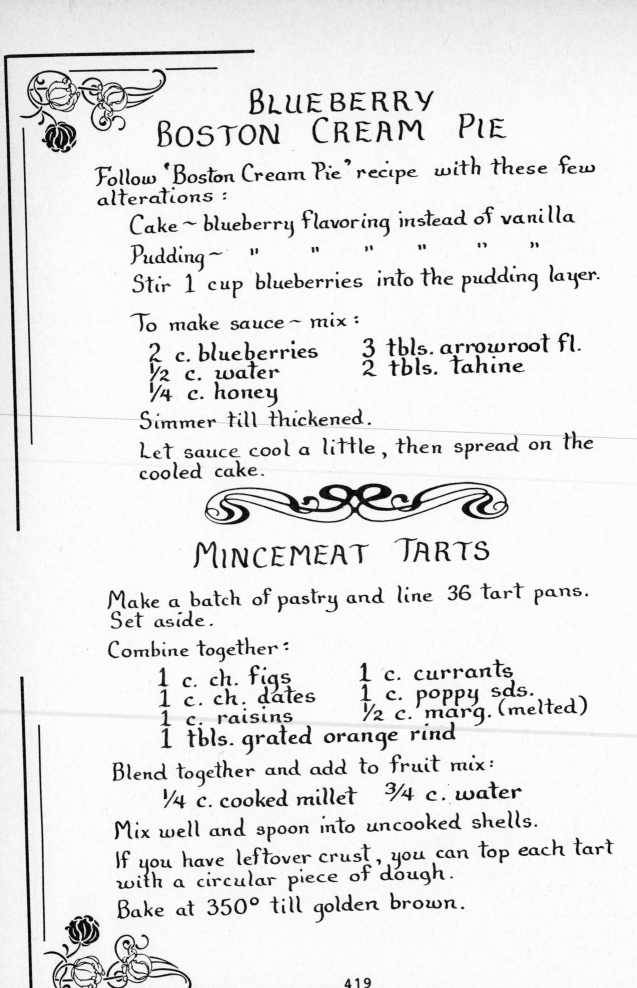

BLUEBERRY BOSTON CREAM PIE

Follow 'Boston Cream Pie' recipe with these few alterations :

Cake ~ blueberry flavoring instead of vanilla

Pudding ~ " " " " " "

Stir 1 cup blueberries into the pudding layer.

To make sauce ~ mix :

2 c. blueberries	3 tbls. arrowroot fl.
1/2 c. water	2 tbls. tahine
1/4 c. honey	

Simmer till thickened.

Let sauce cool a little, then spread on the cooled cake.

MINCEMEAT TARTS

Make a batch of pastry and line 36 tart pans. Set aside.

Combine together :

1 c. ch. figs	1 c. currants
1 c. ch. dates	1 c. poppy sds.
1 c. raisins	1/2 c. marg. (melted)
1 tbls. grated orange rind	

Blend together and add to fruit mix :

1/4 c. cooked millet   3/4 c. water

Mix well and spoon into uncooked shells.

If you have leftover crust, you can top each tart with a circular piece of dough.

Bake at 350° till golden brown.

ORANGE CUSTARD PIE

First make: 2 cups Tofu Whip Cream #2
Chill for 1 hour.

Prepare 'graham cracker crumb crust' for 2 pies.
Bake and set aside to cool.

Simmer in a pot for 15 min. :

6 c. orange juice   8 tbls. agar agar
¼ c. honey   pinch of salt
grated rind of 1 orange or lemon

Let orange juice cool for 30 min.
Blend till well aerated.
Let cool in a large glass or steel bowl.

When mixture has started to gel (40~60 min.),
add the tofu whip cream and beat for 1~2 min.
with a wire wisk. Pour into the cooked pie
crusts and chill.

This can be made using pineapple, cherry, pear,
or most any other type of fruit juice.

BUTTER TARTS

Prepare dough and fill 16 tart pans. Set aside.

Wash: 1 c. raisins (or currants).

Scald with boiling water. Let soak for 10 min.

While the fruit is stewing, combine:

⅔ c. honey   ½ tsp. vanilla
3 tbls. marg.   ¼ tsp. nutmeg
1 egg (beaten)   1 tbls. flour

Drain fruit well and add the honey mixture while
fruit is still hot.

Spoon filling into the uncooked tart shells and
bake at 350° for 25 min.

PHEYLONIAN PINE TARTS

We always make a good size batch of these at Christmas.

Being as these are a special occasion treat, use your best pastry, such as "Shanola's Danish Pastry." Fill 36 tart pans with crust and bake till golden.

To prepare filling, combine in a saucepan:

8 c. water	4 tbls. agar agar
1 c. millet	1 tbls. almond ext.
½ c. maple syrup	or vanilla ext.
4 tbls. marg.	¼ tsp. salt

Bring to a boil and simmer for 30 min.

When cooked, blend pudding and fill tart shells 4/5TH full. Let cool and prepare topping.

In a cast iron skillet, melt:

    ¼ c. marg (or butter)

Add: 2 c. pine nuts   ½ c. maple syrup

Simmer on a low heat and stir constantly. Cook till golden brown. Be careful they don't burn because they sure are expensive.

Sprinkle with Grand Marnier (optional), stir well, and spoon a little on each tart, making sure each gets an equal portion of nuts and sauce.

These are delightful treats to have on hand for family and friends at special times of the year like Christmas, Thankgiving and Easter.

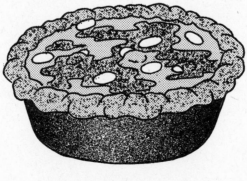

Peach Tarts au Grand Marnier

Prepare dough and line 16 tart pans. Fork the dough (so it won't puff) and bake at 325° till golden brown.

Blanch:

    8 ripe peaches (drop into boiling water and simmer till the skins slip off easily.)

Cut peaches from the pits in ¼" slices.

Combine in a pot:

    peach slices   ¼ c. maple syrup
    ¼ c. water

Simmer with a lid on for 15 min.

Meantime ,, combine:

    ½ c. soy milk
    ¼ c. Grand Marnier
    1 tbls. arrowroot flour

Stir into the peaches and simmer till thickened. Let mixture cool for 20 min.

Pour into cooked tart shells and chill.

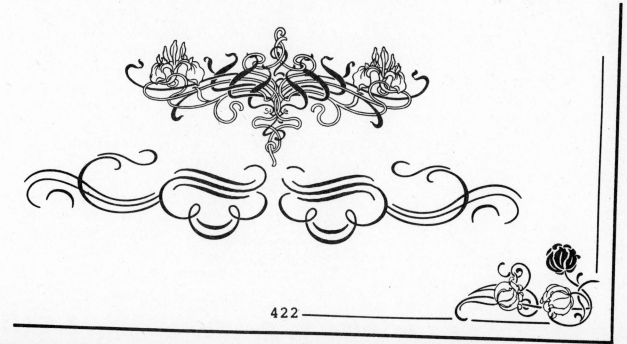

Pie Crusts

We have presented a number of different types of pie dough,,,from the very rich, to simple and wholesome. The recipes are essentially straightforward, however, there are a few points in general about pie crust which I have not mentioned within each recipe.

- All dry ingredients and wet ingredients should be thoroughly mixed before being combined. When they are mixed, the wet should always be poured into the dry.

- When mixing the dry ingredients, mix the oil (or soy margarine) into the flour thoroughly. Do this by rubbing handfuls between your hands. When mixed, a squeezed handful should stick together in a ball.

- If there are eggs in the liquid ingredients, they should be well beaten before being added to the other liquid ingredients.

- The most important step in making pie dough is combining the wet and dry to form the dough. It needs to be consistant, yet you don't want to knead the dough at all. Over-handling or overworking of pie dough makes it tough and unflaky.

- Pour a small amount of the liquid into the dry and stir it in gently with your finger. (Purse your hand with fingers spread like a garden claw is.) Stir only till the liquid is absorbed. Add more liquid and repeat while the dough is moist enough to form a soft ball. Only use enough liquid as you need to hold it together. Often, some of the dough will naturally form grapefruit-sized balls as you work it. These can be removed as they form. Continue adding liquid till all is done.

- Most dough should be refrigerated for an hour or so before using, but it is not necessary.

- Pie dough freezes quite well,,,particularly Shanola's Danish Pastry or the less rich Danish pastry. Whenever I make pastry, I make a triple or quadruple batch and freeze some. It has come in handy countless times when we had family or friends drop in unexpectedly. Freeze in plastic bags or containers.

SHANOLA'S DANISH PASTRY

Shanola's pies are truly the best I've ever tasted, and whenever I use this, or her "less rich" danish pastry, I've never been dissappointed. This is a rich pastry that is light and flaky and melts in your mouth. Excellent for specialty desserts.

Dissolve : 3 tbsp. honey
      in   ½ c. lukewarm water

Sprinkle with :

     1 tbsp. dry active yeast

Let stand for 10 min.

Meantime, sift :

     2 c. flour   ½ tsp. salt

Shred on a fine grater, into the flour :

    ½ lb. chilled butter or frozen marg.

(after every few passes on the grater, mix the flour into the grated marg. or butter.)

Once all is shredded, work flour between your hands until there are no lumps.

Beat : 1 egg

Add to yeast mixture.

Add liquid to the flour, a little at a time ,, working with fingers. As lumps form, set them aside and add more liquid to the remaining flour. Repeat until all is dough. Gently press dough lumps into one ball, shape lightly, but do not knead.

Let chill for 1 hr.

Dough is now ready for whatever you have in mind.

If you only need half the dough, place the remainder in a plastic bag or container and refrigerate or freeze.

Less Rich Danish Pastry
(DOUBLE BATCH)

A very good pastry ,, not quite as rich as the previous recipe , yet it is light and flaky.

Dissolve together :
- 4 tbsp. honey
- 1¼ c. lukewarm water

Sprinkle into water :
- 1 tbsp. dry active yeast

Let stand for 10 min.

Meanwhile, sift together :
- 5 c. flour
- ½ tsp. salt

Shred into the flour :
- 1 cup frozen marg. or chilled butter

Beat and add to the yeast mixture :
- 2 eggs

Add liquid mix to the flour a little at a time and form into a soft ball. Chill for 1 hr.

YEAST RAISED CRUST

A good all round crust, be it for dessert or part of a main meal. It is light, yet not too sweet.

Dissolve : 2 tbsp. honey

     in : 1¼ c. lukewarm water

Sprinkle in : 1 tsp. dry active yeast

Let stand 10 min.

Sift together :

       5 c. flour   1 tsp. salt

Form a well in the flour and add :

     ⅔ c. oil

Work the oil into the flour until no lumps remain.

Beat and add to the yeast mixture :

     2 eggs   2 tbsp. honey (opt.)

Work liquid into the flour to form dough. Do not knead dough. Chill.

SLIGHTLY RAISED VERSION

Sift together :

     2 c. flour   ½ tsp. salt

     1 tsp. bak. pwd.

Mix in a separate bowl :

     1 egg (beaten)   ¼ c. oil

Add liquid to flour mix and work with your hands till well crumbled.

Sprinkle with cold water, while mixing with fingers. Add only enough water to form a soft ball. Do not knead. Roll to desired size and thickness.

Because of the baking pwd., this dough should be used when made. Cook remaining strips for munching.

GRAHAM CRACKER CRUST

This recipe makes 2 graham cracker crumb crusts.

Using graham crackers,, crush with a rolling pin till you have :
>   2 cups of crumbs

Combine :
>   ¼ c. oil or melted margarine
>   2 tbls. honey or maple syrup
>   1 tsp. lemon

Pour liquid into graham crumbs and mix till crumbly again.

Divide in half and press into 9" pie plates.

Bake for 8~10 min. at 325°, or pour in a filling and bake till cooked.

UNLEAVENED PIE CRUST

Sift together :
>   2 c. flour   ½ tsp. salt

Add to flour :
>   ⅓ c. oil

Work flour with hands till there are no lumps.

Sprinkle with cold water while mixing with your fingers. Add only enough to form a soft dough.

Do not knead. Chill or use immediately.

PUDDINGS

These are some of the healthiest desserts that can be made. For special occasions, when you have guests, pour 'em into a cooked pie shell.

These puddings contain no milk products. Most are made using millet as the base, combined with different fruits and flavorings while others utilize the versatility of tofu.

MILLET BASED PUDDINGS

Iilah originated this millet base pudding as a dairy free filling for his Christmas Tarts a la Pine Nuts. His mother can not eat any milk products and yet he needed a custard type pudding. Well, what Iilah came up with was so good,.. it has since revolutionized many of our recipes, from sauces and main courses to a whole series of delightfully tasty puddings.

Any millet cream pudding can be prepared in about 10 mins. working time,, while doing other cooking.

This recipe will give you the basic proportions to which you can create many different puddings.

VANILLA PUDDING

Combine in a saucepan:

8 c. water	1 tbls. vanilla ext.
1 c. millet	2 tbls. marg. (opt.)
½ c. honey	¼ tsp. salt
4 tbls. agar agar	

Bring to a boil and simmer for 30 mins.
Cool for 15 mins.
Blend 2-3 cups at a time. Re-mix the blended batches and pour into pudding cups.

To list the many different puddings we make with this millet base would only be a duplication of the many recipes listed under our 'Cream Pie' section.

Once you understand the proportions of this pudding, you can alter it to make whatever flavoring of dessert you can imagine.

Alter the proportions according to what you are adding:

- Use less honey if adding a sweet fruit.
- Use less water if using juicy fruit.
- Use more sweetener if using sour fruit.

Any of these 'Pie Fillings' from the 'Pie Section' can be simply poured into pudding cups.

Do some experimenting. I'm sure you'll find some interesting combinations yourself.

Puddings can be garnished with:
  grated coconut
  tofu whip cream
  fresh fruit
  roasted nuts

TOFU PUDDINGS

Each of these puddings are made with tofu and fresh fruit or flavoring,, using agar agar as a setting agent.

STRAWBERRY ~ TOFU PUDDING

Blend: 4 c. strawberries
         (add ¼ c. water if needed)
Pour blended strawberries into a bowl.
Boil: 1 c. water (or apple juice)
         5 tbsp. agar agar
         ½ c. honey
Simmer till agar is dissolved (approx. 10 min.)
Add blended strawberries to agar mixture. Stir.
Liquify in blender:
         1 ~ 9 oz. cube of tofu
         ½ of the strawberry mixture
Pour pudding into bowls and repeat with another cube of tofu and the remaining strawberry mix. Chill.

PINEAPPLE ~ TOFU PUDDING

Combine in a saucepan:
         1 19 oz. can of crushed pineapple
         1 c. water
         4 tbsp. agar agar
Bring to a boil and simmer for 10 mins.
Add: ¼ c. honey
         1 tbls. lemon juice
Use: 2   9 oz. cubes of tofu
Blend 1 cube of tofu with half the pineapple mix. Pour into bowls. Repeat with other half. Garnish with roasted coconut.

MAPLE VANILLA PUDDING

Simmer in a saucepan for 10 min. :

      3 c. water   4 tbls. agar agar

Remove from heat and add :

      ½ c. maple syrup
      1 tbls. vanilla extract

Use : 2   9 oz. cubes of tofu

Blend half of the agar mix with 1 chunk of tofu. Repeat with other half.

Pour into dessert bowls.   Top with butter-roasted walnut halves. Chill .

CAROB TOFU PUDDING

Simmer in a saucepan for 10 min. :

      3 c. water   4 tbls. agar agar
      ½ c. carob pwd.

Remove from heat and add :

      ½ c. honey   2 tsp. lemon juice

Use : 2   9 oz. cubes of tofu

Blend half the agar mix with 1 chunk of tofu. Repeat and pour into bowls.

Top with Tofu Whip Cream and chill.

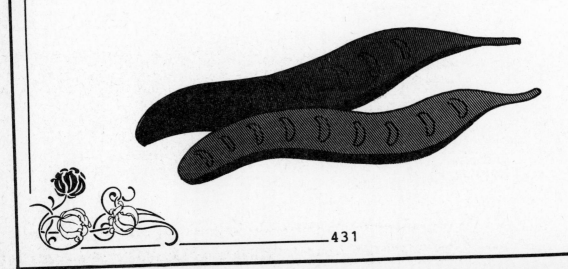

BLUEBERRY - TOFU PUDDING

Boil in a saucepan for 10 min.:

1 c. water   5 tbls. agar agar

Combine in a blender :
1 c. blueberries
½ c. honey   (or less to taste)

Add boiled water and agar to blueberries, blend.

Remove half of the mixture from the blender.

Use: 2   9 oz. cubes of tofu

Blend 1 cube of tofu with each half of the blueberry mixture.

Fold into the pudding:
½ c. blueberries

Pour into bowls and chill.

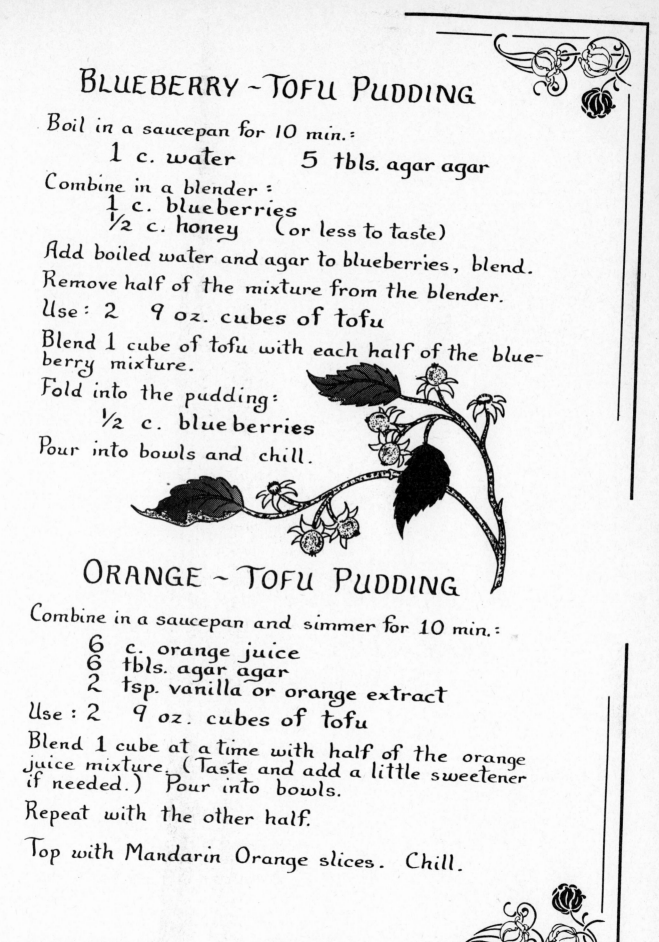

ORANGE ~ TOFU PUDDING

Combine in a saucepan and simmer for 10 min.:

6 c. orange juice
6 tbls. agar agar
2 tsp. vanilla or orange extract

Use : 2   9 oz. cubes of tofu

Blend 1 cube at a time with half of the orange juice mixture. (Taste and add a little sweetener if needed.) Pour into bowls.

Repeat with the other half.

Top with Mandarin Orange slices. Chill.

PARFAITS

These are attractive desserts to serve and fun to eat.

They can be made in a hundred and one different combinations.

To give you ideas, we have listed some of our most favorite combinations. To make these we utilize combinations of the different cream puddings, tofu puddings and jellos. The addition of fresh fruit or nuts between the layers is very nice also.

Ideally,, these are most attractive served in parfait glasses,,however, any tall thin glass or clear, hard plastic cup will do.

List of Puddings to Alternate

Vanilla Cream	Strawberry Tofu
Carob Cream	Orange Tofu
Carob~Mint Cr.	Pineapple Tofu
Lemon Cream	Blueberry Tofu
Coconut Cream	Cherry Pie Filling
Banana Cream	Apple Jello (or any variety of fresh juice jello)
Pineapple Cream	
Mocha Cream	

When making parfaits:

~ use half or $2/3^{RD}$ of choosen recipes if you think the whole quantity of each will make too much.

~ keep each mixture warm till ready to layer so they don't cool and set.

~ let each layer cool just long enough so the next layer will not mix.

~ always finish with fruit, nuts or something attractive as a final layer on top.

~ repeat each layer 2 or 3 times.

Parfait Combinations

★ Carob Cream Pudding
kiwi slices
roasted coconut

Maple-Vanilla Pudding
kiwi slices
roasted coconut

Repeat

★ Carob-Mint Pudding
banana slices

Coconut Cream Pudding
banana slices

Repeat and finish with
Carob filling, trimmed
with upright banana
slices.

★ Blueberry Tofu Pudding
blueberries

Vanilla Cream
blueberries

Repeat, ending with the
vanilla cream pudding
and blueberries

★ Strawberry Pudding
strawberry slices

Pineapple Pudding
strawberry slices

Repeat ending with
vanilla pudding and
strawberries

★ Maple-Vanilla Pudding
honey-buttered walnuts

Cherry Pie Filling
honey-buttered walnuts

Repeat

★ Lemon Cream Pudding
kiwi slices

Orange Tofu Pudding
kiwi slices

Repeat

★ Banana Cream Pudding
Carob chips

Carob Pudding
carob chips

Repeat

★ Grape Jello
green seedless grapes
(halved)

Vanilla Cream Pudding
green seedless grapes
(halved)

Repeat

Parfaits, cont.,

★ Pineapple Tofu Pudding
fresh cherry halves

Cherry Tofu Pudding
fresh cherry halves

Repeat and top with
tofu whip cream

★ Orange Jello
roasted coconut

Lemon Cream Pudding
roasted coconut

Repeat

★ Blueberry Jello
fresh blueberries

Tofu Whip Cream
fresh blueberries

Repeat

★ Mocha Pudding
honey-roasted pine nuts

Maple-Vanilla Pudding
honey-roasted pine nuts

Repeat

★ Apple Jello
strawberry slices

Apple Tofu Whip Cream
strawberry slices

Repeat

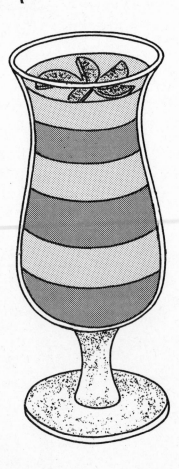

RICE PUDDING

An age old favorite which is very healthy „for young and old alike.

Keeps well in the refrigerator for many days.

In a large bowl, mix:

6 c. cooked rice   2 eggs (beaten)
1 c. soy milk pwd.   1 tbls. vanilla
4 c. water   1 c. raisins (washed)
¼ to 1 c. honey (to your own taste)

Mix well and turn into an oiled casserole dish.

Bake at 400° for approx. 40 min., or till solid throughout and golden brown on top.

Serve with fresh nut milk, soy milk or a scoop of tofu whip cream.

APPLE CANTON
(APPLE JELLO)

One of our favorite desserts, as it is light and nutritious. When set, it can be eaten as is, with fresh fruit, granola and soymilk or with tofu whip cream.

Boil: 4 c. apple juice
      4 tbls. agar agar

Let simmer with a lid for 5~7 minutes, till the agar is completely dissolved.

Pour into dessert bowls and let cool to room temperature, then refrigerate.

Any fruit juice or combination of juices can be used in this dessert. Experiment and have fun with your own ideas.

How Sweet It Is

Sugar vs. Honey, Natural Malts and Syrup, Amasake, Maple
        Syrup, etc.

In most recipes involving a sweetener, I have stipulated either honey or maple syrup.

Sweeteners of all types are essentially natural (with the exception of artificial sweeteners) in that they are all derived from a plant source,, however, what constitutes a healthful sweetener is dependent upon the process by which it is produced and how it reacts internally.

White sugar, fructose, and glucose, in general, are known and considered to be highly refined products which retain none or very little of their original source. They consist of concentrated individual sugars which have been isolated and fractioned from their whole food source by processes of enzymatic or chemical hydrolysis, heating, filtration, or separation methods. Sweeteners of this nature are very quickly absorbed into the blood stream and can cause rapid upsurges in the blood sugar levels, which are inevitably followed by a dramatic drop in blood sugar causing depression and the need (or craving) for more sweet. Because of these metabolic fluctuations, it contributes to increased blood pressure, high possibility of blood clotting, and numerous other degenerative diseases. These sweeteners have negligible nutritional value.

Honey and maple syrup are the most widely used forerunners of the natural sweeteners. Although more wholesome by nature and by process,, they are both very concentrated sweets which are not terribly well balanced and should be used in moderation.

Alternative sweeteners such as barley malt and rice syrup are becoming increasingly popular for a variety of reasons. They are derived from a whole grain source,, are more naturally produced with minimal tampering,, and when consumed, have a gentle, more balanced effect on the body's metabolism,, supplying a prolonged energy source without the immediate blood sugar increase which other sweeteners have.

Either of these sweeteners can be substituted in most recipes,, however, volume for volume, these are less sweet. If you prefer your desserts lightly sweetened,, just substitute the same quantity,,, or for a comparable sweetness, increase the volume by half and decrease the water or some other liquid ingredient by half the amount of extra malt or syrup.

Amasake is relatively new on the market. It is a grain sweetener made by innoculating cooked brown rice and water with rice Koji. This is allowed to ferment during which time the carbohydrates are converted to a subtle sweetness. This mixture is then blended to produce a naturally sweet, thick, pulpy liquid. This can be used as a replacement for honey or maple syrup in recipes, or can be diluted and strained to make some very pleasant drinks. If being used as a substitute for honey,, make similar alterations as described for substituting barley malt or rice syrup. It is perhaps the most balanced of all sweeteners, but takes a little getting used to.

And then there are fruit juices. We have used juices as the sole sweetener in various different desserts. This not only supplies the sweetness,, it usually is done to add a particular flavour,, e.g. apple, cherry, pineapple, etc.

Beware of artificial sweeteners. They are completely synthetic and are extremely detrimental to your health. Ironically,, the producers of these sweeteners advise that they should not be used by children under 6 or pregnant women,,, yet they are "safe" for everyone else. I am not aware of the chemical composition of the many different sweeteners,, but the original one, Aspartame, was discovered and patented by a man who was a refrigerant mechanic. He accidentally had some refrigerant fluid touch his lips, and when he tasted it, it was extremely sweet,,, hence, a new industry was started.

To summarize,,, all sweeteners should be used moderately in accordance to what you feel comfortable cooking with.

CAKES

Cake is a delicacy which always hits the hearts and stomachs of every family, especially when it's light, fluffy and just sweet enough so's you can eat more than 1 piece.

The cake recipes in this book are not like "Duncan-Hines" because we make them with whole grain flours and a minimal amount of alum-free baking pwd., but they sure are good.

Each recipe simply calls for 'Flour'. We use primarily durham flour as it is non-allergenic and mucus-free, however, you can use soft, unbleached, whole wheat flour or whatever else is your preference.

A Bit about Cakes

Use a light oil, such as sunflower or safflower, so it won't impart undesirable flavors.

When mixing the cake ingredients always add the liquid to the dry part. 'Make a well' in the flour and add some liquid, stir or beat, moving always in one direction. Add more liquid and continue beating, repeat till all is added and batter is well mixed and creamy.

Always have the oven preheated so the cake can be put to bake as soon as it is mixed. Baking pwd. starts working as soon as it's mixed with the liquid and the cake will lose some of its levity if it sits around.

Even alum free baking powder is not a healthy ingredient,, however, used in moderation once or thrice a month, won't kill you. You should never use commercial baking pwd. because it contains aluminum oxide which is quite toxic and accumulates in your system because the body can't expel it. There are baking powders without alum, available through most health food stores.

This first recipe is Lilah's mother's basic cake recipe which we simply call "Shanola's Plain Cake", but don't let the name fool you, because its such a good recipe that we use it as the base for all other varieties of cakes that we make.

SHANOLA'S PLAIN CAKE

Sift into a large enough bowl:
2 c. flour	⅛ tsp. salt
2 tsp. baking pwd. (heaped)	

Beat till fluffy and bubbly:

2 eggs

Add to beaten eggs:
1 c. honey	¼ c. oil

Beat well and add:
¾ c. soy milk	2 tsp. vanilla ext.

Add liquid mix to the dry ingredients. Stir till well mixed and no lumps remain.

Pour into an oiled cake pan (9" x 9") or a bread loaf pan.

Bake at 350° for 35~40 min. (knife test)

LESS SWEET PLAIN CAKE

We use this basic recipe,, which has less honey, when we are making a cake with fruit added, so it won't be overly sweet.

Follow 'Shanola's Plain Cake' recipe and reduce the honey to:

½ c. honey

and increase the soy milk to:

1 c. soy milk

441

PINEAPPLE UPSIDE~DOWN CAKE

Open: a 19 oz. can of pineapple rings (or prepare the equivalent amount from a fresh pineapple).
Retain all liquid in a measuring cup.

Combine in a 9"x 13" cake pan:

¼ c. marg.　　　½ c. honey

Place in preheating oven till melted.

Meantime, sift together:

4 c. flour　　　½ tsp. salt
4 tsp. bak. pwd.

Mix separately:

6 eggs　　　2 tsp. vanilla ext.
⅔ c. honey　　2 c. liquid (use pineapple
½ c. oil　　　　juice, plus soy milk
　　　　　　　　for the difference)

Pour liquid into the dry ingredients, mix well.

Arrange pineapple slices in the melted honey and marg. and sprinkle with:

¼ c. flour

Pour batter over the pineapple slices, level evenly.

Bake at 350° for 30~40 min.

Let cake cool completely, then turn upside~down onto a serving tray.

Serve as is,, with a natural vanilla icecream,, or with a hot lemon sauce.

To add a creative, extra touch for a special occasion,, dry roast and tamari 1 cup of walnut halves and arrange in the spaces around the pineapple slices, before you add the batter.

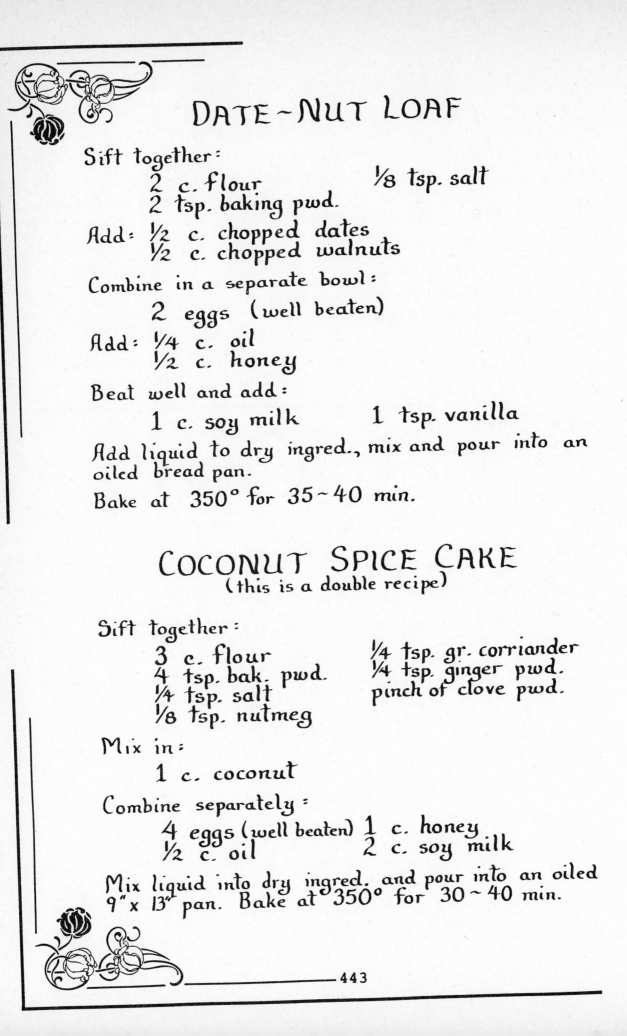

DATE~NUT LOAF

Sift together:
    2 c. flour   ⅛ tsp. salt
    2 tsp. baking pwd.

Add: ½ c. chopped dates
      ½ c. chopped walnuts

Combine in a separate bowl:
    2 eggs (well beaten)

Add: ¼ c. oil
      ½ c. honey

Beat well and add:
    1 c. soy milk   1 tsp. vanilla

Add liquid to dry ingred., mix and pour into an oiled bread pan.

Bake at 350° for 35~40 min.

COCONUT SPICE CAKE
(this is a double recipe)

Sift together:
    3 c. flour   ¼ tsp. gr. corriander
    4 tsp. bak. pwd.   ¼ tsp. ginger pwd.
    ¼ tsp. salt   pinch of clove pwd.
    ⅛ tsp. nutmeg

Mix in:
    1 c. coconut

Combine separately:
    4 eggs (well beaten) 1 c. honey
    ½ c. oil   2 c. soy milk

Mix liquid into dry ingred. and pour into an oiled 9"x 13" pan. Bake at 350° for 30~40 min.

SHANOLA'S MERINGUE CAKE

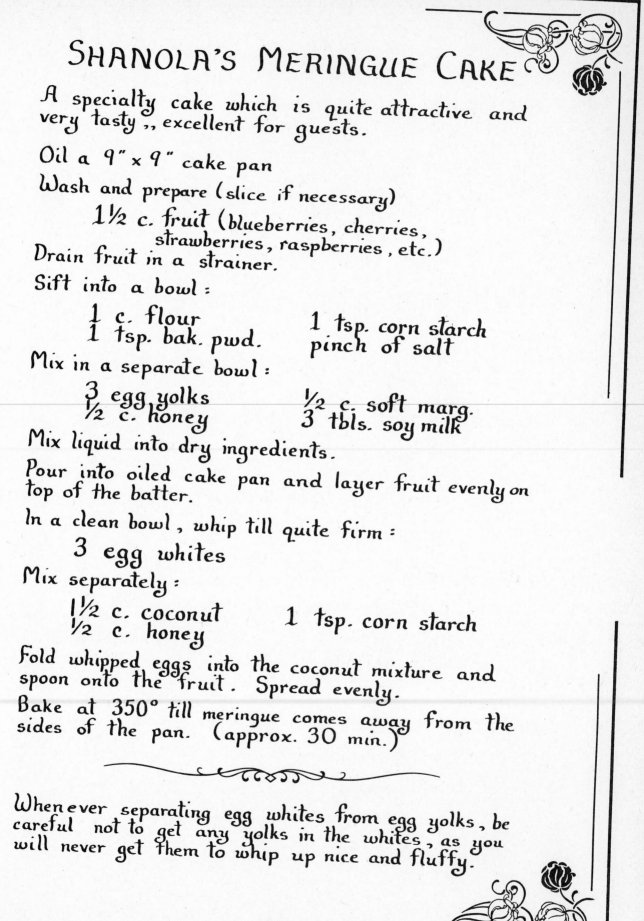

A specialty cake which is quite attractive and very tasty,, excellent for guests.

Oil a 9" x 9" cake pan

Wash and prepare (slice if necessary)

    1½ c. fruit (blueberries, cherries, strawberries, raspberries, etc.)

Drain fruit in a strainer.

Sift into a bowl:

1 c. flour	1 tsp. corn starch
1 tsp. bak. pwd.	pinch of salt

Mix in a separate bowl:

3 egg yolks	½ c. soft marg.
½ c. honey	3 tbls. soy milk

Mix liquid into dry ingredients.

Pour into oiled cake pan and layer fruit evenly on top of the batter.

In a clean bowl, whip till quite firm:

    3 egg whites

Mix separately:

1½ c. coconut	1 tsp. corn starch
½ c. honey	

Fold whipped eggs into the coconut mixture and spoon onto the fruit. Spread evenly.

Bake at 350° till meringue comes away from the sides of the pan. (approx. 30 min.)

Whenever separating egg whites from egg yolks, be careful not to get any yolks in the whites, as you will never get them to whip up nice and fluffy.

SPONGE CAKE

A very rich cake „ but one worth having once or twice a year.

You need a sponge cake pan for this recipe.

Sift together :

    1½ c. pastry fl.   ½ tsp. salt
    1½ tsp. bak. pwd.

Separate and beat well :

    3/4 c. egg yolks (approx. 8 eggs)
    1 whole egg

Add to eggs :

    3/4 c. honey   1 tbsp. orange juice
    1 tbsp. grated orange rind

Bring to a boil :

    3/4 c. water

Sprinkle dry ingredients into liquid mixture and fold in gently (Do not stir or beat.)

Add boiling water and stir just till liquid is mixed.

Pour into sponge cake pan and bake at 325° for 55 ~ 60 min.

Cool well and turn onto a serving platter.

A sponge cake is delicious as is, however it can be trimmed with numerous toppings:

    Hot Lemon Sauce
    Fruit Glaze
    Strawberry Cream Sauce
    Lemon Glaze

SPICE CAKE

Light and spicy, not too sweet.
Preheat oven to 350°.
Combine in a bowl:

  2 eggs (well beaten)

Continue beating and add:

  ½ c. honey   ¼ c. oil

Then add:

  1 c. soy milk   2 tsp. vanilla

Sift into a separate bowl:

  2 c. flour (durham or whole wheat pastry)
  2 tsp. baking pwd.
  ½ c. walnuts   ¼ tsp. ginger pwd.
  1 tsp. cinnamon   ¼ tsp. salt
  1 tsp. corriander   pinch of clove pwd.
  ¼ tsp. gr. nutmeg

Add liquid into the dry ingredients. Beat till well combined. Pour into an oiled and floured 9" cake pan.

Bake till cooked (approx. 30~40 min) Knife test.

BRAN MUFFINS

Mix: 2 eggs (beaten)   ¼ c. oil
  ⅓ c. honey   2 c. soy milk
  ¼ c. molasses

Sift: 2 c. flour   ½ tsp. salt
  3 tsp. baking pwd.

Add: 2 c. bran   ¾ c. raisins
  2 c. grated carrot

Combine wet and dry ingredients and spoon into oiled muffin tins. Bake at 350° for 20~25 mins. Cool before removing from pans.

STRAWBERRY SHORTCAKES

A light, fluffy cake batter designed to be cooked in a shortbread mold pan. When cooked, serve with strawberries and tofu whip cream.

Sift together:

3 c. flour	1/8 tsp. salt
3 tsp. bak. pwd.	

Combine separately:

3 eggs	1 c. honey
1/2 c. oil	1 c. soy milk
	1 tsp. vanilla ext.

Mix liquid into the dry ingredients.

Spoon into cake molds and bake at 325° for 15 to 20 min., till golden. Cool before removing.

CARROT~BRAN MUFFINS

The addition of carrot makes for a nice moist muffin.

Sift together:

2 c. flour	1/4 tsp. salt
3 tsp. bak. pwd.	

Add and mix into sifted flour:

2 c. bran	3/4 c. raisins (washed)
2 c. carrot (fine grate)	

Combine separately:

4 eggs (well beaten)	1/2 c. oil
1/3 c. honey	1 3/4 c. soy milk
1/4 c. molasses	

Oil muffin tins or line with cup cake papers.

Add liquid into the dry ingredients. Mix well and spoon into tins. Fill 2/3 full.
Bake at 350° for 20~30 min.

BANANA BREAD

I could never figure why they call this bread, because it always tastes like cake to me.

Preheat oven to 350°.

Combine in a bowl :

4 c. flour
3/4 c. soy milk pwd.

2 tbls. baking pwd.
1/2 tsp. salt

Whip till fluffy :

2 eggs

Add: 3/4 c. oil

1/2 c. honey

Blend: 1 1/2 c. banana

3/4 c. water

Combine liquid ingredients and mix well.

Oil and flour 2 bread loaf pans.

Mix the liquid ingredients into the dry. Pour into the pans. Bake till done (approx 30~40 min.)

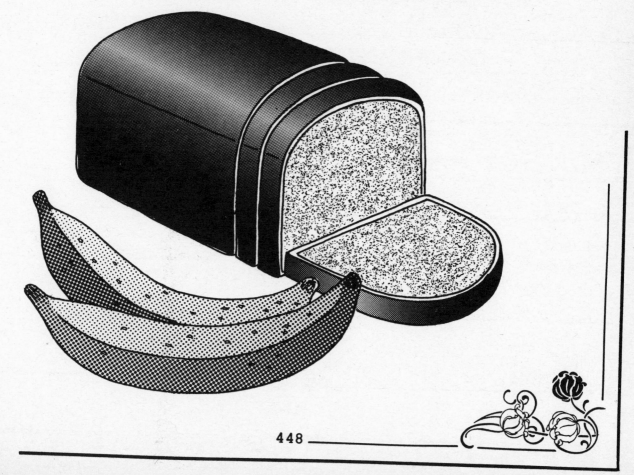

SHANOLA'S CARROT CAKE

Moist, nutty and just nicely sweet.

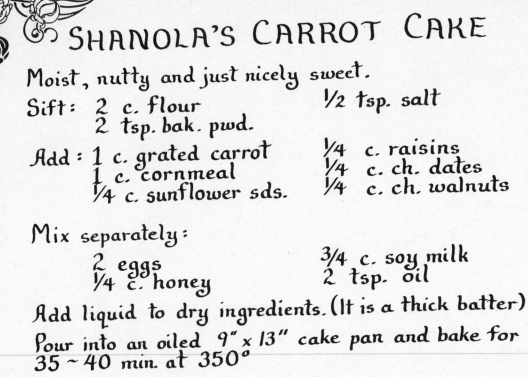

Sift: 2 c. flour   ½ tsp. salt
       2 tsp. bak. pwd.

Add : 1 c. grated carrot   ¼ c. raisins
       1 c. cornmeal   ¼ c. ch. dates
       ¼ c. sunflower sds.   ¼ c. ch. walnuts

Mix separately:

       2 eggs   ¾ c. soy milk
       ¼ c. honey   2 tsp. oil

Add liquid to dry ingredients. (It is a thick batter)
Pour into an oiled 9" x 13" cake pan and bake for
35 ~ 40 min. at 350°

ZUCCHINI ZIP LOAVES

Sift together :
       1½ c. flour (durham)   1 tsp. bak. soda
       1 c. whole wheat fl.   ½ tsp. bak. pwd.
       2 tsp. nutmeg   1 tsp. salt

Add : ½ c. wheat germ   ½ c. ch. nuts

Mix separately:

       3 eggs (well beaten)   1 tsp. vanilla ext.
       1 c. oil   1 c. honey
       2 c. zucchini (grated on a ¼" grate).

Add liquid to the dry ingredients , mix well.
Pour into an oiled bread loaf pan and bake at 350°
for 1 hour.

In the summer, grate and bag 2 cup batches of fresh
zucchini from your garden. Freeze them and utilize
in this recipe as a treat for your family year round.

GLAZED PINEAPPLE SQUARES

Open and drain thoroughly, retaining all the juice:

1 19 oz. can crushed pineapple

Squeeze any excess juice from the pineapple as extra moisture will make the cake bottom soggy.

Oil a 9" x 9" cake pan and arrange pineapple in bottom.

Sift together:

2 c. flour	¼ tsp. salt
2 tsp. bak. pwd.	

Mix separetely:

2 eggs (well beaten)	1 tsp. vanilla ext.
½ c. honey	1 c. liquid (use ⅓ of
¼ c. oil	the pineapple juice and
	soy milk for the difference)

Add liquid to dry ingredients and mix well.
Pour batter over pineapple and bake at 350° for 30 to 40 min. Remove from oven and let cool for 30 min.

Put into a small saucepan and heat:

remaining pineapple j.	1 tbsp. honey

Mix in a cup:

¼ c. water	2 tbsp. arrowroot fl.

Add to the pineapple juice and simmer till thickened and clear.
Let cool for five min., then pour evenly over the top of the cake. Let cool before cutting into squares.

Variations of the Above

Use this basic recipe with any canned or fresh fruit like :

blueberries	peaches	apples
cherries	pears	

In the case of fresh fruit where you have no liquid, simply blend some fruit with water, sweeten and thicken.

BLUEBERRY COUS COUS CAKE

This is a cake of a different sort. It is an unleavened dessert, so it is ideal for people who find baking pwd. not suitable in their diet. Although it has a heavier texture than any other type of 'cake', it is very good tasting. It is lightly sweetened, and all things considered, quite a healthy dessert treat.

This recipe utilizes an ingredient called 'cous cous.' It is a product similar to bulghur that is made from either whole wheat or durham wheat. Both are suitable, however, we prefer the type made of durham wheat.

In a saucepan, bring to a boil:

    6 c. apple juice or apple cider
    1 tsp. vanilla extract

Oil a 9" x 13" cake pan.

Sprinkle bottom of pan with:

    1 c. washed raisins
    ½ c. lightly roasted sesame sds.

When the apple juice is boiling, add:

    3 c. cous cous   ⅛ tsp. salt
    2 c. blueberries

Stir well and pour gently into cake pan.

Bake at 350° till liquid is gone (approx. 20 min.)

While cake is cooling, combine in a saucepan:

    2 c. blueberries   ⅓ c. honey
    1 c. water   3 tbls. arrowroot fl.

Bring to a boil, stirring constantly till thickened and clear. Pour evenly over top of the cous cous cake.

Chill and keep refrigerated.

This recipe can be varied by using many different kinds of fruit.

CARROT SQUARES

A healthy, munchable snack which is not too sweet.

In a large bowl, mix:

3 c. flour   1½ tsp. cinnamon
½ c. ch. walnuts   1 tbsp. bak. pwd.
½ tsp. salt

Mix well and add:

2 c. finely grated carrot

Combine separately:

3 eggs (well beaten)   ⅓ c. honey
⅔ c. oil

Add liquid to dry mixture and stir well. (It is a stiff batter.)

Spread into an oiled 9" x 13" pan.

Bake at 325° for 20~30 min.
When cool, cut into squares.

Bon Apetite, Mes Enfants

Now, don't yawl go getting me wrong with what I'm about to write,,, and know that I'm not on a personal crusade against the ice cream conglomerates or any other food processing plant,,, because, for a fact,,, the stuff put into most of today's commercial ice creams equates the toxic chemicals put into everything else being processed for you and your family. These are just a few of the chemicals proven to be widely used throughout all of the three worlds:

BUTYRALDEHYDE: Is one of the main ingredients of rubber cement,,, and is also used as a nut flavour for nutty ice creams, pies, etc.

AMYL ACETATE: Was originally created to be an oil paint solvent, and has since found its way into the chemical food industry as a cheap, simulated banana flavour, to be used in drinks, pudding, ice cream, etc.

BENZYL ACETATE: Is a nitrate solvent, alchemized into aromatic hydrocarbons, to be used as a powerful cleaning solution in the commercial dry-cleaning business. It is also used as a strawberry flavour in most drinks, popsickles, ice creams, candies, jams, etc., etc.

ALDEHYDE C17: This is an inflammable liquid which is used in aniline dyes, plastics, and rubber. Lately, it can be found in most cherry flavoured ice creams, popsickles, drinks, candies, and syrups.

ETHYL ACETATE: This is a well respected industrial cleaner being used in the leather and

textile business. When used in an unpro-
tected environment, its vapours are known
to cauze cronic lung, liver, and heart
damage,,, yet,,, dear people,,, it's
allowed to be used as a pineapple flavour
in ice creams, frozen drinks, baking,
etc., etc.

PIPERONAL:
This is the main ingredient in a product
designed specifically to kill lice. It
is also sold as a low priced, simulated
vanilla extract available in most food
stores. It is also used in most commercial vanilla ice creams, cookies, cakes,
icings, etc., etc., etc. Obviously,,, it
works,,, because who's got lice today?

DIETHYL GLUCOL:
Now this one takes the cake. Because it
is not only used as an emulsifier for
bulk and texture in most ice creams,,, it
is widely used in place of eggs in many
other commercial products, as well. This
is the same chemical used in antifreeze,
as well as in most paint removers. Ever
wonder why ice creams aren't as cold as
they used to be when you were a kid 30
years ago?

ASPERTAME:
This is a chemical originally manufac-
tured for use as a coolant running
through the pipes of your refrigerator.
A scientist discovered, by accident, that
this chemical possessed a very sweet
taste - Voila,,, low-calorie, artificial
sweetener!

Folks,, I'm not going on with this,,, because these few chemicals being so widely used don't begin to equate the usage of the thousands of other chemicals utilized in the food and drug industry.

All I can say is,,,, "Cancer, anyone?"

The choice is really yours,,,

Go ahead,,, take your kid out for a nice banana split. Prove to 'em you love 'em,,,, heck, one more can't hurt. My God, people, stop,,, please stop askin' for more!

HAMENTASHEN

Prepare a batch of pastry dough (page 426) or use this traditional recipe.

Sift together:

3 c. flour	1/8 tsp. salt
2 tsp. bak. pwd.	

Mix together in a separate bowl:

3 eggs (well beaten)	1/2 c. honey
1 c. oil	3/4 c. water

Add liquid to the dry ingredients. Work gently into a soft dough. Do not knead.
Roll to a 1/4" thickness and cut into 3" rounds.
Fill with a heaped tbsp. of filling. Fold up 4 sides into a pyramid and pinch dough along edges to seal.

HAMENTASHEN FILLING

PRUNE OR DATE FILLING

Combine and stir well:

or
1 lb. stewed prunes (pitted and chopped)
1 lb. dates (pitted, chopped and mixed with 1/4 c. boiling water)

1 c. scalded raisins	
1/2 c. ch. nuts	1/2 c. cooked bulghur
1/2 c. honey (opt.)	juice & rind of 1 lemon

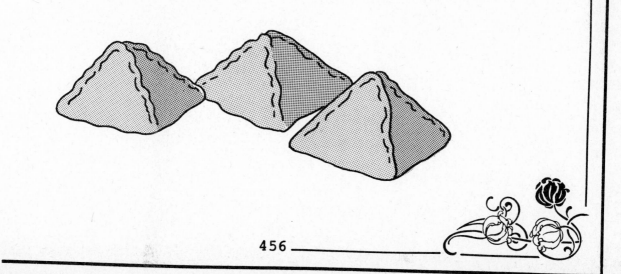

Poppy Seed Filling

Soak overnight :

 2 lb. blue poppy sds.   8 c. boiling water

In the morning, drain well and oven dry slightly.

Add : 1 lb. walnuts

Pass thru a food grinder with the 'nut-butter' attachment on (you want the mixture to come out 'pasty'.)

Stir well.

 1 c. honey   juice of 2 lemons

Mix well and spoon into pastry.

AMASAKE BROWNIES

Moist and flavorful with the subtle sweetness of amasake.

Preheat oven to 350°.

Mix together in a bowl:

 1 egg (well beaten)   ¼ c. oil
 ⅔ c. amasake   1 tsp. vanilla

Mix together :

 1 c. flour   ⅓ c. carob pwd.
 ⅔ c. walnuts   1 tsp. bak. pwd.
  (chopped)

Combine the two mixtures and pour into an oiled 9" x 9" pan. Bake for 25~35 min. Knife test.

SHANOLA'S RAISIN SQUARES

These are great munchables and good lunch box treats as they are not oozy or sticky.

Combine in a saucepan and simmer for 10 min:

    1 c. raisins   ¼ c. honey
    1 c. water

Stir in: 1 egg yolk   1 tsp. vanilla ext.
        1 tbsp. marg.

Simmer for 2 min. Stir occasionally.

Mix: 1 tsp. arrowroot flour
     ¼ c. water

Add to the raisins and simmer till thickened. Turn off the heat and cover to keep warm.

Oil a 9" x 13" cookie tray. Roll ⅛" thick crust and line bottom and sides.

Pour raisin mixture onto crust and spread evenly. Top with another layer of crust. Fork top with a decorative design and bake at 350° till pastry is golden brown. (approx 25~30 min.)

Cool and cut into elongated squares.

Try this recipe using other fruits such as:

     currants   dried apricots (soaked)
     figs   dates

~alter sweetness to taste.

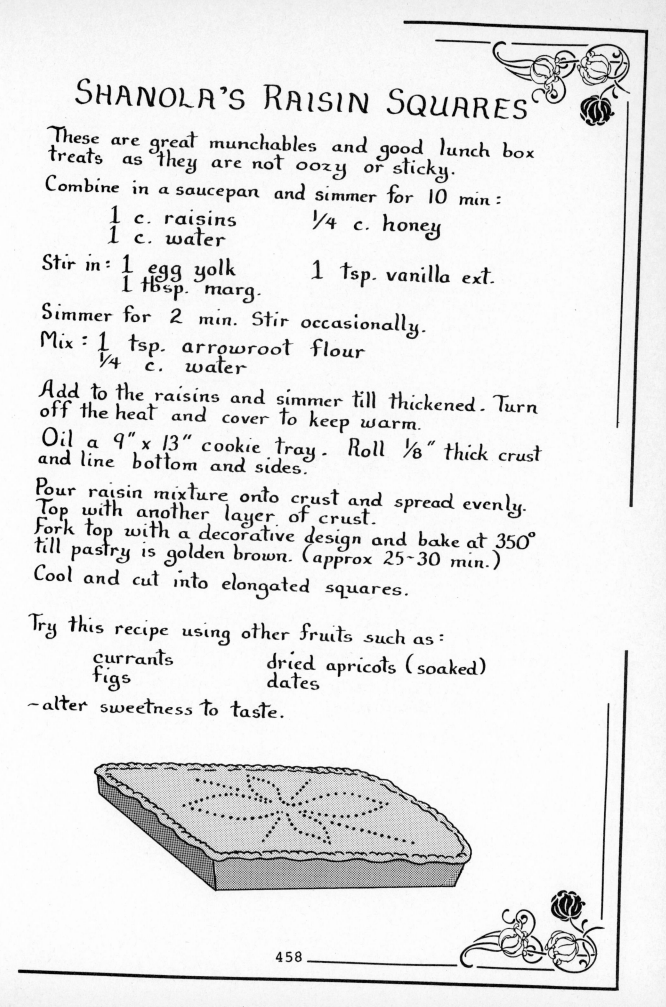

CAROB BROWNIES

Combine together:

1½ c. honey	½ tsp. salt
3/4 c. oil	1 tbsp. lemon juice
1/4 c. tahine	1 tbsp. vanilla
1 egg (well beaten)	

Combine in a separate bowl:

2½ c. flour	1 c. walnuts
1¼ c. carob pwd.	1 tsp. bak. pwd.
3/4 c. coconut	

Add liquid mixture to dry ingredients. Mix well. (It is a very stiff batter.)

Oil a 9" x 13" cake pan and spread mixture evenly in it. Bake at 325° for 30 min.

Watch it doesn't burn. It's hard to tell because of the dark brown color. Knife test for dryness.

POPPY SEED ROLL

Premake: 1 batch of pastry dough.

Simmer: 2 c. blue poppy sds.
2 c. water

When water is boiled off, add:

1 c. honey	1 tbsp. lemon juice
1 c. ch. walnuts	1 tbsp. vanilla
1 tbsp. marg.	

Roll pastry to 12" width about 1/8" thick. Spread with poppy sd. mixture and wrap dough into a roll. Place on an oiled tray and cut 2/3 of the way thru at 1" intervals. Bend roll into a half moon shape to spread each cut. Bake at 350° till golden.

CARROT SQUARES

There are a number of innovative recipes for utilizing the pulp left over from juicing carrots. This is one of our favorites.

When you know you are going to make carrot squares, you don't have to extract as much of the juice, turn off the machine as soon as the last carrot goes thru.

Mix together in a bowl:

2½ c. flour
1½ c. carrot pulp
1 c. raisins
½ c. soy milk pwd.

1 tsp. ginger pwd.
1½ tbsp. bak. pwd.
¼ tsp. salt

Mix with your fingers till all the lumps of carrot are crumbled into the flour.

Mix in a separate bowl:

3 eggs (well beaten)
¾ c. honey
1½ c. soy milk (or carrot juice)

½ c. oil
1 tsp. cinnamon

Stir liquid into dry ingredients.
Oil a "9" x 13" cake pan. Add batter.
Bake at 375° for 30~40 min. Knife test.

APPLE CRISP

Peel, core and slice:

    4 lbs. apples

Squeeze and mix into the apples:

    1 tbls. lemon juice
    (this keeps them from going brown)

Combine in a saucepan and mix till dissolved:

    1 c. apple juice   **2 tbls. kuzu**

Add: **½ c. raisins**   **1 tsp. vanilla**
    ¼ c. barley malt   **¼ tsp. salt**

Heat mixture on a flame tamer, stirring constantly till hot and thickened. Simmer for 5 min.

Oil a 9" x 13" pie pan.

Layer in the apples. Pour hot mixture over the apples and set aside. Preheat oven to 350°.

In the same saucepan,. heat till liquid:

    ½ c. rice or barley malt
    ⅓ c. oil

Mix in a bowl:

    1½ c. rolled oats   **½ c. chopped walnuts**
    ½ c. flour   **¼ tsp. salt**

Add the melted malt and oil. Mix till it becomes crumbly. Sprinkle over the apples and bake for 35 ~ 40 min.

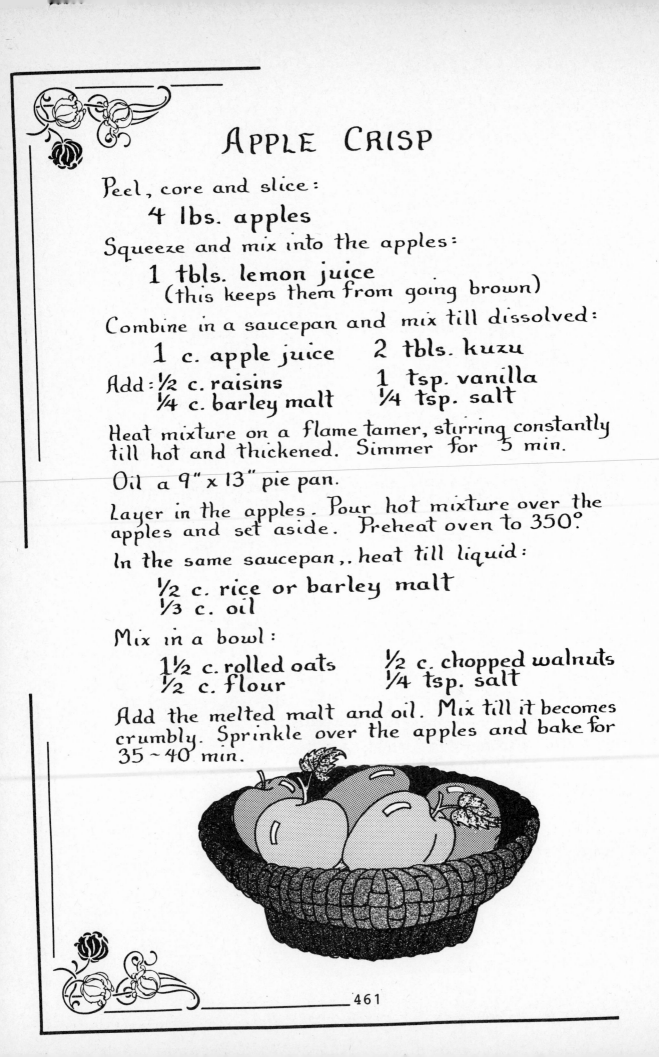

MUNDEL BREAD

Sift together :

4 c. flour	½ tsp. nutmeg
2 tsp. bak. pwd.	½ tsp. salt
1 tsp. cinnamon	

Add : 1 c. chopped walnuts or almonds

Combine separately :

4 eggs (well beaten)	¼ c. soy milk
1 c. honey	1 tsp. vanilla ext.
¾ c. oil	

Add liquid to the dry ingredients. Mix just enough to make a soft dough. Do not knead. Shape into 3 rolls about 2" thick. Place on an oiled cookie tin. Bake at 350° for 30 min.

Remove from oven and slice into 1" pieces, separate slightly and return to oven to dry. 300° for 15 min.

A tahine ~ maple syrup sauce is nice to dip them in.

APPLE ~ CURRANT SQUARES

Premix a batch of pastry and set to chill.

Oil a 13" x 9" cookie tray.
Roll dough ⅛" thick. Cover bottom and sides of pan.

Layer with : 3 c. applesauce (natural or sweetened)
1 c. currants (washed)

Top with another ⅛" thick crust.
Bake at 350° for 30 min., or till crust is cooked.

Cool and cut into 2" squares.

Try this recipe with other fruit sauces: pear, peach, stewed figs, dates or apricots.

Instead of currants use : raisins, walnuts, almonds or poppy sds.

COOKIES

Most of these cookies are made using little or no leavening, so they are not the "fluffy, dissolve in your mouth", type of cookies. Those kinds of cookies are made using lots of sugar, lard or butter, baking soda and other ingredients that are very unhealthy.

To meet a half way point, we use a little egg in most recipes,, rather than use so much oil and to help minimize the amount of baking powder needed. (We prefer not to use baking soda, as it is twice as bad on the digestive tract than the powder is.)

For those of you who do not eat eggs,, you can leave them out and add oil for the same amount of egg. (approx. 2 tbls. oil per egg.)

Cookies should not be eaten daily,, and the same goes for pies, cakes and all the other fine treats in this 'Dessert Section',, but eaten moderately, in conjunction with seasonal fruit, fresh or cooked, won't hurt.

COCONUT~RAISIN COOKIES

Mix: 2 c. flour
     1 c. coconut
     1 c. bran
     5 tsp. bak. pwd.
     2 c. raisins
     ½ tsp. salt
     1 tsp. cinnamon
     ½ tsp. nutmeg

Mix separately :
     2 eggs (beaten)
     1½ c. honey
     1½ c. oil

Add liquid into dry ingredients and mix well.

Drop by spoonfuls onto an oiled cookie sheet. Fork into rounds about ¼" thick.

Bake at 325° till lightly browned (approx. 20 min.)

OATMEAL COOKIES

Combine :

     2 c. oatmeal
     2 c. flour
     1 c. chopped dates
     1 tsp. bak. pwd.
     1 tsp. salt

Mix in a separate bowl :

     2 eggs (well beaten)
     1 c. oil
     1 c. honey
     ½ c. soy milk

Add liquid into dry ingredients and mix well.

Drop by spoonfuls onto an oiled cookie sheet. Fork into rounds about ¼" thick.

Bake at 325° till lightly browned (approx. 20 min.)

When using a fork to flatten cookies,, the batter will not stick to the fork if you dip the fork into a cup of cold water in between each cookie.

Space cookies an inch apart from each other, when they cook,, they expand slightly.

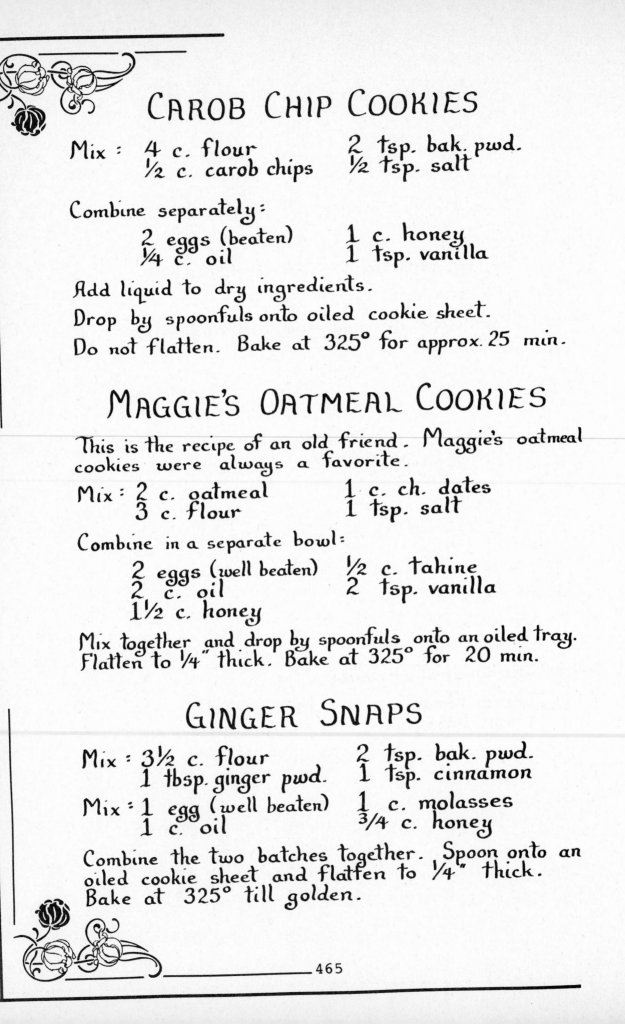

CAROB CHIP COOKIES

Mix : 4 c. flour   2 tsp. bak. pwd.
      ½ c. carob chips   ½ tsp. salt

Combine separately :
      2 eggs (beaten)   1 c. honey
      ¼ c. oil   1 tsp. vanilla

Add liquid to dry ingredients.
Drop by spoonfuls onto oiled cookie sheet.
Do not flatten. Bake at 325° for approx. 25 min.

MAGGIE'S OATMEAL COOKIES

This is the recipe of an old friend. Maggie's oatmeal cookies were always a favorite.

Mix : 2 c. oatmeal   1 c. ch. dates
      3 c. flour   1 tsp. salt

Combine in a separate bowl :
      2 eggs (well beaten) ½ c. tahine
      2 c. oil   2 tsp. vanilla
      1½ c. honey

Mix together and drop by spoonfuls onto an oiled tray.
Flatten to ¼" thick. Bake at 325° for 20 min.

GINGER SNAPS

Mix : 3½ c. flour   2 tsp. bak. pwd.
      1 tbsp. ginger pwd. 1 tsp. cinnamon
Mix : 1 egg (well beaten) 1 c. molasses
      1 c. oil   ¾ c. honey

Combine the two batches together. Spoon onto an oiled cookie sheet and flatten to ¼" thick.
Bake at 325° till golden.

PEANUT BUTTER COOKIES

A delicious, crumbly cookie.

Cream together:

 ½ c. crunchy peanut butter
 ½ c. honey
 ¼ c. oil
 ½ tsp. vanilla   ¼ tsp. salt

Add and mix in:

 1¼ c. durham or wh. wheat pastry flour

Preheat oven to 350°.

Drop by spoonfuls onto an oiled cookie sheet. Flatten to ¼" thick and bake for 10~12 min.

MOLASSES COOKIES

Preheat oven to 350°

Cream together:

 ⅓ c. barley malt   ½ c. soy marg.
 ½ c. molasses   1 egg (well beaten)

Combine in another bowl:

 1½ c. flour   ½ tsp. salt
 2 tsp. bak. pwd.   ¼ tsp. ginger pwd.

Stir the molasses mixture into the flour.
Fold in:

 ½ c. raisins   1 tsp. vanilla
 ¼ c. apple juice   ½ tsp. apple cider
                              vinegar

Drop by spoonfulls onto an oiled cookie sheet. Flatten to ¼" thick with a wet fork. Bake for 10~12 min.

DAD'S FAVORITE COOKIES

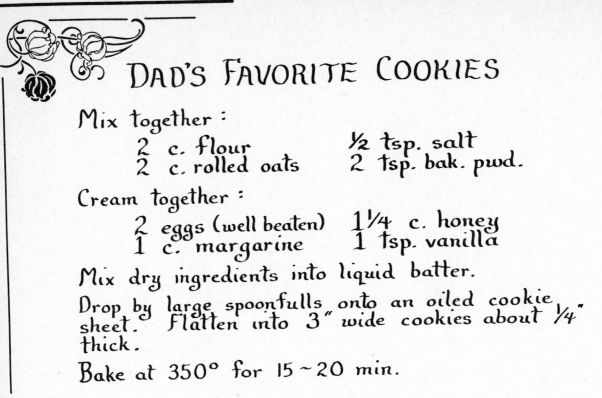

Mix together :

2 c. flour	½ tsp. salt
2 c. rolled oats	2 tsp. bak. pwd.

Cream together :

2 eggs (well beaten)	1¼ c. honey
1 c. margarine	1 tsp. vanilla

Mix dry ingredients into liquid batter.

Drop by large spoonfulls onto an oiled cookie sheet. Flatten into 3" wide cookies about ¼" thick.

Bake at 350° for 15~20 min.

BUTTER~ALMOND COOKIES

Sift together :

4 c. durham or wh. wheat pastry flour
2 tbls. baking pwd.

Cream together :

1 c. melted soy marg. or butter
¾ c. honey
1 egg
3 tbls. lemon juice
1 c. chopped almonds

Preheat oven to 350°

Drop by spoonfuls onto an oiled cookie sheet. Flatten to 2" cookies about ¼" thick.

Bake for 8-12 minutes, till golden brown.

OATMEAL COOKIES

There are numerous oatmeal cookie recipes around. This recipe was shown to me by our friend Terri. It's full of goodies „ not too sweet and makes a very tasty, hardy cookie.

Combine in a bowl:

2 c. rolled oats
2 c. flour
3/4 c. coconut
1/4 c. lightly roasted sunflower sds.
1/4 c. lightly roasted almonds or walnuts

1/2 tsp. cinnamon
1 tsp. salt
1 tbls. baking pwd.

Preheat oven to 325°.

Combine in a pot:

3/4 c. barley malt   1/4 c. apple juice

Heat till the barley malt is liquid (1-2 min).

Add: 1 c. oil   1 tsp. vanilla
1/2 c. currants

Remove from the heat and mix well.

Add liquid to the dry ingredients. The mixture should be fairly stiff. If too dry add a little more apple juice.

Drop by spoonful onto a well oiled cookie sheet and flatten with a wet fork to 1/4" thick. Bake till golden brown. Remove from the oven and loosen from the pan while hot, otherwise they tend to crack if loosed when cooled.

ICINGS

Everyone enjoys icing on their cake,, muffins, brownies and invariably, on the finger.

Each of these icings are smooth and sweet. Sure to please even the fussiest palate.

CAROB ICING

Cream together:
½ c. honey	½ c. marg. (¼ lb.)

Add: ½ c. soy milk pwd.   1 tbls. lemon juice
    ¼ c. tahine   (eliminates chalkiness)
    ¼ c. carob pwd.   1 tsp. vanilla

Mix well and spread on cake or brownies.

Refrigerated, this will last a week or more. It can also be frozen in small batches.

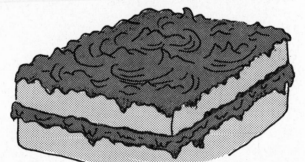

BASIC TAHINE ICING

This icing is not as firm as others,, yet it is very good on cake, or as a dip for mundel bread.

Cream together:
    1 c. amasake   ½ c. margarine
    ½ c. soy milk pwd.   1 tsp. vanilla
    ½ c. tahine

Chill slightly before spreading the icing on the cake so it will firm up a little.

VANILLA TOFU ICING

Premake: 1 batch of Tofu Whip Cream #1
Chill in the refrigerator for 1 hour.
Mix together:

    ¼ c. honey   2 tbls tahine
    ¼ c. soymilk pwd.   1 tsp. vanilla

Fold tofu whip cream into the tahine mixture.
Spread on your dessert or cake.

MAPLE SEA FOAM ICING

When you need a deliciously, light and elegant icing, try this recipe. Our friend Mehlam,, showed me how to make this for Shanola's birthday, as she is a maple syrup fan. This is also a very nice icing for a wedding cake.

In a medium sized pot, boil to the thread stage:

    1 c. maple syrup

(watch that it doesn't boil over and stir it frequently. Test by dribbling a little into a cup of cold water. When it forms a thread, rather then dissolving, it is cooked enough.)

Remove from the heat.

Separate and whip till fluffy and stiff

    2 egg whites (they whip up better
          at room temperature).

Continue beating the egg whites while dribbling a thin stream of the cooked maple syrup into it. Continue beating till all the syrup is used and and the icing is a spreadable consistency.

Let cool slightly, then spread. Keep chilled.

PEACH SAUCE

Combine in a saucepan:

    1 c. apple juice   1 tbls. agar agar

Bring to a boil and simmer with a lid for 5~7 min.

Mix: ¼ c. water   2 tbls. arrowroot fl.

Add to the apple juice and simmer till thickened and clear.

Add: 2 c. peaches (blanched to remove the skins, then cut from the stones in 1" wedges.)

Blend till smooth:

Add: 1 c. peaches (blanched and cut from the stone in thin, ¼" slices)

Bottle and refrigerate. Shake well before using.

This will keep in the fridge for 5 to 7 days.

Ideal for serving over ice cream, cake, etc.

LEMON GLAZE

Ideal to top cake, dessert loaves or pudding.

Combine in a saucepan:

    ¼ c. lemon juice   ¼ c. water
    ¼ c. honey or   2 tsp. arrowroot fl.
    maple syrup

Bring to a boil, stirring constantly, until clear and thickened.

Use the glaze while hot. Cool and serve.

STRAWBERRY - SHORTCAKE SAUCE

Use either fresh strawberries or ones which have been thawed from your freezer.

Combine in a saucepan and simmer for 5-7 minutes.

2 c. water   2 tbls. agar agar

Mix: ¼ c. water   2 tbls. arrowroot fl.

Add to the boiling water and simmer until thickened and clear.

Add: 4 c. strawberries   ½ c. honey

Blend in two batches and bottle.

When chilled,, shake well or reblend.

Tasty when poured over cake, fresh fruit, ice cream, crepes, etc.

As an alternative to honey, replace the 2 cups of water with apple juice and the ½ cup of honey with ½ cup of amasake.

BUTTER'D ALMOND TOPPING

Sauté in a skillet till lightly browned:

1 c. chopped almonds   4 tbls. marg.

Add: ¼ c. honey   1 tbls. almond ext.

Mix: 1 tbls. arrowroot fl.   ¼ c. water

Add the arrowroot and water to the skillet and simmer till thickened. Use while hot.

TOFU WHIP CREAM #1

Ideal for people who can't or don't want to eat real whip cream. It is a very delicious substitute.

Use on top of pies, puddings or fresh fruit.

Unless you have a food processor, the easiest way to make this is in smaller batches in the blender.

Blender batch:
Crumble into the blender:

    1 9 oz. cube of tofu (1 cup)

Add: 1~2 tbls. honey   ½ tsp. vanilla
       3~4 tbls water   ½ tsp. lemon juice
       1 tbls. oil   pinch of salt

The use of lemon eliminates the 'chalky' taste.

The amount of water you use is the trick to making a good tofu cream. If you add too much it will be runny,, more like a sauce,, yet you need enough so it will blend. I use a chopstick to help move the tofu in the direction of the blades,, but be careful and keep the chopstick tight to the sides, or you will have a few wood chunks in your whip cream. Doing this I can use less water and achieve a thicker cream.

If you have a food processor,, you can make a double or triple size batch, using a minimal amount of water.

There are many different kinds of tofu available, on the market. Depending on whether it is 'firm' or 'soft' tofu will make a difference in the amount of water needed to make it blend properly.

Also,, buy your tofu as fresh as possible and change the water it soaks in daily, unless it is in an airtight sealed package.

TOFU WHIP CREAM #2

This method involves a little more preparation, yet it is easier to blend. This version will make a whip cream that will set firmer.

Keeps well in the refrigerator for 4~7 days.

Combine in a small pot:

½ c. water   1 tbls. oil
1 tbls. agar agar   1 tsp. vanilla
2~4 tbls. honey   pinch of salt

Simmer on a flame tamer with a lid till the agar is dissolved. (approx 5~7 min.)

Crumble and measure into a measuring cup:

1 c. of tofu

Blend the tofu with the agar mixture. Pour into a bowl and let set for 5~10 min. Whip with a wire wisk till fluffy. Add on top of pie, cake or pudding. At this point you can create some nice designs in the cream and they will set.

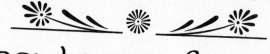

HOT LEMON SAUCE

Excellent on top of cake or bread pudding.

Combine in a saucepan:

3 c. water   2 tbls. lemon rind
¼ c. millet   ¼ tsp. salt

Bring to a boil and simmer for 20 min.

Mix: ¼ c. lemon juice   ½ c. honey
        1 tbls. arrowroot fl.   1 tbls. marg.

Add to the saucepan and simmer for 10 min.

Blend and keep warm till ready to serve, or reheat in a double boiler.

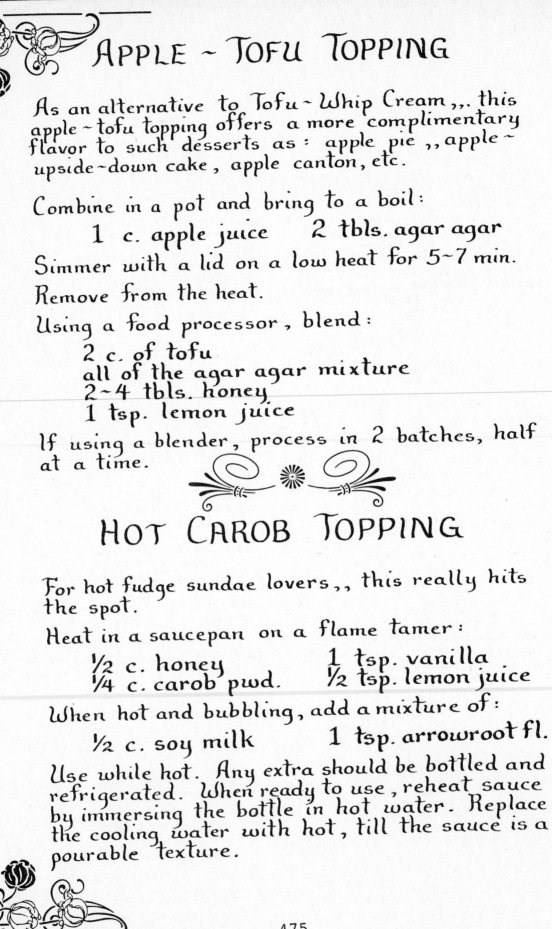

APPLE ~ TOFU TOPPING

As an alternative to Tofu ~ Whip Cream ,,. this apple ~ tofu topping offers a more complimentary flavor to such desserts as : apple pie ,, apple ~ upside ~ down cake, apple canton, etc.

Combine in a pot and bring to a boil :

1 c. apple juice   2 tbls. agar agar

Simmer with a lid on a low heat for 5~7 min.

Remove from the heat.

Using a food processor, blend :

2 c. of tofu
all of the agar agar mixture
2~4 tbls. honey
1 tsp. lemon juice

If using a blender, process in 2 batches, half at a time.

HOT CAROB TOPPING

For hot fudge sundae lovers ,, this really hits the spot.

Heat in a saucepan on a flame tamer :

½ c. honey   1 tsp. vanilla
¼ c. carob pwd.   ½ tsp. lemon juice

When hot and bubbling, add a mixture of :

½ c. soy milk   1 tsp. arrowroot fl.

Use while hot. Any extra should be bottled and refrigerated. When ready to use, reheat sauce by immersing the bottle in hot water. Replace the cooling water with hot, till the sauce is a pourable texture.

Index

PHEYLONIAN PRODUCTION KOHR.
PROUDLY PRESENTS

ALPHA, MU, OMEGA - Written by: Iilazzandroff N. Chickalo
Intro by: Kjo Dindee

* A World Class Documentary having the potential impact needed to mildly bring the good, the bad and the ugly back to their common senses before it's too late to do it all together.

* It is a book of simple answers, taking everybody's sensitivity on the subject of God and Kreashon into account.

* Includes explanations of who built the three and four sided pyramids on Mars, and of whose face was found there carved in stone with a one mile distance between cheekbones, with a tear coming down its left cheek.

* Aside from the renowned burial site of the Famed Boy King, discover the real hidden mysteries which have been kept secret for countless centuries within the Valley of the Kings.

* What was the real story about the Ark of the Covenant?

* **For the first time:**

  - The Great, mysterious 'Missing Link' in man's evolvement is unfolded.

  - It speaks of the Eighth Wonder of the World and of why it has been kept a secret for so long.

  - Here's proof of how many mythical characters and animals have turned out to be far more real than most have been led to believe.

  - Know exactly who it is God has come to make right about all that's been done, and exactly of who's been made to be wrong all this time.

  - True life tales of dragons and a giant whirlpool atop an 11,000 foot mountain crater lake; Run-ins with Ancient Eygptian Giant Killer Bees, Electric Mountains of blue, yellow and pink crystal; hidden tunnels of gold, and much more.

* It is not a book based on any one religion, sect, cult or personal animate or inanimate concept. On the contrary, if one was to say "Ahh, this book is full of it.", one would be found to be correct and should smile when saying it, for that it is. Yet, compared to the Great Books written, it is nothing shorter than an 'ENOUGH ALREADY'!

$24.00 ea.

A PHEYLONIAN ODYSSEY - Written by: Iilazzandroff N. Chickalo
Illustrated by: The Philoxians

This odyssey is a rarely experienced adult story book about children, who, after being taught of their atomized spirit bodies are to partake in a wonderful Astral Adventure.
From atop a pyramid they get wisked away on a light beam to the ancient haumlands of Vohlantia, where Heyose and Chaunda are about to begin an adventure to the Great Wizard's Castle. It is an ancient story derived from the tablets of old and is designed to stimulate the subconscious minds of all who read it. As well, it allows people a simple in, when wanting to explain and guide their family and friends to better understand their own ancient heritage and reason for being.
Our story begins on Earth and moves quickly, without need of star ship, to Vohlantia where lives the Great One and His Family. Soon after their arrival, our spirited adventure begins with a secret message brought to Heyose and Chaunda by special courier from the lands under the sea. So, off they go through the enchanted forest where unicorns, narwhales, wee folks, tigers, dragons, magic carpets and the Great Wizard himself become enthralled with our dynamic duo as they prepare for their first Earth encounter aboard the Great Mother Ship.

A gift to be enjoyed by people of all ages.
"AN HEIRLOOM EDITION'
$22.00 ea.

Folks, this is a special hand written manuscript unlike any other in the world. It is a family participation book to be cherished and appreciated years later, when viewed by those who painted and colored in it.

* Everyone in the family can participate in coloring the 32 Dee-lightful illustrations which are readied for any media from acrylics or pastels, to watercolors, coloring pencils or markers.

* A removable, full color slate from the original/book is enclosed.

Please include postal handling as indicated

	ONT.-QUE.	MARITIMES, MAN., SASK.	B.C., ALTA., or YUK.,N.W.T.	U.S. of A.
1 Book	4.00	5.00	6.00	6.00
2 Books	5.00	6.00	9.00	7.00

For Wholesale and Distribution Quantities Please Write For Further Information

"MAJIK KARPET KREASHONS" CATALOGUE - $4.00 ea. (incl. shipping)

A full color catalogue outling all of the unique and original products which the Pheylonian Production Kohr privately produces:

Pure Beezwax Candles
Life Lite Survival Candle

Waxems
Fooshins

To My Children Plaque
and much more.

(Updates will be forwarded as products are available)

With each catalogue sent, we will include complimentary multipurposed Waxem's with instructions and recipes -value $3.79.

Pheylonian Production Kohr. R.R. 1, Marlbank, Ontario /Canada, K0K 2L0 1-613-478-6070

About the Authors

TAWLIA AND IILAZZANDROFF CHICKALO have been a team in the joyous arts of life, common sense, and oneness for some 14 years now . . . and throughout their world travels they have lectured, taught, and exemplarated this rare enchantment with thousands upon thousands of people who have had the good fortune to be introduced to this spirited duo. Many times, Iilah has been invited to speak privately to the faculty of many different universities throughout the world about the true meaning of life and of one's purpose for being, and of the necessary tools needed to consciously activate one's inner atomic self into a harmonious blend with the arrogant vibrations of the outer self.

This is where Tawlia comes in with the Grits of Life . . . because if it weren't for proper diet . . . one's spirited self would never come to such a sense of allowing reality to be whole and true. It's amazing to see what she can do for real and of how the grits of her kitchens help to cause the fullness of everyone's day to be real in spirit. ii . . . ya're what chew eat . . . and what she done put on paper, gonnah make yawl feel mighty fine about yourselves, once you get to be doin' it for real as well . . . from the grits on up. ii . . . it's not what you know that makes a Master out of you . . . it's what's done with it . . . "Tawlia, me 'at's off to ya, cuz yer quite the gal ". I'm sure people are gonna be pleased and happy you took the time to share such a rewarding wholesomeness.

Wish to know more about the authors? Well . . . they are simple folk, born to fine parents like the rest of you. To honestly know more of what they are involved with, and of what's to come, let your hearts and minds open to their heavenly haum cookery, books, musics, and way of life. Truly, it is one worth expanding on, and bettering to every degree. You might say it's a deelite making their acquaintance in some little way.

Folks . . . all I could say is . . . "Ahh, yer in for a rare treat".

Kjo Dindee